Strawberry Days

Strawberry Days

HOW INTERNMENT DESTROYED A JAPANESE AMERICAN COMMUNITY

David Neiwert

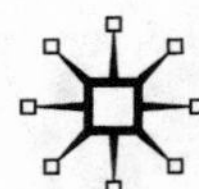

STRAWBERRY DAYS

First published 2005 by
PALGRAVE MACMILLAN™
175 Fifth Avenue, New York, N.Y. 10010 and
Houndmills, Basingstoke, Hampshire, England RG21 6XS.
Companies and representatives throughout the world.

PALGRAVE MACMILLAN is the global academic imprint of the Palgrave Macmillan division of St. Martin's Press, LLC and of Palgrave Macmillan Ltd. Macmillan® is a registered trademark in the United States, United Kingdom and other countries. Palgrave is a registered trademark in the European Union and other countries.

ISBN 1-4039-6792-X

Library of Congress Cataloging-in-Publication Data

Neiwert, David A., 1956–
Strawberry days : how internment destroyed a Japanese American community / David A. Neiwert.
p. cm.
Includes bibliographical references and index.
ISBN 1-4039-6792-X
1. Japanese Americans—Washington (State)—Bellevue—History—20th century. 2. Japanese Americans—Washington (State)—Bellevue—Social conditions—20th century. 3. Japanese Americans—Washington (State)—Bellevue—Biography. 4. Ethnic neighborhoods—Washington (State)—Bellevue—History—20th century. 5. Bellevue (Wash.)—Social conditions—20th century. 6. Bellevue (Wash.)—Ethnic relations. 7. Bellevue (Wash.)—Biography. 8. Japanese Americans—Evacuation and relocation, 1942–1945—Case studies. I. Title.

F899.B39N45 2005
979.7'77'004956—dc22

2004060107

A catalogue record for this book is available from the British Library.

Design by Letra Libre, Inc.

First edition: July 2005
10 9 8 7 6 5 4

Printed in the United States of America.

Contents

Acknowledgments vii

Prologue Good Earth 1
Chapter 1 The Clearing of Bellevue 9
Chapter 2 Strawberries 47
Chapter 3 "A Jap is a Jap" 97
Chapter 4 Exile 141
Chapter 5 Going for Broke 175
Chapter 6 The Long Road Home 201
Epilogue The Internment: Race, Memory, and Meaning 235

A Note On Sources 251
Notes 254
Bibliography 273
Index 276

Acknowledgements

Because this text was written over many years, beginning with its origins as a month-long series in the Bellevue *Journal American* and continuing with its long project life as a book in progress, there have been many people who have contributed to its development at its many various stages. It will be impossible to remember them all, and all I can do is beg forgiveness from the many helping hands that may have been overlooked.

I owe a deep debt of gratitude to Ron Chew and the staff of the Wing Luke Asian Museum (notably Beth Takekawa) who played a significant role in connecting me with many of the original interviewees from 1992, as well as a good deal of research material made available through their exhibit that year commemorating Executive Order 9066.

Similar thanks are also due to the many interviewees, all of whom are listed in "A Note on Sources." But very special thanks must be paid to Ed Suguro, who connected me with a number of former Bellevue Nisei; Rae Takekawa, who sat in and helped facilitate many of the interviews with her father; and Al Yabuki, who spent many hours driving about Bellevue with me and showing me where old farms and buildings had once been. The deepest debt, perhaps, is owed to Tom Matsuoka, who had endless patience for my many questions, and who made the story a book worth writing.

Along the way, I also owe thanks to my erstwhile colleagues at the *Journal American*, especially former city editor Mary Rothschild and former editor Jack Mayne, who helped make the original project happen. Subsequently, I'd like to thank Michael Duckworth, the acquisitions editor at University of Washington Press, who shepherded the manuscript through several different peer reviews; and the several anonymous peers who read this text in its many earlier versions.

I owe many thanks to the respective staffs at the University of Washington Special Collections, the UW Microform and Newspaper Collections, the

UW Government Publications Library, and the Museum of History and Industry (especially Dr. Lorraine McConaghy) in Seattle; and at the Washington State Archives in Olympia.

Thanks is also due to the many people who helped finish the text, especially my editors at Palgrave, Brendan O'Malley and Airié Stuart, and their assistant, Melissa Nosal; Palgrave history editor Alessandra Bastagli; copyeditor Rick Delaney; indexer Rebecca Francescatti; and production chief Donna Cherry. Thanks also to my proofreaders, Evie Kara and Carrie Monaghan, and especially Lisa Dowling, my wife and constant reader throughout its many versions.

Finally, but perhaps most significantly, I owe an eternal debt of thanks to the Densho Project and its staff, particularly executive director Tom Ikeda; interview programs manager Alice Ito; and staffers Dana Hoshide, Leslie Arai, and Geoff Froh. Their work was indispensable in helping give this text its final shape.

Dedicated to my daughter, Fiona,
in hopes that her generation does not forget.

Prologue

Good Earth

THE SOIL ON JOHN MATSUOKA'S LITTLE FARM IN BELLEVUE, Washington, was black and rich with loam, and he liked to show it to you, cupping it in his hand and letting it trickle like coal dust through his fingers. This used to be a lake bottom and then a wetland, and the result was this dark, fertile earth.

"It's wonderful soil," Matsuoka said. "And you should see what it produces."

When I visited his farm in the summer of 2000, he set about showing me. He'd wade into a furrow and begin pulling up potato plants, whacking off the green leafy tops and collecting the remaining tubers in a box. Going from furrow to furrow, he gathered all kinds: brown Russets, Yukon golds, reds, even some strange-looking purple potatoes.

He dug up some with bite marks in them. This was his latest farm problem: "Rats," he said. "And the worst part is, they just take one bite out of the potatoes and then go on to the next one. They ruin more that way." He considered setting out some traps, but he wouldn't even consider poison: "I won't use anything that might get into the food."

Having filled the box with about a sack's worth of potatoes, he set it aside and headed over to the rows of corn growing in the adjoining plot. Again, he had about three different varieties, only evident by the differing heights of the stalk rows. All of the stalks towered above Matsuoka, who was never a big guy to begin with, and at age 85 had probably lost a few inches over the years.

He could recall a time when he tried his hand at a different kind of agriculture, working the sugar beet farms of southern Idaho during World War II, as a way of getting out of the nearby internment camps where he and thousands of other Japanese Americans were exiled. Unlike the 5- or 15-acre tracts he'd worked all his life, suddenly he was in the middle of monstrous 500-acre farms.

"They were big," he said. "And then, it was heavy—you know, like loading the hay on—well shucks, you're shoving up fifty and sixty pounds up higher and higher, you know. Then, there was a Caucasian guy on the other side—I'm on this side and he's on that side. Pretty soon the pile of hay on the wagon was getting pretty up there. And then he comes around and says, 'How in the hell are you getting that hay up there?'"

"He knows I'm not as strong as he is. And I says, 'Oh, I stick the fork in that pile and then I put the butt on the ground, right next to my foot. Get it straightened up, and then I shoot it right straight up and on there.' 'Oh!' Of course, he's strong enough to get, just fork it and heave-ho, you know, but he knows darn well I can't do it."

Matsuoka laughed at the memory.

He reached up, rustled through the stalks, and carefully selected and cut off four ears, then sauntered back to where he left the box and tossed them in. "Here," he said, handing me the box. "Take that home and have it with your dinner." Generosity is his second nature.

Tucked away on a bench of land above Lake Sammamish, Matsuoka's was a tiny farm by any measure, totaling only about four acres. But he got everything out of it he could. In addition to the potatoes and corn, he also grew lettuce, cabbage, and cucumbers. They were not big crops, but they were of extraordinarily high quality. He sold to the local, somewhat upscale QFC supermarket chain: "They take everything I grow."

He dug around in the lettuce, took out a knife, and lopped off the upper half of a leafy head, exposing the core. He pointed to a brown spot in the middle of it, a product, he said, of a hot spell that hit around the Fourth of July. He had to be more selective that year about which heads he took to market, but he'd learned how to detect the tainted lettuce. He only wanted to sell his best. It kept his customers happy.

That's how it always was for Matsuoka: not just surviving, but thriving by being a better farmer than the next guy, by growing better food on less land. That's how it always was for Japanese American farmers generally.

Matsuoka had another farming job during the war that got him out of the internment camps—this time in rural Michigan. He and his wife transferred out of Minidoka, the big camp in southern Idaho, when an old friend in Ann Arbor hooked them up with a Michigan farmer who needed help on his spread—the farmer mainly ran a chicken and egg business, and needed someone to run the produce side of things. Matsuoka agreed to come out and run the farm on a shared-profit basis.

It was a new experience for Matsuoka, who had to spend the first year learning how to network with small grocers instead of simply hauling his goods to a packing shed, as he'd always done. But he proved a quick study.

He recalled how in his second year there with a big batch of tomatoes, he enlisted the help of local 4-H youngsters to pick them early, with the promise that they could take home any red tomatoes if they'd pick his green ones as well. This raised a few eyebrows with his neighbors.

But there was a method to his seeming madness: "I found out that the first heavy frost was in the first week of September, and I had all my green tomatoes picked and in the barn. And that was a lot of tomatoes. And then the frost hit, and down went the tomatoes. And then I was peddling other things there, and the grocery guy, he had his own garden, oversized garden: 'I got my own tomatoes.' But when the frost hits the tomatoes, it gets the brown spots on them, and then pretty soon that brown spot deteriorates and it will spoil your tomato if you don't eat it. And he says, 'But I can't understand how come my tomatoes have got brown spots.' And I said, 'That's because they got hit by the frost.' 'Oh?' 'Yeah. Next week, my tomatoes will be ripe, and I'll show you what I mean.'

"So I brought him in my tomatoes. And he looked at them and he says, 'How come yours is without blemish and mine's got all these brown spots?' 'Because you're a grocery man and I'm a farmer.'

"And there was that 28-pound lug box that the tomatoes come packed in. It was selling for $2 when I picked the green tomatoes. And then when the frost hit, and two weeks later, that box of tomatoes went up to $18.

"We made a bundle. And of course, you know, when they got their split, they couldn't give it up. And then on top of that I had dry onion in the corn bin. . . . Another Japanese farmer wanted to use my truck. So I said, 'Well, you can use it. Right after the first of January I want you to take my dry onion and sell it, irregardless of what the price is.' That was in November. I told him, and he said, 'OK, OK.' And the price of that dry onion from November to January went up two times. So we made another chunk of dough." He laughed at that memory, too.

Matsuoka had been farming this particular plot since 1950, back when it was a larger, 40 acre farm and he made his living from it. But it's been more of a hobby for him since the late '50s, when he decided to quit farming and take a job at the Bellevue Post Office. The land's owner, Armondo Desmond, also decided to get out of farming.

"I knew I'd have plenty of time in the summer, too much time," Matsuoka recalls. "So I told 'Mondo, 'I'll have to—the kids don't want to work on a farm anymore, so I guess I'll have to give it up. But I'd like to have about four acres to play around.' 'Fence off what you want, and pay me what you want.' So that's how come I cut off that four-acre piece there, and went to work for the Post Office.

"Gee, I farmed from stem to stern. I don't know how I did it."

The farm was adjacent to a small lake and wetlands that were ideal park property, which they became. Eventually, Matsuoka had a different landlord: the city of Bellevue.

"After three years of paying taxes and the Parks Department offered to buy the low grounds for wetlands, [Desmond] sold out, so he wouldn't have to pay the taxes. 'But,' he said, 'as long as John is farming, you'll let him farm there.' So now I've been paying my rent to the Parks Department.

"At the beginning, I told them, 'What are you going to do when I quit?' 'Oh, we'll make wetland out of it.' But then in the meanwhile, there's such demand for farmland, because there isn't any, so they decided to keep the farm farm, so that whoever wants to rent it can rent it. I was happy because it's a shame to let a ground like this go to a wetland. It produces beautiful stuff."

In fact, the summer of 2000 was the last year John operated the farm. Later that autumn, he decided to call it quits at fifty years, and turned the farm over to the Bellevue Parks Department.

The old farm is worth preserving for another reason: It is a genuine relic of Bellevue's past. Look around the farm at the surrounding landscape and the contrast becomes clear.

No longer bounded by woods and other farms, large housing developments are on all sides of the farm and the little park at Phantom Lake. Most of the homes have been built in the last 20 years, and many of the neighborhoods are built with uniform architecture that makes all the homes look nearly alike. In some of the neighborhoods, above-ordinary wealth is obvious, but the graceful Victorian manses so common to Seattle are almost nowhere to be found in Bellevue. It is relentlessly modern. These vast residential tracts represent Bellevue's identity of the past half-century as a suburb, providing homes to a workforce that commuted across the floating bridges of Lake Washington to Seattle.

Viewed from an even broader perspective, modern Bellevue reveals itself as more than a mere suburb; it has become a modern megalopolis. At its downtown core, gleaming steel-and-mirror buildings rise up 30 stories and more, imitating on a smaller scale the massive skyscrapers that form the Seattle city skyline just a few miles away, westward across Lake Washington. City streets sprawl five and six lanes wide, and a major freeway with innumerable lanes and exits and on-ramps bisects the city north to south. To the north, on the city's borders, is the sprawling Microsoft campus, home to the world's most powerful software corporation and 10,000-plus of its workers. There also is a bounty of other high-tech companies in Bellevue, large and small. Most of the people employed by these firms live on the Eastside, which is the name Seattle-area residents give to the several communities on the eastern side of Lake Washington, the 30-mile-long body of water occupied on its west side almost entirely by Seattle.

Bellevue is the crown jewel of the Eastside. The Eastside as a region also encompasses Kirkland, Redmond, a large part of Renton, Issaquah, Bothell, and Woodinville, as well as the outlying areas on the Sammamish Plateau. But Bellevue is both the suburbs' commercial and cultural center, the hub city that gives them an identity.

Bellevue is, in fact, the embodiment of a phenomenon that *Washington Post* columnist Joel Garreau calls the "Edge City": modern metropolises arising on the shoulders of former suburbs. It fits Garreau's description: it has a workday population that renders it a work center rather than a residential one; it is perceived locally as a destination for a range of daily activities, from work to shopping to entertainment; it contains more than 5 million square feet of office space and 600,000 square feet of retail space; and it was essentially a mixed residential and rural area 30 years before.[1]

Bellevue is like most such cities in several other key areas: for most of its short life as a city, its racial homogeneity has been striking. It is predominantly white, almost as if by design. But the very forces that have driven the city to metropolitan status have simultaneously altered this demographic; minorities are making significant inroads here, and the city now boasts in pure numbers its largest minority population ever.

The city's white population in the 2000 census was 74.3 percent of a total 109,569 residents—an appreciable change from the 1990 census, which found that 86.5 percent of Bellevue was white. Of the rising minorities, by far the largest component is Asians, who constitute 17.4 percent of the population, up from less than 10 percent in 1990.[2]

This is palpable to even a casual observer at the heart of the city's commercial district, Bellevue Square Shopping Center, the most venerable and the most prestigious of the Eastside's shopping malls. The large number of Asian faces has become remarkable, particularly in a setting that in most people's memories has been the essence of white suburban culture. There are annual Japanese festivals at the mall, and Asian Americans of every age are abundant at any time.

Indeed, Japanese money has played a significant role in Bellevue's transformation in the past 20 years. Much of it has come from the presence of Nintendo of America's headquarters (virtually adjacent to the Microsoft campus), particularly since a number of the company's key executives reside in Bellevue, and both they and the workers who collect Nintendo's significant payroll live on the Eastside and tend to spend their incomes there. Moreover, Japanese partners have helped build a number of major projects in the downtown core, often with the help of developer Kemper Freeman, who also happens to own Bellevue Square.

There is both irony and a certain kind of justice in this outcome. Because even in the days before Bellevue was known as a white enclave, it was known as a "Jap town." In those days, Bellevue's chief identity—built around a fabled annual Strawberry Festival—was inextricably woven with the people who grew and sold the fruit. The Japanese American community gave Bellevue its personality, not to mention economic vibrancy; indeed, it was largely their labors clearing the land that had made Bellevue livable in the first place. And when they were driven out—in a fit of hysteria borne of deep rooted prejudice and conspiracy theory hobgoblins—the city lost much of its distinctive original character. One of the key players in that persecution happens to be one of Bellevue's most significant city fathers: Miller Freeman, the man who masterminded Bellevue Square, and grandfather of the current owner.

More important, in the process, the displacement of Japanese Americans at a crucial point in the city's development made it possible for Bellevue to transform from a rural village to a modern, mostly white, suburb. Some of this was by design, and some by historical accident. Oftentimes, the racial prejudice that was a commonplace in the early part of the twentieth century was thoroughly interwoven with economic competition and capitalistic Social Darwinism, to the point of being indistinguishable. The conjunction of these forces in a perfect storm of governmental overreaching and mass hysteria destroyed what had once been a vibrant and well-integrated minority community.

There has been much discussion in recent years regarding whether the internment of Japanese Americans during World War II was justified, particularly in light of the events of September 11, 2001, and a fresh desire to resort to "racial profiling" measures to ensure the nation's security. The story of the Bellevue farming community puts flesh and blood to this argument, and demonstrates with great clarity the reality: what the government inflicted upon Japanese Americans in 1942 was not just a horrendous waste of national resources in a time of war, one that damaged the integrity of the Constitution, but it was in the end an atrocious wrong, morally, civically, and otherwise.

It destroyed the livelihoods and careers of thousands of citizens, based on an unconstitutional mass presumption of guilt. It humiliated a whole population of largely loyal and patriotic citizens by identifying them with the national enemy. It forced them to lose their possessions, their property, their businesses, all without even a hint of compensation. It uprooted families, destroyed their close-knit structures, and laid waste to whole communities like the one in Bellevue.

This is the story of the rise and fall of that community. It was fairly representative of the average Japanese American's lifestyle; at the time of the evacuation in spring 1942, most Nikkei were employed in agriculture. Some two-thirds of the first-generation Issei immigrants worked in farming, while a majority of second-generation Nisei relied on agriculture for a living, either farming themselves or working in shipping and transport.

John Matsuoka's farm was the last vestige of those days, the final tiny remnant of the city's former face, of a time when a drive around the Bellevue countryside revealed a broad community of Japanese faces, all farming little tracts, living in relative harmony with their white neighbors, sweating and striving like all American dreamers to make a better life for themselves. Matsuoka's older brother, Tom Takeo Matsuoka, was among the foremost of them.

The internment changed all that forever, all along the Pacific Coast. It wiped out most of the small farming communities that had been providing a bounty of fresh produce for white consumers for over a generation, almost uniformly displacing them with the relentless spread of modern suburbia. It made for a kind of progress, of course. But there was a price—moral and civic—to be paid for it.

Chapter 1

The Clearing of Bellevue

Tom Matsuoka had a long history in Bellevue with an abrupt ending. He arrived at a time when the original Japanese American community was taking root, and he played a key role in making it grow. Matsuoka was a Kibei—born American, educated in Japan, and then returned to the States—who wound up marrying a Bellevue farm girl. The couple became leaders in the community, especially in making the farming economy of the Eastside flourish. It was a place that gave him many happy memories.

One of his sharpest memories, though, was of the last day he lived in Bellevue: December 7, 1941. He could remember it like it was yesterday, even though it had been more than 60 years. But then, he liked to say, time is elastic like that: "It seems like both a little time ago and a long time ago." At other times he would remark in amazement at how quickly his 98 years had flown by.

Matsuoka led the quiet life of an exiled retiree in Ridgefield, a village on the Columbia River in southwestern Washington, some 170 miles from the city he had a hand in founding. His walk in his later years was slightly stooped, and he moved slowly, carefully, about the yard of his little home. But Matsuoka's mind remained lively, his memory keen. His eyes would dance, and he often smiled as he recounted the stories of his past. The skin of his face was almost preternaturally smooth despite a lifetime of working in the sun, wind, and rain, like a statue worn by the elements.

Matsuoka had a small house tucked away on a side street on the edge of town, and devoted most of his time to tending what once was a large and productive garden, though he scaled back the size of it as the work of tending it

Figure 1.1. Tom Takeo Matsuoka at his Ridgefield, Washington, home in 1998. Courtesy of David Neiwert.

grew more taxing. In his 90s, he spent more time inside. His house was neatly cluttered with mementos collected over the past century.

Even at a smaller scale, he was good at growing things. Before he lived in Ridgefield, he ran a farm in Montana. He lived there for nearly 50 years.

And before that, he lived in Bellevue. He had come to the quiet farming town across Lake Washington from Seattle as a young man, was married there, was raising his children, and had a prosperous business. He was a community leader, admired and depended upon by hundreds of people, both Japanese and white. He organized and coached baseball and basketball teams. He was a central figure in Bellevue's thriving produce export industry.

It all ended, suddenly, with a knock on the door in the dead of night.

Although Tom Matsuoka's time in Bellevue is now only a distant memory, in many ways he personified the story of the Eastside's Japanese community and the role it played in Bellevue's beginnings. Most local histories have tended to give at best a brief nod to the Japanese community's presence.[1] Yet for most of its early years, while it still was an unincorporated town, 10 to 15 percent of

Bellevue's population, perhaps more, was Japanese. By 1941, there were 60 families and over 300 people of Japanese descent among a total Bellevue population of slightly less than 2,000. Outside of the Puget Sound and Yakima areas, such a presence by any minority was rare in rural Washington.[2]

The relatively small numbers also belie the significance of their contributions to Bellevue's development. Foremost among these was that, by converting the landscape from stumplands to arable farming tracts, the Japanese made the landscape fit for human habitation. Subsequently, the farms they built out of this cleared land and the bounty they created gave Bellevue much of its original identity.

When the Japanese first arrived in the 1890s, Bellevue was a wilderness of dense, virgin old-growth forest. The forests attracted logging crews from across the lake in Seattle, where timber was the dominant industry. The logging was brutal, difficult, and dangerous labor, but there were plenty of jobs to be had, though not always enough white men to do the work. That's where the Japanese immigrants came in.

The first wave of Asians to arrive on American shores came primarily from China. Drawn by the California Gold Rush of 1849, the hard working Chinese immigrants were at first welcomed with open arms, since they filled an important niche in the mining camps. Rather than jostling for a place among the other gold seekers, the Chinese made their fortunes by providing services necessary for the mining camps to flourish: laundry, food, and general labor. Their presence, considered indispensable, was praised by California's governor and was sought at public functions.[3] Chinese manual labor also proved invaluable in building the West's railroad system.

But the welcome lasted only as long as things were plentiful. As Henry Kittredge Norton observed:

> Thousands of Americans came flocking in to the mines. Rich surface claims soon became exhausted. These newcomers did not find it so easy as their predecessors had done to amass large fortunes in a few days. California did not fulfill the promise of the golden tales that had been told of her. These gold-seekers were disappointed. In the bitterness of their disappointment they turned upon the men of other races who were working side by side with them and accused them of stealing their wealth. They boldly asserted that California's gold belonged to them. The cry of "California for Americans" was raised and taken up on all sides.[4]

Worse yet, the completion of the Central Pacific Railroad in 1869—symbolized by the driving of the Golden Spike—threw thousands of Chinese workers into the already crowded labor market, adding to the intensity of resentment over the competition they represented. As early as 1862, anti-coolie clubs had formed in San Francisco, and they spread like a virus to every ward in the city.

By decade's end, Chinese constituted 10 percent of California's population, and the resentment festered. The first of many large "anti-Oriental" mass meetings occurred in San Francisco in July 1870; anti-Chinese agitation had become the most important issue in the state. It gathered steam for the next 12 years, led largely by labor organizers who used the Chinese worker issue as the chief recruiting tool for their fledgling movement. The issue culminated in the Chinese Exclusion Act of 1882, barring further immigration from China.[5]

All Asians already were prevented by law from ever attaining American citizenship. The 1790 Immigration Act specified that naturalization was available only to "free white persons"—language originally intended to ensure that African Americans and Native Americans were excluded from citizenship (in 1870, Congress updated the naturalization statutes to include Africans), but applied with equal vigor to Asians as they attempted to immigrate. Of course, any children of those immigrants born on American soil were entitled to full citizenship, though their parents might be barred, and this birthright would play a major role in later anti-Asian agitation.

A belief in the supremacy of the white race—and the need for racial segregation—was an often explicit, and always implicit, feature of the inflamed rhetoric aimed at excluding the Chinese. Speakers at rallies appealed to "racial purity" and "Western civilization" and described Asians in subhuman terms, simultaneously posing the most dire of threats, with a none-too-subtle sexual undertone. Moreover, agitators claimed, they were innately treacherous, as in a Knights of Labor pamphlet circulated in 1878:

> By his industry, suavity and apparent child-like innocence, seconded by unequaled patience and the keenest business ability, the Chinaman is always the winner. Let white men set over him whatever guards they may, he can surpass them in threading the by-ways of tortuousness. Dr. S. Wells Williams, in his standard work on China, "The Middle Kingdom," makes these remarks on the untruthfulness of the Chinese: "There is nothing

> which tries one so much, when living among them, as their disregard of truth; or renders him so indifferent to what calamities may befall so mendacious a race. An abiding impression of suspicion rests upon the mind toward everybody here, which chills the warmest wishes for their welfare. Their better traits diminish in the distance, and the patience is exhausted when in daily proximity and friction with this ancestor of sins."[6]

The harsh words were accompanied by action. Chinese became targets of violence, which ranged from young boys yanking on queues—they often were taught at a young age that this was a cute prank[7]—to numerous assaults, murders and acts of mob brutality. The most notorious of these was a night-long rampage by a white mob in the sleepy town of Los Angeles in 1871, which ended with some 20 Chinese men shot and hanged.[8]

Chinese had emigrated up the Pacific Coast to the Oregon and Washington territories as well, and racial agitation soon followed them. Anti-Chinese activism in Washington reached a fever pitch in 1885–1886, when the Territorial Legislature passed a law barring Chinese ownership of property. The new law in hand, a cadre of Seattle-area agitators—comprising largely labor, progressive, nativist and utopian elements—demanded that city officials expel all 350 or so of Seattle's Chinese residents, who occupied the logging town's first Chinatown east of Pioneer Square's red-light district. Some cooler heads, notably Judge Thomas Burke and Mayor Henry Yesler, tried to prevail. However, they also agreed that the Chinese had to go—albeit in a legal fashion.

For the local agitators—who included utopianist George Venable Smith, later the founder of the Puget Sound Co-Operative Colony on the Olympic Peninsula[9]—this approach was much too slow. So on February 7, 1886, a mob rounded up virtually every Chinese person in Seattle and began herding them toward the dock at the foot of Main Street, intending to put them aboard a waiting steamer for passage out of town. However, a contingent of local police and the volunteer Home Guard met the agitators at the pier and prevented the forced expulsion of their frightened captives, at least for a day.

Some 200 Chinese embarked for San Francisco the next morning. However, another 150 or so were forced to remain behind to catch the next boat, due six days later. As authorities tried escorting these Chinese back to their homes, the mob erupted in violence. Police fired into the crowd, and five members of the mob fell; one died. Martial law was declared by the governor and President Grover Cleveland.

Eventually, as all but a few Chinese left Seattle within the ensuing weeks, the passions cooled. And the city's nascent Chinese community nearly disappeared, at least for the time being.[10]

With American borders closed to Chinese immigrants, demand for the cheap labor they had produced along the Pacific Coast rose, and other Asians fit the bill nicely. This was particularly the case for the Japanese, for whom two centuries of self-imposed isolation had ended with Admiral Perry's famous visit to Japan's shores in 1853. On its heels came the Meiji Restoration (1868–1912), a revolution that toppled the Tokugawa shogunate, "restored" imperial rule, and transformed the country from a feudal state into a modern one. Though these upheavals caused some social and economic dislocation and a certain eagerness to emigrate—particularly in rural areas, where the government's program of forced conscription into the armed services was extremely unpopular—much of the outflow was actually a product of Japan's longstanding patterns of internal migration, combined with the new government's conscious decision (indeed, its determination) to begin looking outward and become involved with the rest of the world. In 1866, the government of Japan opened its doors and allowed citizens to emigrate to America—though at first, students were the only citizens allowed to move abroad, mainly for the purpose of learning how to build "big ships" and make "big guns." But in 1884—two years after the United States excluded the Chinese—common laborers became eligible to leave, thanks largely to the pleadings of the Hawaiian immigration board, which was desperate for workers in its sugar fields.

These immigrants, nearly all of them male, were in the centuries-old tradition of the Japanese *dekaseginin*—that is, workers who left home for work. And following the same patterns of migration that had been established in Japan over those centuries, the first wave of them was primarily comprised of *mizunomi*, landless people and tenants who migrated more frequently and readily than the landowners, or *honbyakusho*. The family ties of the *mizunomi* were also less stable, lending often to a lifestyle of frequent migrations from village to village.[11]

Thus it was a collection of rather footloose wanderers who first came from Japan to America's shores in successive emigrations after 1884, when the Japanese government finally opened the door for laborers to emigrate. The vast majority of these first immigrants were drawn to Hawaii and its burgeoning sugar industry during the 1890s; and by the turn of the century many more of them were taking up residence in the coastal United States, particularly in the Northwest, where railroad, timber, and fishing jobs were abundant.

Most of these early Japanese immigrants—who, like the Chinese, were excluded by the 1790 Immigration Act from becoming naturalized citizens—came to the United States fully intending to return home to Japan eventually, hoping in the interim to make their fortunes. And they came in substantial numbers; from a total population of 148 Japanese in the United States in 1880 (most of them students), their numbers climbed to 2,039 in 1890 and then soared to 24,326 by 1900. However, it is worth noting that these numbers were minuscule compared to immigration from Northern Europe during the same period; in 1900 alone, there were nearly 400,000 such immigrants arriving in America.[12]

The Japanese who came through Hawaii had been recruited to work in the labor-starved sugar cane fields. From there, they leapfrogged to the continental United States, where they found a labor market on the Pacific Coast eager for their services. Still others arrived on North American shores directly from Japan. A network of "boardinghouse keepers" who doubled as labor contractors, ranging along the Pacific Coast, actively recruited young Japanese men to come to America for work; upon arrival, the keepers would put the immigrants to work at cut rates, usually in the local farm fields.[13] During the 1890s, a substantial portion of these were in the Pacific Northwest—there were major Nikkei (that is, Japanese-descended) communities in Seattle and Tacoma, both of which featured bustling *Nihonmachi*, or "Jap towns," as they were called by whites; in Seattle, it eventually came to be known as the International District or Chinatown. There were also substantial Japanese communities in mill towns like Port Blakely on Bainbridge Island, and in farming communities like the White River Valley. Many of the Northwest emigrants eventually moved southward to California, swelling the numbers of Japanese arriving there, which soon outpaced their numbers in the Northwest.[14]

As it happened, most of the lasting popular conceptions about the nature of the Japanese immigrants came from workers in this first wave—that is, that they were clannish and disinclined to take up "American ways"; that none of them intended to stay, but rather planned to go back to Japan once they'd hit it rich; and that their unswerving loyalty was to Japan. The reality, however, was that within only a few years of the opening of Japan's doors to outward migration, the picture became more complex as subsequent emigrants began trickling in from rather different segments of the culture. Nonetheless, this initial image became more or less chiseled into whites' conceptions of the Japanese, and it played a significant role in the race-baiting that followed.[15]

Indeed, some of the same voices that had once been heard agitating for Chinese exclusion now raised a cry against the fresh tide of Asian immigration coming from Japan, and from Korea as well. Among the first to sound the alarm against the "Jap menace" was Dennis Kearney, the Irish-immigrant firebrand who had led the Workingman's Party to short-lived third-party successes during the fight for Chinese exclusion but who had since dropped from view. Given a fresh threat to trumpet, Kearney made the most of it, decrying to a San Francisco crowd in 1892 "the foreign Shylocks" behind the latest wave of immigrants. He also raised the specter of sexual paranoia in a fashion that became common in subsequent years, warning that "Japs . . . are being brought here now in countless numbers to demoralize and discourage our labor market and to be educated . . . at our expense. . . . We are paying out money [to allow] fully developed men who know no morals but vice to sit beside our . . . daughters [and] to debauch [and] demoralize them."[16] Kearney's campaign, however, came to naught and he receded to obscurity.

Sentiments like his, though, flourished wherever Japanese immigrants showed their faces. In Washington state, a working force of about 400–500 Japanese laborers had established their presence in the White River Valley south of Seattle, which at the time was dominated by dairy and produce farms. In 1893, the local *White River Journal* published an editorial headlined "STOP THE JAPS," which included this observation:

> It is a common occurrence in these days to see from six to a dozen Japanese leave the trains and, loading themselves like pack horses, strike out for some one of the valley ranches. Though there is little as yet said about them we know that the sight is distasteful to the working men of this region.

The paper's campaign made little impact at first—most of the farmers apparently welcomed the hard-working Nikkei—but a year later it weighed in with another editorial declaring that "The Japs Must Go." According to its account, some 50 people gathered in a room over a local store to discuss what to do about the influx of Japanese workers, the main objection being "the starvation wages which the Japs were willing to work for." The result was that the first anti-Japanese organization in the state was formed, and this time, the campaign had its desired effect. Eventually, a "citizens committee" passed a well-publicized resolution calling on all the valley's white farmers to discharge their Japanese help by May 1, 1894, and apparently most of them complied. Most of the Japanese dispersed to other locales, and the few who remained kept a low profile.[17]

The anti-Japanese sentiments lingered and caught fresh life in 1900, when the presence of the Japanese had become unmistakable. In April of that year, the steamer *Riojun Maru* arrived in Seattle with some 1,000 Japanese men hoping to find work. The Hearst-owned *Post-Intelligencer* reported steadily on the stream of "little brown men," and noted that labor organizations were demanding that federal authorities enforce the exclusion laws—except that there were no such laws for Japanese immigrants.[18]

On April 20, the first large anti-Japanese meeting in the United States occurred when a group of over 100 citizens from the South King County town of Renton gathered to prepare and submit a petition to the county commissioners protesting the presence of Chinese and Japanese laborers on county road and bridge crews. Their efforts were rebuffed when the commission explained that those crews were hired by private contractors who were free to employ whosoever they pleased.[19]

Once stirred to life, the racial animus hovered like a poisonous cloud. Anti-Japanese sentiment wound up playing a role in that year's election in Tacoma, Washington's second-largest city located south of Seattle. Tacoma unionists tried to spur a campaign to urge Congress to exclude all Asians, but backed away when it became clear that such a move might cause the Japanese government to retaliate by cutting off millions of dollars in trade. Still, whites were seen handing out fliers to laborers on their way to the polls, declaring: "FELLOW WORKINGMEN BEWARE! Do you know why 1,500 Japanese are in Tacoma? . . . These Japanese are to take the place of our own white laborers in mills and factories in the event of the election of Louis D. Campbell as mayor of Tacoma, who will provide the necessary protection to the employers to carry such an outrage into effect." The scare tactics failed; Campbell was elected, and Japanese workers continued to arrive.[20]

An incident in Sumner, in rural Pierce County not far from Tacoma, on the eve of the election revealed the violent undercurrent of the agitation. A group of whites, spurred on by local politicians who also were using anti-Japanese rhetoric as an election ploy, marched upon a boardinghouse for Japanese hops pickers "and threatened to kill them if they didn't leave." As the mob fired shots into the house, the unarmed workers fled for their lives; fortunately, no one was killed.[21]

All along the Pacific Coast, rumors were running rampant that the Chinese Exclusion Act, up for renewal in 1902, was going to be undermined or done away with completely by insidious legislative forces from the East Coast. Combined with continuing alarms over the arrival of Japanese, sentiments were ripe for a resurgence in anti-Asian fearmongering. Leaping onto that particular stage with gusto was San Francisco's mayor, James Duval Phelan.

A banker and native son, born in San Francisco in 1861, Phelan was elected mayor in 1896 as a Democrat and his tenure was largely undistinguished. But in 1900, he caught national attention when the city's Board of Health "discovered" an ostensible victim of bubonic plague in the Chinatown district. Phelan declared a quarantine and blamed conditions among the Japanese and Chinese. The "plague scare" was widely reported in the nation's press, and Phelan had to scramble as local businessmen descended on him to protest that the scare was ruining their trade. The mayor quickly backed down and blamed the health board's overzealousness. In fact, the only problem a health board inspector had been able to observe among the Japanese was that he found three Japanese men in a single tub in a local bathhouse; evidently, the inspectors were unaware that this style of washing was common in the men's homeland.[22]

Phelan also was the featured speaker at a mass rally against the Japanese, organized on May 7, 1900, in San Francisco largely by local unions. He sounded a note that would continue to ring for nearly half a century:

> The Japanese are starting the same tide of immigration which we thought we had checked twenty years ago. . . . The Chinese and the Japanese are not bona fide citizens. They are not the stuff of which American citizens can be made. . . . Personally we have nothing against the Japanese, but as they will not assimilate with us and their social life is so different from ours, let them keep at a respectful distance.[23]

Phelan was defeated in the 1902 election, for reasons more to do with labor unrest than with the "plague scare" fiasco, though that was hardly the end of his career. Nor did his nascent campaign against the Japanese go away. In early 1905, the *San Francisco Chronicle*—previously the model of Republican restraint, but in the midst of a fierce newspaper war with William Randolph Hearst's *San Francisco Examiner*—began running a series of shrill articles decrying the growing presence of Japanese in the city's midst. The headlines shrieked:

THE YELLOW PERIL—
HOW JAPANESE CROWD OUT THE WHITE RACE

JAPANESE A MENACE TO AMERICAN WOMEN

BROWN ARTISANS STEAL BRAINS OF WHITES[24]

The campaign continued for months, during which the Asiatic Exclusion League was born in San Francisco, dedicated to repelling all elements of Japanese society from the city's midst. Its statement of principles noted that "no large community of foreigners, so cocky, with such racial, social and religious prejudices, can abide long in this country without serious friction." And the racial animus was plain: "As long as California is white man's country, it will remain one of the grandest and best states in the union, but the moment the Golden State is subjected to an unlimited Asiatic coolie invasion there will be no more California," declared a League newsletter.[25] As one speaker at a League meeting put it: "An eternal law of nature has decreed that the white cannot assimilate the blood of another without corrupting the very springs of civilization."[26]

Anti-Asian animosity came to the fore in the wake of the Great San Francisco Earthquake of 1906. First, James Phelan—placed in charge both of the local Red Cross and several city committees—spearheaded a drive (ultimately unsuccessful) to remove Chinatown, destroyed in the quake, south of the city to Hunters Point.[27] Then in October, the city's school board, acting under pressure from the Asiatic Exclusion League, decided to order all Japanese children—previously intermingled with white children—to begin attending the city's Chinese-only school. When news of this reached Japan, a nation whose pride and military might were riding high in the wake of its victory in the Russo-Japanese war, an uproar ensued. Many sabers were rattled on both sides, with threats of war between the two nations rumored for weeks as a result of the school board's slight.

Finally, President Theodore Roosevelt defused the situation by negotiating what became known as the "Gentlemen's Agreement," completed in March 1907: Roosevelt persuaded the Board of Education to back off and allow Japanese children to continue attending general public schools, while in turn the Japanese government would agree to halt issuing any further passports to its laborers trying to reach America. Thus came to an abrupt end the first great wave of Japanese emigration to America.

There was one exception permitted: Japanese workers already in the United States could send home for their wives. It seemed like a minor and humane concession at the time, but within a few years it became the focus of a fresh wave of racial antipathy.[28]

Just as anti-Chinese sentiment had traveled up the coast to the Pacific Northwest, so did the campaign against the Japanese. And just as it had in California, much of the agitation in the region revolved around a singular, charismatic figure. His name was Miller Freeman.

Freeman was a slender, handsome man of medium height, with angular features and a piercing gaze. He came from true pioneer stock; his mother was killed by an accidental shotgun blast while the family traveled by covered wagon from Ogden, Utah—Freeman's birthplace, in 1875—to Butte, Montana, in 1879. His father, the descendant of a Virginia plantation owner (he and numerous relatives served in the Confederate Army), was a peripatetic publisher who set up shop in the mining town for a few years, and then moved to Yakima, Washington, in 1884, and from there to the Puget Sound town of Anacortes in 1889. Young Miller helped in the shop, learning the mechanics of the trade and developing a newspaperman's sense of writing. The elder Freeman went broke in the Panic of 1893 (a financial crisis in which over 15,000 companies and 500 banks failed, many of them in the West), and in 1897 Miller struck out on his own.

Beginning with only $3 in cash and a bicycle on which he could ride through the countryside to sell subscriptions, Freeman started up a farming newspaper called *The Ranch*. Soon he was branching out, and by 1903 had started up another trade paper called *Pacific Fisherman*, a move that would become the focus of Freeman's affairs for the rest of his life. By 1912 he had a whole parcel of other trade publications to his name: *The Town Crier*, *The Washington Farmer*, *Pacific Motor Boat*, *The Pacific Coast Dairyman*, and *The Oregon Farmer*.[29]

It was from the pages of these papers—particularly *Pacific Fisherman* and *The Town Crier*—that Freeman launched his crusade against the Japanese. It began with a fight over salmon. In 1904, Freeman ran an item in the fishing industry paper detailing Japanese plans to fish the waters off Alaska. Freeman described the events in his memoirs:

> Early the following spring a group of fishermen appeared in my office, headed by Jim Barron, who operated the Thlinket Packing Company at Funter Bay in Southeast Alaska. He then reported that two Japanese schooners were operating in the bay, which of course was American territorial waters. There appeared to be no United States government office in Seattle qualified to act in the matter, so I sat down at my typewriter and drew up a communication addressed to the United States Department of State and the Department of Commerce and had all those present sign the document. I then forwarded it to Washington, D.C. The then President was Rough Rider Theodore Roosevelt, who ordered the cutter "Perry" to Funter Bay, where the schooners were seized and their personnel imprisoned, and later deported. There was no diplomatic note-writing, and no war.[30]

According to Freeman, he then prevailed upon the U.S. Bureau of Fisheries to establish regulations forbidding "aliens ineligible for citizenship"—in other words, all Asians, but specifically the Japanese—from fishing in Alaskan waters, and the states of Washington and Oregon soon followed suit.[31] Freeman apparently believed the incident played a role in inspiring Roosevelt to pursue the "Gentlemen's Agreement" two years later. As he later described it: "I got on the warpath of wholesale immigration of Japanese to the Pacific Coast in 1907, and joined up with others in making such a rumpus about it that Theodore Roosevelt finally took it upon himself to notify Japan that colonization of our Pacific Coast areas would have to be stopped."[32] However, there is nothing in the historical record that would indicate Freeman's advocacy played any role at all in Roosevelt's actions.[33]

There was one central reason why Freeman saw Japanese immigrants as a greater threat than any other: the "Yellow Peril." Like many of his contemporaries, Freeman ardently adopted a conspiracy theory, which posited that the Japanese emperor intended to invade the Pacific Coast, and that he was sending these immigrants to American shores as shock troops to prepare the way for just such a military action, and lay the groundwork for acts of sabotage and espionage when the signal was given. As his counterpart in California, James Phelan, put it in 1907, the Japanese immigrants represented an "enemy within our gates." Freeman frequently cited a 1909 book promoting this theory, Homer Lea's *The Valor of Ignorance*, which detailed the invasion to come and its aftermath.[34]

Freeman saw the rising rivalry over Alaska's salmon fishery as an early salvo in this coming war. He declared in the pages of *Pacific Fisherman:* "If we follow the false doctrines preached by the pro-Japanese press, we will soon be making Japan a present of the Pacific Coast in order to preserve our friendly relations and build up a large American-Japanese commerce for Nippon steamships to handle."[35]

Driven by fears of an invasion, Freeman's career soon moved into a military phase. After reading a 1910 article in *Harper's Weekly* calling for the formation of a Naval Militia in Puget Sound, he sprang into action.[36] Freeman contacted the Secretary of the Navy and offered to spearhead the drive to form just such a body, comprised of ships provided by the navy and a phalanx of yachting volunteers. He organized a meeting at the Seattle Yacht Club and lined up a muster roll and sent their names off to the U.S. Navy. In short order, the state Legislature made the naval militia an official entity, and Freeman was named its commander. The U.S. Navy provided the militia with an aging, modestly seaworthy ship dubbed the *Cheyenne*, and Freeman spent the next several years organizing drills and preparing for the Japanese invasion.[37]

Such an event was nearly inevitable, in Freeman's view. He warned his recruits that they should enter the naval militia fully expecting to see battle action. "I want to warn you all that a conflict of arms with Japan is highly probable," he told the *Seattle Times*, adding: "The safety of the nation is in the people and the people must be aroused to action if our coast is to be saved from devastation by a foreign enemy."[38]

Freeman sturdily denied that his campaign was driven by racial animus, saying that he "harbors no enmity toward the Japanese. They are a wonderfully bright people, frugal and industrious. But they are Orientals. We are Caucasians. Oil and water do not mix."[39]

Kanju Matsuoka had no notions regarding any plans by the Emperor to invade the United States. He simply wanted to work—so badly that he was even willing to marry a cousin.

A farmboy from the village of Ishikawa in the Kumamoto region of the southern Japanese island of Kyushu, Matsuoka was drafted into the Japanese Army in 1898 and promptly shipped off to join the Japanese forces that had just taken Taiwan from China. But drilling in the hot sun, he suffered a sunstroke and was given an honorable discharge.

"So my dad was really disappointed," recounted Tom Matsuoka, "and he come home. And that's why it happened to be he thought about moving to Hawaii. Because in Hawaii, the sugar company, they were recruiting for the labor in Japan, you know. Well, my dad went to the recruiting place. They said, 'No, no more, no more, that's all filled up. If you were married and a family, maybe you'd have a chance to go.'

"Well, he come home and—'How am I gonna do it, get married? I have to find a woman!' So I guess the whole family talked: 'If you want to go to Hawaii that much, why, the only that is left is his cousin,' my mother, you know. That was the way they get married. They went to the consul to Hawaii because, if married people, why, they could come to Hawaii." It was an unusual arrangement, but not unheard of.

The couple arrived in Spreckelsville, Maui, in 1902, and Kanju went to work for Sam Damon's sugar cane operation there. That didn't last long; after a few months, Kanju rented a small farm and began growing vegetables. The young couple loved their life on American soil and planned to remain. So when, on August 1, 1903, Tori Matsuoka gave birth to her only child, they gave the bright-eyed little boy a twinned name, indicating his dual American and Japanese citizenship: Tom Takeo Matsuoka.

However, their happiness was short-lived. "My mother got sick in Hawaii," Tom Matsuoka said. "In those days, you couldn't find a good doctor. She got pleurisy. Nowadays, there's nothing to it; nowadays, they just open up your back and pump it right out. But in those days, nobody knows such a thing. So they figured out that maybe in Japan, there was more chance to take care of it. That's why mother took me, and we went back to Japan."

They returned to Ishikawa in 1905, where despite being back in familial surroundings, Tori Matsuoka's pleurisy worsened. She died in September 1906, and Tom remained at the farm to be raised by his grandfather.

Kanju Matsuoka had not remained in Hawaii when his wife and son returned to Japan. Enticed by the promise of dollar-a-day wages, he gave up the little vegetable farm in Maui and signed on with recruiters from the Great Northern Railroad, who were seeking laborers for crews to build a new line between Seattle and Chicago. He arrived in Seattle in late 1905 fully expecting to head out to the inland West somewhere on the rail crews, but thanks to his laconic personality, it didn't work out that way.

The railroad, Tom Matsuoka said, had arranged for rail cars to meet the laborers at the docks, at which time they would be sorted out and boarded directly onto a train that would take them to their eventual destinations. "And some people they really rush, rush, rush going to the train. And my dad [says], 'Oh well, long as we came here, you don't have to rush. They pick up.' He said he was very much [one] of the last bunch to get on the train. Well, then the train, they start, and pretty soon just stop and they cut [the last] car off [at a designated work station] and then the train [would] go on. Well, that's how it is. That's why the guys [who] get on the train late, they don't go too far."

While his rail-crew work station would be at Green Lake, just to the north of Seattle, those who had rushed to be first aboard the train wound up in remote and often inhospitable locales like the Hi Line of Montana. Tom laughingly recalled his father's own perspective: "'That time I was pretty smart to get on the last so I didn't have to go to Montana!'"[40]

Matsuoka was just one of the thousands of Japanese immigrants who began pouring into the Pacific Northwest in the late 1890s, drawn in particular by the railroad work. Employed as section hands and engine watchmen, their pay was meager, ranging from 85 cents to $1.50 per day. Many of the rail workers got along by cutting back on food expenses, with a regular diet consisting of thin soup, rice, and a faux soy sauce (made by burning flour and mixing it with water, sugar, and salt).[41]

If they weren't working on the railroad, there were plenty of jobs to be found at sawmills, logging camps, and canneries. By the time the Gentlemen's Agreement took effect, there were some 3,000 Japanese workers in sawmills in the Puget Sound region (notably at the huge Port Blakely mill on Bainbridge Island), and a couple thousand more employed at canneries, where they took the place of the now-excluded Chinese work force on which the industry had previously relied. Many took up farming, often beginning as day laborers and then moving up gradually, renting out small tracts and growing vegetables and fruits.[42] The largest of these communities by far took root in the White River Valley, where a tiny contingent of remaining Japanese laborers had succeeded eventually in obtaining their own little fruit and vegetable farms, and this in time provided the footing for a substantial population, many of whom eventually moved into dairy farming.[43]

It was during this period that the nature of Japanese immigration began to change substantially. Whereas the footloose *mizunomi* immigrants were wedded to a transient lifestyle and likely had hopes of making their fortunes and returning home, the landed *honbyakusho* came from much more stable backgrounds and were more open to the possibility that a move to America might be permanent. This, after all, was in keeping with the internal migration pattern within Japan that had been in place for centuries, particularly during the Tokugawa Period (1600–1868). Within the tradition of the *dekaseginin*, the first to occupy new niches and markets in labor or manufacture typically were *mizunomi*, followed in turn by *honbyakusho*, who were more inclined to view their new homes as permanent. (Such a pattern indeed had transformed Tokyo from a sleepy fishing village into a major metropolis during the Tokugawa period.)

Just as the lack of economic or familial center encouraged the *mizunomi* to migrate, so ironically did the powerful core traditions of family, or *ie*, encourage migrations among the *honbyakusho*. The successor to the family name, household, property and fortune was by tradition the eldest son in the *ie*, which meant that any younger sons who desired either independence or material wealth had to leave home and establish themselves elsewhere. These latter migrations did not happen by whim, but instead were the products of interfamilial networks; the carefully cultivated contacts of the *ie* would usually find a position for the would-be *dekasegi* and place him securely before he ever left home. This also meant that the resulting chain migrations usually involved very specific locales; many of the emigrants to a new market would often come from one or two regions where the first migrations occurred.

This pattern continued when the emigrants' horizons expanded to include the United States. When the Hawaiian government negotiated the first agreement with Japan to allow emigration to its sugar cane labor market, its special agent, Robert W. Irwin, was directed by former Japanese business associates to the rural southwestern Yamaguchi, Kumamoto, and Hiroshima prefectures, or *ken*, because people of those *ken* were "not timid or afraid to go to faraway places" and were "sound and law abiding." Because of the chain migrations that resulted from these initial contacts, over the ensuing 40 years of Japanese emigration to America, the vast majority would come from these three largely rural *ken*.[44]

Out of these patterns emerged a second class of émigré, officially recognized by the Japanese government in 1896 as *imin*, or immigrant, implying greater permanence and distinguished from the previous designation of *dekaseginin*, or traveling workers. In the cities, these tended to become shopowners and bankers; in the mill towns and rural areas, they generally established themselves as homeowners and farmers with their own economic sub-communities.

Kanju Matsuoka was almost perfectly representative of the *imin:* a younger son from a respected landholding *ie* in Kumamoto; a *honbyakusho* eager to strike out on his own, placed in Hawaii through familial contacts; and finally, recruited out of those fields to the United States by railroad crew bosses. Though at times he considered returning home, Matsuoka's goal was to earn enough to set himself up on a farm and settle down. According to Tom, he had come to view the United States as his new home, even if it meant a few years leading a transient lifestyle.

Matsuoka spent a year on the rail crew at Green Lake, and received word of Tori's death the next fall. He couldn't afford to return for her funeral. Distraught and apparently feeling adrift, he quit the railroad and went from job to job at the local sawmills, living in poor conditions so he could save up for his long-term goals.

"He had a rough time when my mother was dead," Tom recalled. "So I guess Dad was thinking about going back to Japan. Well, then they said that if you farm, you make a fortune. So he started farming on Vashon Island. They said they cleared up the field in Vashon and started strawberries. Then, they had pretty good money. That's how dad started. I think he rented five acres and cleaned up the land and started strawberries."

This line of work wasn't immediately profitable. "Second year, a little bit you get crop," said Tom. "And third year, finally you start [getting a] very good crop."

It was also harder than he expected. "Well, he started, and he found out that [for] just a bachelor, [it was] pretty hard farming, because in the morning and nighttime, you have to cook and wash the dishes. So this way, he thought that maybe it [was] impossible to stay on the farm. He wanted company. So he wrote to Japan, and wanted a wife. Would they send a wife?

"Well, in the meantime, they had a few Japanese missus[es] over in this country already. And one missus going back, she [was] pretty close to our old place in Japan. So I guess that she told him, my dad, 'Oh, I'm going to find somebody.' That's why it was that she found her." Her name was Tatsuno Tatayama, and she too hailed from Kumamoto.

Like nearly all Japanese marriages, it was arranged by the friendly go-between—and according to Japanese law and custom, this was a legal marriage even before they had met. So when his new wife arrived on Vashon Island in 1910, the only idea of what the other looked like came from the photographs they exchanged: "Well, they didn't know each other," Tom said. "It's called a picture bride."

Kanju Matsuoka's arranged marriage was, once again, representative of a larger trend in Japanese immigration—one bound to raise white hackles along the coast. Under the conditions of the Gentlemen's Agreement, Japanese laborers already in America in 1907 could send for their wives back in the homeland. However, the vast majority of Japanese laborers were single men. Spurned by whites as "unassimilable" and thus unacceptable marriage partners, they usually chose to resort to the "picture bride" method of marriage by proxy, perfectly legal under Japanese law. But the steady stream of these women arriving on American shores—and, moreover, producing equally "unassimilable" Japanese children with the citizenship rights given to anyone born on United States soil—would come to be seen by those who had pushed for Japanese exclusion as yet another instance of Oriental cunning and betrayal.

For Kanju Matsuoka, however, the arrival of his new wife was too little, too late. A severe economic downturn in 1910 put him out of business as a strawberry farmer; he was forced to move off Vashon Island and take a job at a sawmill in a small town near the base of Mount Rainier called Barneston.

"In 1910, they had a real farmers' depression," says Tom Matsuoka. "My wife's mother used to tell me they had the same thing in Bellevue. The strawberries, you can't sell. But if you take the vine and stamp it down, the plant will get weaker, and maybe there'll be less crop next year [to reduce harvest costs]. She used to tell me she'd put the gunny sacks on her shoes, and she'd have to smash the strawberries.

"My dad, he was broke. Yeah. They couldn't stay. They just had to throw everything away, and he went back to the sawmill."

Directly east across Lake Washington from Seattle another rural community was proving hospitable to Japanese immigrants. Locals called the village Bellevue.

Before the arrival of white men, the lands along the eastern shore of Lake Washington were a dense forest of primeval old-growth wilderness—so dense that they were largely uninhabited even by Native Americans who dwelt in the Puget Sound region. A village called Satskal built by the Duwamish tribe was located at what was then the inner reaches of Mercer Slough, and a pair of Duwamish longhouses once occupied a spot on Yarrow Bay, but the tribe's main population lived on the lake's southern reaches, in modern-day Renton.[45]

The first white dwellings mostly belonged to speculators from Seattle looking for cheap land that might turn a profit. William Meydenbauer and Aaron Mercer both staked out land and built log cabins in the area that would become Bellevue in 1869. Meydenbauer's homestead was at the mouth of the bay in the lake that bears his name today, while Mercer's crude dwelling was set up on the western side of the slough named after him. Both moved away within a few years' time, and for the next decade or so only a handful of trappers and loggers were the land's occupants. Permanent settlers arrived in 1879, and a community began building in earnest in 1882. Most of the homesteaders made their living logging—taking the trees first from their own lands, then moving on to other lands. Logs were plentiful and they sold cheap, so the loggers had to work long days to make a decent living.[46]

One of those first settlers was Isaac Bechtel, who in 1889 also became one of the first fatalities on the Eastside. Beatrice Mathewson of Renton, his granddaughter, was told the story as a young girl: "My grandfather came here in about 1882. He came from Canada. And he was here for awhile before he sent for the rest of the family, then my grandmother came. She had five children at that time.

"He was killed in an accident where he was working. There was a logjam, they were I think shooting them down to the lake, and he got up on top to separate them, the logs split up and he fell in and they crushed him. And the oldest [child] was about 16 at the time, I think." Bechtel's widow, Isabel, remained in the little home overlooking Meydenbauer Bay, running the post office her husband had established there in 1886.[47]

One telling has it that she christened the town when two visiting postal inspectors insisted on giving the post office a name, and selected Bellevue because of the lovely view from her home. However, it is more likely that the name was first given to the nearby school, built in 1883, by the man who donated the school's windows, after the town of the same name in Ohio.[48]

The family remained in the home for as long as it could. Bea Mathewson's mother, Barbara Bechtel, not only was born in the little cabin overlooking the lake, but it was there that she gave birth to her first son, Russell. Barbara Bechtel had married a Medina boy named Robert Whaley in 1907, and they moved a little southward in 1909 to the lakeside village called Beaux Arts, which sprang up as an artists' colony overlooking the passage between the mainland and Mercer Island. A carpenter by trade, Whaley built many of the homes in the village.

"They had four children when they moved there," recalled Bea Mathewson. "And the first house burned down, and the oldest daughter died as a result of that fire. This was about 1913. Don't know why the house burned—I mean, it was middle of the night, and the bedroom was upstairs. Everybody jumped out of the window or off the steps or balconies, or something, except this one girl, she wouldn't jump, so she was—my brother told me when she came out, she was like a pillar of fire. So she did finally jump, and she only lived a week afterwards."

The Whaleys built a new home in Beaux Arts and stayed there until 1919; Beatrice was born in 1915. Isabel Bechtel, the family matriarch, eventually lost the old home on the lake: "It was not a homestead," explained Bea Mathewson. "He [Isaac Bechtel] bought it, like 25 cents an acre. She didn't pay the interest on the loan or anything and eventually lost it all. . . . It was just one of those things, you know."

Because Bellevue was directly opposite Seattle across the middle of Lake Washington, it remained a relatively isolated community, inaccessible except by long routes around the northern or southern ends of the lake. The largest town on the Eastside by far was Issaquah, which had sprung up in the 1880s as a logging and mining community; it was situated on the main highway that took Seattle travelers east and west over the Cascade Mountains. To the north, the town of Kirkland—envisioned and built in 1888 as a booming steel center that never came to be—was home to several hundred residents. A little farther east, some 300 people made up the farming and logging town of Redmond. Bellevue was mostly known as the dock site for the ferry that brought picnickers from Leschi Park in Seattle to the park at Peterson's Landing in Meydenbauer Bay.[49]

Populated at first solely by whites, the village progressively grew. To support the sawmills that sprang up to handle the steady supply of timber the settlers produced, a grocery store, a blacksmith shop, and other signs of an established community began to appear. The Northern Pacific Railroad, running north to south and passing next to the small inland body dubbed Lake Sturtevant, was finished in 1904. And with the railroad came faces of different color—Japanese faces.

The first rail line into the Bellevue area was built in 1900, running north from the Newport area up to Wilburton, where a sawmill had been built. But it was built on spongy ground and had to be relocated farther inland. By the time Northern Pacific was done in 1904, the line ran all the way through to the north end of the lake. Several Japanese men were employed on these crews, notably a fellow named Yoshiya Kubota, who worked as a crew foreman and a timekeeper for the crews. Haruji Takeshita followed shortly, arriving in 1901 to take a timekeeper's position. Numerous Japanese laborers—most of them transient—came and went with the crews.[50]

The sawmills also attracted more Japanese laborers. Like other Asians of the time, the Japanese were segregated from the Caucasian population. Logging camp maps from the Eastside (and other areas as well) are dotted with little squares denoted as "Jap house"; these were often ramshackle huts that squeezed as many Japanese workers into them as the square footage might allow. The Japanese spoke little English, and had little opportunity to learn it; then again, if they were capable of cutting down trees, no one cared very much. Most of these workers moved on when the sawmills—finished with cutting through the rich timber supplies on the Eastside—closed shop and moved on. Those mills that remained were forced out of business in 1916, when their access to Lake Washington was cut off after the opening of the Seattle Ship Canal lowered the lake some seven feet.[51]

Another early Japanese arrival was Jusaburo Fujii, who beginning in 1898 worked as a cook for the owner of an Alaskan cannery business. This businessman also owned several acres of land in the Clyde Hill area that he had cultivated with strawberries. Fujii was placed in charge of the strawberry operation, and he organized crews of Japanese laborers to come from Seattle and help work the fields. Some of them wound up remaining in Bellevue and trying their own luck at berry farming.[52]

This, however, was easier said than done. In the wake of the sawmills, most of the open land in Bellevue comprised vast tracts of stumps. These weren't ordinary stumps, either, but the Northwest old-growth variety—large, stubborn, and deeply rooted. Clearing the land for other uses, like farming and pasture, was a formidable task. So those who owned the land hired laborers from the Japanese logging crews, and from the immigrant Japanese communities in Seattle, to do the work. The Japanese mostly were too poor to buy land themselves, but needed land to ply the trade they knew: farming. So they agreed to clear the land, and in exchange would receive the right to cultivate it for a given length of time, usually five years.

Though there were Caucasians who cleared the land in Bellevue as well, the evidence indicates that the bulk of the land-clearing was provided by Japanese labor. Besides those tracts that they occupied in later years, early records indicate Japanese families leasing the land on clear-and-farm agreements, according to Asaichi Tsushima, whose privately published book written in 1952 recounts the struggles of the early Japanese pioneers.[53] Other histories note that nearly all of the area of Medina called Downey Hill, or Vuecrest, was cleared by Japanese laborers.[54] Land clearing, because of its difficulty and dangerousness—as well as the often meager returns on the labor—was not a popular occupation among Caucasians; a 1919 editorial in the *Seattle Star* complained that too much of Washington's potential farmland was lying fallow because the white landowners lacked the wherewithal to clear its stumps and make it arable.[55] This was not, however, the case in Bellevue, where industrious Japanese farmers had carved out a niche for themselves.

Most of the Nikkei came to Bellevue not so much through Seattle but rather from the White River Valley, where a farming community had established itself early on and was thriving by 1900. As the supply of available farmland dwindled there, more would-be farmers began looking elsewhere. Little communities of strawberry farmers began springing up, including on Vashon and Bainbridge islands, the latter of which already had a flourishing Nikkei community associated with the massive Port Blakely timber mill. Likewise, the fallow lands surrounding Bellevue proved a good place for a farmer to start out. Over the ensuing years, the resulting Nikkei community on the Eastside would continue to have stronger ties to the White River Valley—which was much closer anyway, in terms of travel on the existing roadways—than it would to Seattle's *Nihonmachi*, and in many ways was seen mainly as an extension of its larger neighbor to the south.

Of course, every community is constituted of individuals with their own stories to tell. The stories of the Bellevue Nikkei were in most ways perfectly typical of Japanese American farming communities along the entire Pacific Coast. Some labored only a year or two before giving up. Others stayed and raised families.

TATSUNOSUKE HIROTAKA was a big, strong man who took a job clearing 10 acres of land in Bellevue in 1902. Shortly after his arrival, he sent for his wife, Chiyono, to join him from their family home in Hiroshima; she became one of the first Japanese women to live in Bellevue. They left their first son behind to be raised with family in Hiroshima. Their first daughter, Kazue, was born in 1907, the first second-generation Japanese—or Nisei—child born on the Eastside; Tokio, their second son, was born in 1910. In all, they had two sons and three daughters.

The family did not stay put for many years. After Tatsunosuke's six-year lease on the first farm expired, they moved on to the Clyde Hill area, which attracted a number of Japanese because of the wealth of stumplands ripe for clearing and ultimately cultivation. Tats Hirotaka cleared ten-acre sites in Clyde Hill and in Conway Place, moving the family with him each time. Finally, by saving pennies, he was able to afford to buy a piece of land in 1918, and settled his family in the Midlakes area, where they remained for more than half a century.

HIKOTARA ARAMAKI arrived in 1904, from Kumamoto via Seattle. "He was young and raring to go," recalled his son, Akira. "And Japan was poor, and there was no hope. So they all hear about this United States. He came, he and another fellow who lived in Woodinville, they came from the southern part of Japan, and they left Yokohama.

"They landed in Vancouver, B.C. They walked to Seattle [a distance of 150 miles], hiding in the daytime in the brush, and walking at night, in December. It rained every day. They were tough."

Aramaki found farming and land-clearing work to his liking, and settled into a spot owned by another Japanese man in the Clyde Hill area. Like other Japanese bachelors, he finally tired of the single life, and arranged to be married to a "picture bride" through a traditional Japanese go-between; she arrived in Bellevue in 1910. They moved twice before settling on a farm in the Midlakes area that, like Tats Hirotaka, he purchased in 1918. His first son, Akira, was born in 1913; in all, they had four daughters and two sons.

TOKUO NUMOTO came to Bellevue to work as a gardener for a local white landowner in 1904. A year later, he leased a strawberry farm from another landowner in the Clyde Hill area and soon began clearing land for farming on the side. Like other farmers, he experimented with crops, and found wintertime holly tree cultivation to be especially lucrative, since it gave him something to market in normally quiet months. He formed a partnership with Edward Tremper in the Yarrow Point area, where he ran a combination strawberry and holly tree farm.

Numoto purchased a tract of land in Yarrow Point in 1909 that he promptly turned over to his younger brother, Tsuruichi, who had joined him from Japan with his wife. Tsuruichi Numoto turned the farm into a modest success with steady crops of lettuce, celery, and cabbage, which he sold by making a weekly 30-mile trek to the Pike Place Market in downtown Seattle. His son Cano was born in 1910.

ITARO ITO, according to people who knew him, was one of the town's characters; he had a ready smile, a cheerful disposition, and "he liked to help everybody," according to his daughter Sumi. He arrived in Bellevue in 1905 and cleared five acres due north of the Bellevue townsite. His wife, Shimeno, arrived in 1910. They raised a family of four daughters and three sons there and at farms in the Downey Hill and Highland areas.

"Our family was not a rich family," recalled Tosh Ito, their third son. "So we always borrowed money on the basis of paying it back at crop time, at harvest time. That was more or less the ritual from year to year. You borrowed it in the winter, and you paid back when you sold your crops. Very hand-to-mouth, and sometimes it was just the hand."

Since Itaro was the eldest son in his family, he was held responsible, under Japanese tradition, for the well-being of his parents back home in Fukuoka. When his father died in 1918, he sent back his two oldest daughters to tend to their elderly grandmother, and they remained in Fukuoka thereafter. Sumi, their third daughter, was born in 1920; Tosh was born in 1922. Chiye, the fourth daughter and youngest child, was born in 1923.

RYUTAN KURITA'S first job in Bellevue was as a houseboy for a white landowner, where he worked from his arrival from Shiga in 1906 until 1909, when he began cultivating a five-acre strawberry tract on the edge of Bellevue that he purchased, making him one of the first Japanese landowners in the town. His wife joined him that year. He enjoyed some prosperity, so in

Figure 1.2. Strawberry harvest entailed a combination of family and hired labor. The Numoto family, harvesting at its second farm in 1925, included Yoshi Numoto, kneeling at far left; Frank Yabuki, third from left; Cano Numoto, third from right; and Tsuruichi Numoto, second from right. The remainder were day laborers hired from Seattle. Courtesy of the Eastside Heritage Center/Cano Numoto Collection.

1911 he purchased a larger plot a little farther north along the highway to Kirkland at Northeast 10th Street. He became a leader in the Japanese community and was a president of the Farmer's Association. In 1915, though, he encountered some rough waters, and sold the title to his old Bellevue tract to a farming company. In the process he became a mortgagee—a move that would have fateful consequences.

ASAICHI TSUSHIMA arrived at age 20 in Bellevue in 1908 with no work and no money in his pocket. He lived with another Japanese man in a barn on the farm managed by Gumpei Hirayama, where they worked as laborers in the strawberry fields. When an oversupply of strawberries in 1909–10 resulted in a financial disaster for Eastside farmers, Hirayama gave up the business and moved to Seattle.

Tsushima picked up stakes and went to work in an apple orchard, as well as doing gardening work for his white neighbors, all the while living in a tent in the Clyde Hill area. He, too, arranged for a wife through a go-between in his hometown of Okayama. When Nami Tsushima arrived in 1912, however, it became immediately clear that the arrangement wasn't for the best. He was smaller and not as handsome as the man in the picture, and she likewise was, in his view, less attractive than she had been described. Worse, in his opinion, was that she was even less ladylike.

"She was very independent, very feisty," recalled their daughter, Michi Nishimura. "She used to smoke, which was very unusual for Issei women. She and my dad were never very . . . they weren't a loving couple. And so she went her way and he went his."

It was a loveless marriage, and Michi, their only child, was adopted at birth from a family friend. "And I think Papa was disappointed that I was not a boy. My natural mother was a good friend from back in Japan who now lived in Bellevue, and she had two children already and couldn't afford any more. So when she was pregnant with me, they made arrangements that they would pay for whatever expenses she had, and I would be given to them whether I was a girl or a boy. Papa, I'm sure, would have preferred a boy. He was that way; a traditional Japanese."

Nami wound up getting work as a house servant to some of the wealthy families that owned waterfront property on Hunts Point. "She would go out and stay there with them," said Michi. "Later she got a job on a farm, and she just stayed out there and worked."

Asaichi leased a small tract on Hunts Point in 1917. "We had a very small farm. We used to raise vegetables, and people would call, and order something, and then we'd get it ready, and they would come pick it up. Or sometimes I would walk down to Hunts Point and deliver the vegetables to them. Every once in awhile I'd have to go around, I remember, and take them their bills.

"Our operation wasn't big enough for other helpers other than a couple of Filipino men who were crew. We had a little shed where they lived. A lot of people had tractors, or horses, and trucks. We never did. We had electricity, but no bathroom. Running water, but an outhouse.

"My family, we were never a very open family. We never really talked to each other like kids nowadays do. Even more so than other Japanese. We were more reserved, and we weren't open with each other."

Asaichi Tsushima still kept a high profile in the community. He organized the community's Japanese-language school and taught Japanese to the local youngsters for several years. And he tried to help organize the Japanese farmers. He also kept a record of his Japanese neighbors, and years later put it together into a small book that lists more than 200 Japanese men and their families who came to Bellevue.

HICHIRO MATSUZAWA first arrived on the Eastside in 1906, leaving a wife and son behind in Japan to try making his fortune. He worked on a dairy farm some 20 miles east of Bellevue in Snoqualmie, where his first bout of real misfortune struck.

"While he was working in the dairy," recalled his son, Joe, "why, he was feeding a bull in a bullpen. And the bull got him down—he was kind of a mean animal—and he got him down and crushed his chest, broke some ribs. And I guess punctured his lung. But he finally got ahold of the ring in the bull's nose and got out.

"But from then on, that was the beginning of his health [problems] . . . the rest of his life. So anyway, he suffered for a couple of years and he decided he'd go back to Japan, and see if he could get better medical attention.

"In the meantime, why, my mother had come over to be with him, but he had already scheduled to go back, so she stayed here. . . . And you can imagine what it was like for her, because . . . it was a social shock to anybody to come over, didn't know the language, didn't know the customs, didn't know anything."[56]

Hichiro came back in 1909, and found work as a gardener for a white family in the Clyde Hill area. He and his wife raised a family of four sons and two daughters, moving from farm to farm in Clyde Hill, and finally settling onto a tract in the Wilburton area, southeast of the Bellevue townsite. But he never fully recovered from the goring, and Joe recalled that he was always sickly.

ENJI TAMAYE ran away from his home in Fukuoka at the age of 14 in 1904 and came to America. He spent his early years wandering the West, from California to Colorado, and eventually worked his way up to Seattle. There he met another Fukuoka native, Kikumatsu Fujikawa, who found work for the two of them at a sawmill in Bellevue.

In 1912, the pair decided to get out of the mills and into farming. They leased a tract in the Highland area of Bellevue, cleared five acres, and began growing vegetables and strawberries. By 1916, Tamaye was ready to strike out on his own; he leased a section of land among other Japanese farmers in the Peterson Hill area and farmed it. Realizing quickly that he couldn't make it on his own, he set about to obtain a "picture bride."

"My father, when he was 28 years old, called back to Japan, they had a young lady that they wanted him to marry," recalled Chizuko Norton, his second daughter. "So he went back and married my mother. And they came back here, and he brought her back here." She arrived in 1918, and they had a small family by Japanese standards: a daughter born in 1920, followed by Chizuko in 1924. They set about growing strawberries.

"The soil was terrible," said Norton. "I remember our parents breaking up these lumps of clay, clay soil I should say. I remember that very vividly."[57]

TOGORO SUGURO found work in 1913 on a Bellevue strawberry farm. He was already familiar with the area, since his first work in the United States upon his arrival from Shizuoka had been at a Redmond poultry ranch. He had since learned how to farm during a six-year stint on Vashon Island. His son, Frank, joined him from Shizuoka in 1915, and they together cleared and farmed a tract in the Midlakes area.

Eventually, they were joined by eight to nine other Japanese families, and the Midlakes area became the heart of Bellevue's Japanese community. Frank and his wife had four daughters and two sons; the youngest boy, Ed, was born in 1935.

HARUJI TAKESHITA, who had worked as a timekeeper on the early rail crews, returned to Japan for his wife, Kuma, and they both came back to Bellevue in 1915. "There were opportunities out here," said their oldest daughter, Mitsuko. "They were clearing land, they cleared the farmlands for everybody. And that's what all those young men were doing. They had all kinds of energy. They were all in their twenties, too."

Thinking, like many immigrants, that they would return to their homeland in a few years, the couple left two daughters behind in Japan to be raised by relatives. And while Haruji Takeshita already had experience clearing the land, for Kuma the job of land-clearing was more than she had expected.

"So then she came," recalled Mitsuko, "and she says, 'Look what you have to do.' She says it was hard, really hard. She says, 'You know, I would have never came if I knew this job was this hard.' She said her legs were swollen like that.

"Of course, the women had to go out there too and log all those trees and everything. But they cleared a plot that was five acres up there at 108th and Main Street. All those Japanese areas up there got cleared."

By 1919, the Takeshitas had saved up enough money to buy a small, 13-acre plot of land in the Midlakes area. Placing the title to the land in the hands of a Japanese American lawyer they knew in Seattle, they set about making a living from "truck farming"—intensively cultivating small plots of land with a variety of vegetables and then transporting them to local markets by truck. In 1921, Mitsuko—the oldest of what would eventually be four American children—was born. Their first two daughters remained in Japan for the rest of their lives.

GONZABURO MUROMOTO emigrated to the United States in 1908, but traveled around the West—to San Francisco, Pasadena, Salt Lake City, Denver and Seattle before finally settling in Bellevue in 1917, clearing land with Asaichi Tsushima and his lifelong friend, Naosaburo Mizokawa, in Fairweather Bay, between Hunts Point and Evergreen Point.

The Muromoto and Mizokawa families became virtual partners, and together farmed several strawberry tracts in the Clyde Hill area. The Muromotos had a daughter and two sons to help, while the Mizokawas had a daughter and son. Kim, the youngest of the Muromotos' sons, was born in 1923.

KAMEJI YABUKI had a different plan than most of his Japanese neighbors when he arrived in 1918. While the strawberry farmers often fell into dire straits during the winter because of a lack of income, Yabuki turned to a greenhouse operation in Kirkland, which he operated with moderate success.

"My father came over, like most of them originally, to the land of opportunity," recalled Rose Matsushita, Kameji's daughter. "To make some money and return to Japan. My father was the second oldest in his family; at the age of 17, I believe, he came to America. His father was an alcoholic, and he racked up a lot of debt. So my dad originally came to earn enough to pay off his father's debt.

"As the years went by, they were paid so little for what they did it took years to pay off his debt. And his brother wanted to come, so he helped him over, helped him establish his own greenhouse."

Kameji's brother, Terumatsu, joined him on the Eastside that same year and set up operations at a greenhouse in the Yarrow Point area. They grew vegetables and flowers year-round and operated an adjacent tract of land as a farm in the summer. Terumatsu and his wife, Hide, raised three sons and a daughter there. Alan Yabuki, his second son, was born in 1921, and the third son, Kiyo, in 1923.

EITARO SHIRAISHI came to the Seattle area to arrange a funeral for his brother, who died in an accident there in 1907. He took a liking to the area and stayed, operating a fruit market in downtown Seattle; his wife joined him there from Kumamoto.

"They got married and found out that there were very many disappointments," recalled their daughter, Mitsi. "It was arranged, and sure, they went through with the marriage, but actually, they didn't know each other. Marrying for love, well, I think the second generation were able to get married for love. And a lot of the (first-generation) Issei weren't; a lot of them were arranged."

Mitsi was born in 1912 in Seattle. But in 1916, Eitaro Shiraishi tired of the mercantile business, and went to work on a farm in the Newport area, where he helped clear land and cultivate peas and strawberries. His family continued to live in the Bryn Mawr area of Seattle until 1921, when the family moved to a farm he had helped clear. The family found it impossible to get ahead, however, and remained leaseholders on their 15-acre tract.

"They waited for us to get our summer vacation from school, so they would have the extra hand," recalled Mitsi. "It was work like tying tomatoes, picking strawberries, putting weevil bait on. It was minor work, but they were happy to get the help.

"My mother had to go out and do more work on the farm than my father. In the summertime, he had a little truck, and he would load it up with his tomatoes or strawberries, and then he would go down to Renton, the grocery stores, about three times a week to sell them. So while he was out in the truck, my mother would have to work the crops. We were all poor in those days. We were really poor."

Collectively, these and dozens of other Japanese families formed a tightly knit community that still, in many ways, adhered to traditional Japanese mores, even as it attempted to adapt to the unique challenges presented by living in America, where their services were welcome but they were despised and discriminated against merely on account of their race. They spoke Japanese among themselves, but encouraged their children to speak English. They often worshipped as they had in their homeland, but many others were fully Christianized converts. They formed Japanese businessmen's associations that emphasized their ethnic identity, but openly embraced American-style capitalism.

In Bellevue, their presence had a singular and widely desired effect: it transformed the landscape from a vast tract of stumplands into a genteel farming community.

"We cleared the land," Tom Matsuoka explained. What is now downtown Bellevue, he said, "that's just about all what I think Japanese people have cleared. If people now, if they think about it, they'd say, that's the craziest thing: But in an acre, there'd be twenty, thirty big stumps, left from when they'd cut the logs. A lot of people were using dynamite. Nowadays, you know when it goes out, but in those days, you had to be on the lookout.

"Then you'd dig the roots out, and cut them with the ax. Then you get the horse to pull. Boy, that's a lot of hard work."

Though most immigrants harbored hopes of making their fortunes as farmers in America—some intending eventually to return to Japan—most found that life in the States was a hardscrabble existence, living hand to mouth, working from sunup to sundown, just growing enough to eat and maybe pay some bills. It was also dangerous work. Some men lost their lives, usually in dynamite accidents. Others were maimed.

Akira Aramaki remembered seeing one of those fatalities. Toranosuke Yamasaki, who had arrived in 1916, was helping a colleague clear land in the Midlakes area. "This Yamasaki, he lit the fuse, then came out" and went

Figure 1.3. Mitsi Shiraishi, with a strawberry flat, on her family's Newport-area farm in 1933. Courtesy of Densho: Japanese American Legacy Project/Kawaguchi Family Collection

home for lunch, Aramaki recalled. "They came back, and it wouldn't go off, and he went up to look at it, and the thing blew up right in his face, and he went up in the air. I saw his body. Half his face was blown off."

Tosh Ito remembered excursions to the Peterson Hill farms, where both his parents were occupied clearing the land to farm it. "I recall them placing me in one of those empty dynamite boxes, and just leaving me back away from the debris when it exploded. It would sail for a long, long way. I recall that then they used horses to pull up the stumps. There was a lot of digging with mattocks. A lot of grubbing."

Once they had cleared the land, they cultivated it. The lots were small, and they were only able to grow small parcels of vegetables and fruits. Perennial crops like strawberries often took a couple of years to establish themselves, and then, after five years or so of farming, the land would peter out. So would their leases. So they would pack up their belongings and move to a new plot to begin the process all over again.

Itaro Ito had been a sumo wrestler back in Fukuoka; he was not a big man, but was renowned for his strength. "My dad prided himself on being tough," Tosh Ito recalled. "He used to do a lot of things that some people found easier ways to do. He used to carry a plow on his shoulders after work.

"We had small pieces of property. He owned some land. But he farmed some other pieces of property that he leased. And he would carry the plow on his back down to the place where he was leasing a piece of property. It wasn't that far, but. . . . "

The Japanese in Bellevue followed a pattern that occurred all along the West Coast: like their countrymen in California and Oregon, they often turned marginal or previously unusable land into productive, valuable farmland, and made their livings by operating small tracts and selling their goods in the city.[58] They also substantially increased the value of the landowners' property in the process.

"It was land that was not cleared, and so nobody could do anything with it," explained Rae Takekawa, Tom Matsuoka's daughter. "It was very poor land, in some places. A lot of the farmers were very poor, too. There wasn't much land there, but what could they do? There were really some tough, tough families, tough making a living. These were families living on the edge. Of course, at that time you didn't have the social welfare programs that I don't know if they'd have used anyway. The other thing is, of course, that you have this awful pride, that you don't take any help."

Faced with open rejection by white American society, the Japanese relied heavily on the culture that most brought with them from their homeland, and in turn became insular and fairly self-contained. Despite the conditions that had forced many of the immigrants to seek their fortunes on the eastern rim of the Pacific, Japan itself remained a considerable military power whose renown was a source of pride even for the agrarian classes that largely made up the immigrants. Moreover, Japanese culture was ancient and thoroughly ingrained in their sensibilities. American culture, in contrast, was strange to them as well as openly hostile. The English language was exceptionally difficult for them to learn, and many were only marginally educated to begin with. As such, most of the first-generation Issei immigrants tended to stick to themselves, forming pockets of Japanese culture wherever they farmed. They continued to speak Japanese and taught the language to their children.

However, even in hanging onto their heritage, the Japanese were constantly adapting to American ways. Many Issei were converts to Christianity; on Bainbridge Island, for instance, there were both Buddhist and Baptist churches for the Nikkei. The bulk of the Bellevue community was Nichuren Buddhist. But even this form of worship represented an adjustment to American ways: it featured congregations, Sunday worship services, hymn singing, and a whole panoply of Christian-style fellowships such as dinners and picnics. These things were unheard of in Japan, with its system of localized temples and monks which wove itself into the fabric of daily life.

Such adaptations helped the Nikkei become a community within a community. In Bellevue, they were scattered around at farm sites from the Mercer Slough in the south to Medina in the north, and out to the Redmond area east of Bellevue. But there remained large pockets, notably in the Midlakes and the Peterson Hill areas, that were solely Japanese farms, and these formed the core of their community.

They developed a Japanese language school for their children, and Buddhist worship services were held at a variety of locales, often someone's home. They also had their own cemetery, where shrines reflecting their native religions were erected. In all, they created an environment where they could continue to be as Japanese as circumstances would allow.

This seeming insularity created resentment and suspicion among their white neighbors, many of whom possessed a singular sense of their own cultural superiority. Whites were widely accustomed, when confronted with a minority culture, to assuming that immigrants would attempt to adopt their Western ways. When Japanese instead clung to their native culture, their fellow Americans often reacted with shock and anger. Whites also continued to hold the upper hand in land ownership—with no small help from the politics of the time—and thus forced the Japanese into a transient lifestyle, moving from farm to farm every three to five years as the land petered out.

The Caucasian suspicion of the "inscrutable" Japanese amplified the situation. Whites often resented the immigrants out of a belief that land was the primary form of wealth in what was still a primarily rural economy, so allowing the Japanese any foothold in the countryside would give root to their alien culture. If an Issei family tried to remain on a tract longer than those few years, it was not unusual if the landlord decided to raise the rent to levels beyond what they could afford.

"They'd rent the land, so they could raise vegetables," said Akira Aramaki. "So they cleared the land. Then, when it got good, then they'd [the landowners] raise the rent, and they'd have to move. The Japanese were moving all the time in Bellevue. That's how they cleared this land."

Tom Matsuoka could remember his first day in America clearly, too.

Summoned by his father, he had undertaken a three-week overseas voyage that began in Nagasaki. The ship pulled into the harbor at Seattle on February 25, 1919. The teenage boy and an older friend joked on the deck about the unlikely prospect of finding their families easily upon arrival.

"There was one man on the boat from Nagasaki, and then he came out on the deck," Matsuoka recalled. "'Now that we will get off and you look and you see father over here.' So I look. I see [my] two brother[s]. That is, I can right away notice that was James and John. So I told him, that is my brother right there. He sure [did] laugh, you know."

His American citizenship simplified his arrival: "We went to [the] immigration office. I passed real fast," he said. "And what the trouble was, I came off [the] boat in Japanese clothes. I didn't have a suit on. My dad said, 'Well, that is the first thing we have to do is go buy the suit.' I remember I bought [my] first suit at below the Smith Building. This was in those days [the] highest, tallest building in Seattle. And I don't know why he went, but anyway I bought the suit right there." The next day, they hit the road for the family home in Barneston.[59]

As exciting as Tom's arrival was for a 16-year-old, it also marked the end of what had been a largely idyllic childhood in the Kumamoto countryside, raised on the family farm by his grandparents. His grandfather grew rice and other Japanese staples and sold them in the town of Ueki.

"Where we lived was really in the woods, you know. It was near the headwaters of the Shira River. That's where the shallow waters that come from the sea come in. We couldn't fish, because you can't row out to fish on the river because it was the headwaters for the Shira. Anyway, we had a one-room school, no high school, just a one-room grade school. I stayed with my mother's family when I came with her.

"I had a pretty good life. My grandpa was a big farmer; he was well-to-do. So I had a pretty good life. I grew up with my cousins. I was the oldest one among the cousins, and I was always bossing. I used to boss them around just because I was the oldest one in the family. In Japan, they had a good life for children in my family.

"I owe lots to my grandpa. He was very strong in his faith. He always taught me about the right way to treat other people. He lived until he was 81, in 1933, which at that time was a really long time. Most people only expected to live until they were 50. I remember when I was a kid he always made sure we did the rituals and worshipped the right way."

When Tom reached 16, he was forced to make a decision that would prove fateful. "In Japan, in school, at a certain age, you just about have to decide which school you go to. There's business college, or manufacturing, or farming, or schoolteacher. And all had a special school. And you had to decide which school you go to. Young men take a test.

"Well, my grandpa wanted me to go to business college. I wanted to go to school for teaching. Well, my dad, he didn't write too much, but at that time, he wrote to us about which school should I go to, and he wanted me to go to the army school. So my grandpa said, you know, that there was too much discrepancy, but I cannot agree with your dad. And dad wrote, and said, if you don't go in the army, then you better come to the United States. So grandpa finally gave up, and he said, you might as well go and see what the place looks like. And if you don't like it, then you come right back."

Tom Takeo Matsuoka did not see Japan again for another 20 years, and even then, it was only to visit.

Chapter 2

Strawberries

KANJU MATSUOKA WENT BROKE THE FIRST TIME HE TRIED HIS HAND at growing strawberries. When he had joined the nascent Issei community on Vashon Island in 1908, strawberry prices were strong, but a little over a year later, just as he was ready to turn a profit, they turned sour practically overnight. The mill work in Barneston, by contrast, was steady and reliable, though just as grueling.

Farming, however, was in his blood. Shortly after Tom arrived in America in 1919, Kanju made up his mind to give it another shot. After all, he had grown up on a farm (albeit one where the main crops were rice and millet) and he believed he was good at making things grow. His two young sons, James and John, were coming of school age, and he knew that the muddy little milltown was no place to raise them anyway. Perhaps most of all, he was not much interested in being a mill worker the rest of his life, and farming offered him a chance to move up in the world.

Tom, meanwhile, had in his first year as an adult in the United States managed to find work in Barneston—first as a snow shoveler, and then as an ordinary millhand. When summer 1920 rolled around, the other Japanese mill workers taught him how to play baseball. He learned how to be a catcher, and he was good at it. He took night classes in English, and gradually acclimated to his new surroundings.

But by that same summer, his father had opted to return to farming by leasing acreage near the town of O'Brien, about 30 miles to the west of Barneston and 30 miles south of Seattle, just between the towns of Renton and Kent. This time, he tried his hand at a different crop.

"You know, the first year he started, he contracted the cabbage," remembered Tom. "Ten acres of cabbage, to the Libby Canning company. Oh, ten acres of cabbage you have to plant by the hand, that takes a long time. He called me. I was in the sawmill, and I wanted to come help, you know. So I went to help, and planted cabbage every day, every day, every day.

"Oh, it started around May, I think. By the Fourth of July, oh, it looked like the tail end, but we're still planting." He shook his head and added laughingly: "Aw, gee. Ten acres is a lot of cabbage, you know."

After the harvest was finished, Tom drove up to Seattle to see if he could find work. He wound up taking a job at another sawmill, this time in the Olympic Peninsula town of Port Angeles. He moved there, and soon found himself embarked on a mixed career as a mill worker and baseball player. At the time, he thought he had put farming life behind him, though he returned to his father's home regularly and pitched in, especially at harvest time.

Growing cabbage provided a barely adequate living, and within a few years, Kanju Matsuoka had shifted to a strategy already adopted by many other Issei farmers in the White River Valley: truck farming. This entailed growing a variety of crops that were harvested at different times in order to get the most out of his little acreage. These crops included lettuce, peas, snap beans, corn, potatoes, and cucumbers, as well as the crop that by then had become the signature of the Japanese truck farmer: strawberries.

Truck farming itself was an important development in the way people obtained their fresh food. Certain technological advances in transporting and storing produce—particularly the arrival of trucks driven by an internal combustion engine and the growth of cold-storage facilities—allowed farmers, beginning in the early twentieth century, to grow personal produce on a larger scale and sell the crops in distant places. This lent itself to the intense cultivation of smaller plots, which was fairly labor-intensive yet still yielded a good profit.

This style of farming was alien to most Caucasians, who often preferred to farm mass crops such as wheat, corn, and potatoes in large tracts, and whose harvesting techniques were increasingly mechanized. Truck farming entailed a great deal of "squat labor" as well as careful attention to detail, particularly in the often specialized requirements of irrigating and harvesting a variety of crops. Whites' disdain for this kind of work was especially evident in their sneering discussions of the Japanese immigrants' willingness to perform it, though such talk rarely if ever evinced any awareness that this kind of labor also put a great deal of the fresh food on their tables.

Moreover, for the Japanese immigrants—hailing as most of them did from rural provinces—this intensive style of cultivation was one with which they were already familiar. Their chief crops in Japan were quite different than those favored by Americans, but the demand for land and water had for centuries placed a premium on intense use of the land and sophisticated irrigation techniques. Japanese agriculture stressed careful management of the land's potential, as well as a close relationship of the family to the land. It also emphasized the value of cooperation among families and the larger community as well.

This cultural background gave the immigrants a remarkable ability to convert previously unusable lands into productive farm tracts that provided large numbers of consumers with a bounty of fresh produce. Nearly all of the favored truck crops were alien plants to most of the immigrants, but they wasted little time in adjusting their talents to the demands of the American market.

This same ability to adapt was important in other ways in driving the Issei into truck farming. For immigrants who were seeking to rise from the ranks of migrant laborers, three main steps—contract farming (cultivating someone else's land for a set wage), share tenancy (essentially a sharecropping agreement in which the resources provided by the owner determined the tenant's share), and cash leasing of white men's properties (usually for a set rate lasting from one to ten years)—provided the best means of climbing the economic ladder en route to becoming a landowning farmer. Japanese farmers increasingly turned to these strategies as anti-Japanese agitation strove to deny the Issei the right to land ownership.

The resulting transient pattern of tenancy was perfectly suited to truck farming, which required little in the way of capital outlays. Also, the perishable crops lent themselves to being grown on leased land that could be vacated quickly, as was often necessary, since Issei farmers at times found their leases abruptly terminated without explanation. In many cases, though, they also preferred moving to a new tract anyway, because the soil on their small plots often seemed to lose their productivity after five years or so, and thereafter required intensive fertilization.[1]

Thus the Issei farmers displayed a high degree of mobility. In many regards this reflected the immigrants' quest for an ideal place to farm, as well as their willingness to try new ventures, unafraid of leaving behind whatever security they may have established. Indeed, several studies have attributed the success of the Issei farmers to this very lack of permanence, since it encouraged an emphasis on new crops and flexibility according to the demands of the marketplace.[2]

This transience also, however, helped feed the existing stereotype about the character of the Japanese immigrants—that they came to America with more or less mercenary purposes, intending to make a quick killing and return to Japan. This, combined with the growth of Japanese language schools within the Nikkei communities, in turn stoked the preconception that they had no intention of "becoming American," and that their ultimate loyalties lay with the Japanese emperor.

By as early as 1905, however, the reality had become a good deal more complicated. While the desire to make a quick profit and return home wealthy remained a prominent theme among the Japanese, more and more Issei were indicating a desire to make America their permanent home and to set down familial roots. This reflected the changing demographic base of the immigrant population; while much of the first wave of Issei were of the footloose *mizunomi* class, the subsequent tides of immigrants tended to come from the landed *honbyakusho*, whose more staid nature was inclined historically to settle down and create permanent communities.

The chief indication of this shift was the preeminence of farming as an occupation for the Issei; by 1910, well over half the Japanese immigrants in America were employed in agriculture in one form or another, and it remained that way until 1942. Farming was an occupation that stressed community and a connectedness to the land, and in itself indicated a desire to establish roots. It also was clear that the goal of the immigrants was to become landowners themselves. Many of the Issei farmers who cleared land often did so on sizeable tracts that suggested an aspiration to long-term occupancy. Moreover, even as they moved around from place to place, the Issei often did so within the communities, or at least the general region, where they already lived, giving them a sense of place despite their mobility.

Kanju Matsuoka, for instance, worked three different farms, but all were within the O'Brien area of the White River valley. "I graduated from high school while we lived in O'Brien," recalled John Matsuoka, who was five years old when his father returned to farming. "First we lived by the riverside, and then we moved, halfway between the river and the grade school, at the Yateses' farm. And then when she sold out to Malmo Nursery, we moved to [a farm] by the railroad track at O'Brien, at Mr. Olsen's farm.

"And as I look back, I can remember, I was 12 and was blowing up these stumps—tree roots, and burning it, so the land would be clear. There were three Japanese farmers in the Yateses' place, and we all cleared farm and used the horse to pile up the stumps and burn it." Once the farmers had made the tract arable, Matsuoka said, the owners sold it out from under them to the nursery. They moved on to the Olsen tract, where they spent the next five years improving the land, but the family became close friends with the landowner, and remained on that tract through the 1930s.

Over the years, the crops grown on the Matsuoka farm, like those of his neighbors, varied widely, largely depending on the market and the shifting tastes of American consumers. The one constant, not just for Matsuoka but nearly all the truck farmers, was strawberries.

The domesticated strawberry has its origins in North and South America. Though it had grown wild in Europe for centuries, it was not cultivated until the thirteenth century. However, new varieties carried from Virginia and Chile in the seventeenth and eighteenth centuries were hybridized, and the resulting breeds were so popular that they eventually completely displaced the wild species in European gardens. They were little known in Asia; the first commercial strawberry crops were not grown in Japan until after 1899, whereas they had been introduced in America as early as 1834.[3]

Nonetheless, strawberries were nearly the ideal crop for the Issei truck farmers. They offered greater potential for profitability per acre of cultivated land than nearly any other crop. They were immensely popular and could be sold in a broad range of markets, including distant ones that were now within reach thanks to cold-storage techniques and rapid transportation. The climate and soil of the Pacific Coast, from California to Washington, were generally hospitable, and cultivating them was unlikely to inspire hostility, since in most of the coastal areas (except Oregon) they were not considered an important crop among Caucasians. This meshed with the Issei tendency to avoid any kind of competition with members of the dominant society that might create conflict.[4]

Most of all, strawberry farming required very little in the way of capital. Often an Issei could get into the business with an investment of only a few hundred dollars.[5] Immigrants primarily needed to locate available land, then invest in the plants and a little equipment, and finally provide time and labor. In this last respect, it also was important to have a family: As one Issei put it, "All you needed to grow strawberries was one horse, one plow, and lots of kids."[6]

Of course, strawberries were the crop of choice for marketplace reasons as well. Demand for the nutritious fruit boomed during the first decade of the 1900s, especially as they became more available and affordable. In turn, they produced substantial profits for anyone who ventured to grow them, especially between 1905 and 1910. An economic recession and overproduction sent prices plummeting between 1910 and 1914. This drove many of the farmers out of business, but more often, the Issei simply adapted by shifting to different crops.

Strawberries were more of an entry point for the truck farmers than anything else. Certainly, they did not provide enough of a living on their own; one survey, conducted in 1926 when berry prices were reasonably strong, found that a typical strawberry farmer could only make $597 a year, which was considered well short of an acceptable family income. But when supplemented with a few other vegetables, such as cabbage, a farmer could add as much as another $500 to his annual income, which was enough to make it over the hump.[7]

In any event, once they had their feet on the ground, as it were, the Issei quickly diversified, adding a broad array of vegetables to their truck farm offerings. Many of them turned wholly to other kinds of agriculture. In the White River valley, for instance, many of the Issei eventually became dairy farmers[8]; in Oregon's Hood River community, strawberry farming very quickly gave way to orchard fruit growing (in no small part because Oregon already was home to a substantial strawberry-growing industry dominated by whites).[9]

Nonetheless, in spite of the downturn in prices that lasted until 1915, strawberries remained a constant of nearly all of the Japanese farming communities, if for no other reasons than that there were always newcomers hoping to try their hand at tilling the land, demand for the berries never abated, and the Issei were remarkably adept at cultivating them. Wherever people bought and ate strawberries throughout the West and even farther inland, the chances were great they were grown by Issei farmers. The very image of the fruit became associated with the Japanese.

In turn, the strawberries themselves deeply affected the Issei communities' basic character. The cultivation and harvesting of the crop placed a premium on families, since in many regards children were ideal farmhands on the small plots; the work was demanding but not strenuous, and smaller people with delicate hands were better suited to picking the low-lying berries.

More important, the plants themselves only had a life of about five years, meaning that at the end of their usefulness, farmers were forced to tear them out and start over. The plants produced pathogens that rendered the soil unfit for cultivation afterwards, though this fact was mostly unknown at the time; today's farmers can simply sterilize the soil to eliminate the toxins, but in the early part of the century, farmers simply assumed the soil had "petered out" and either resorted to heavy fertilization techniques (John Matsuoka, for instance, recalls hauling tons of chicken manure to build up the soil on the Olsen tract) or they moved on.[10]

Thus, the strawberries themselves were an important cause of the Issei farmers' transience, one that tended to complement the ongoing campaign among whites to limit their abilities to climb the social and economic ladder, as well as their sometimes crass exploitation at the hands of white landowners. At the same time, this same transience made the Issei economically nimble and forced them to remain aggressive in seeking out fresh markets and strategies. It also reinforced their cultural inclination toward economic cooperation within the community, leading to the formation of a number of growers' associations that played a fundamental role in getting the farmers' goods to market. All of these were key elements in their ultimate success.

The strawberry paradigm—in which communities formed around farming families comprised largely of *honbyakshu* immigrants who began by cultivating strawberries, and then either branched out or shifted to different kinds of farming—played out in nearly every place where the Issei farmers settled and formed communities. It was notably evident in Washington state, since strawberries were closely associated with the Japanese communities on Bainbridge and Vashon islands; in the White River Valley; and particularly in Bellevue. Elsewhere along the Pacific Coast, it manifested itself in such communities as the Hood River Valley and the town of Russellville in eastern Multnomah County in Oregon; and in California, in such places as Gardena in the south, and in Watsonville, Agnew/Alviso, and Florin in the north. Even in coastal Canada, notably in British Columbia's Fraser River Valley, strawberries played a critical role in founding and shaping the Issei communities.[11]

Several of these communities explicitly adopted the strawberry itself as the main image of their hometowns. Some featured annual strawberry festivals that attracted large crowds of Caucasians, eager to sample the fresh strawberry shortcake that was a staple of such affairs. Gardena had an annual "Strawberry Days," and both Vashon and Bainbridge islands, as well as Bellevue, had their own strawberry festivals, the latter being a massive affair that drew tens of thousands; Mission City in British Columbia marketed itself as the "Home of the Big Red Strawberry." The fruit was a symbol of these communities' pride, and the Nikkei farmers saw the celebrations as a chance to promote not only their skill at growing fruit and its resulting contribution to the general weal, but also their industriousness and citizenship—their good intentions, as it were, as hard working Americans in the making.

Strawberries thus also were a symbol of something deeper: the immigrants' nascent desire to set down roots in America—even if it meant moving every few years to do so. Wherever the strawberry plants appeared, so too did extended Nikkei families, particularly the Nisei citizen children who ardently and readily adopted American ways. With them sprouted the Japanese schools and business associations and baseball teams, all of which became woven inextricably into their communities.

All of this stood in sharp contravention of the popular stereotype of the Japanese as soulless mercenaries who intended to return to their homelands once they had made their fortunes. Latent in the rising fortunes of the strawberry farmers was an aspiration to overcome, through hard work and honest dealings, the mountain of prejudice that kept them from being openly accepted in their adopted country.

If, however, there was a silent olive branch extended to their white neighbors alongside the servings of strawberry shortcake, it was largely ignored. For that matter, it seemed that the more Issei put down roots, the more hostile their white neighbors grew.

A few months after Tom Matsuoka landed in Seattle, a political firestorm erupted in the Northwest over the very presence of people like himself. Japanese immigrants had been hearing the rumblings of blame since the end of World War I in 1918, as veterans returned to a sour economy that offered few jobs, but it came to a head that summer of 1919.

On July 26, the 84-point banner headline across the front page of the *Seattle Star* shouted:

DEPORT JAPANESE
Demanded by Secretary of Veterans' Commission

Beneath the lead-in was a small portrait of Miller Freeman, with a caption: "Sees Menace in Japanese Here." The first paragraph laid out Freeman's case:

> That by getting control of 47 per cent of Seattle's hotels, and by leasing land when forbidden to own it, Japanese violate the spirit of the "gentleman's agreement" between the United States and Japan, was the charge made Friday by Miller Freeman, secretary of the veterans' welfare commission.[12]

The story went on to detail how the Japanese "controlled" 218 of the hotels in Seattle (it would later turn out that "control" included mere managerial status, not necessarily ownership), and worse yet, were taking over all the state's prime farmland: "Practically all the best farming lands in the vicinity of Seattle are in the hands of the Japanese—a condition true of nearly all of the farming land adjacent to all the cities of the Pacific Coast.

"The law forbade foreigners to own land, and the spirit of the law is to prevent them from realizing the profits of our agricultural acreage. Yet these Japanese come here, lease the land, cultivate it, and take the cream. And the spirit of the law and the 'gentleman's agreement' is violated."

As a result of this travesty, Freeman claimed, World War I veterans returning home from Europe were being shut out of the labor market: "By gaining control of business, the Japanese is crowding our returning veterans out of a chance to get a new start." And if the trend continued, he warned, the result would be inevitable: "In the face of the flow of Japanese to the Pacific Coast, white people are ceasing to move here from the East. Eventually the whites will be forced to go elsewhere to make a living. . . . Thus, the Japanese will eventually hold the balance of power in politics on the Pacific Coast. They will vote solid, and will control political affairs. Japan retains control of her people everywhere, notwithstanding that they may be accepted as citizens by the countries of their adoption."[13]

Of course, very little of Freeman's tirade was true, but that last assertion was flagrantly deceptive; thanks to the 1790 Immigration Act restricting citizenship to "free white persons," naturalization was not an option available to the Japanese. The only means by which a person of Japanese ancestry could obtain citizenship was by being born on American soil; but then, as Freeman would make clear on numerous other occasions, even those American-born Japanese were not racial equals and could never mix with white society. They were Japanese through and through, and thus their citizenship was of dubious nature at best.

Despite his later contentions that he had no prejudice against the Japanese, this racial separatism was a cornerstone of Freeman's argument as he presented it in the pages of the *Star*. He voiced it largely by sprinkling his writing and speeches (including his remarks to the *Star)* with popular aphorisms: "The Japanese cannot be assimilated. Once a Japanese, always a Japanese. Our mixed marriages—failures all—prove this. 'East is East, and West is West, and ne'er the twain shall meet.' Oil and water do not mix."

And his conclusion became a political benchmark: "It is my personal view, as a citizen, that the time has arrived for plain speech on this question. I am for a white man's Pacific coast. I am for the Japanese on their own side of the fence. I not only favor stopping all further immigration, but believe this government should approach Japan with the view to working out a gradual system of deportation of old Japanese now here."[14]

Freeman's return to the political mainstage had been brewing for the previous eight years. Out of the state legislature since 1910 and preoccupied with running the naval militia, he had continued making irregular warnings about the dire machinations of the Nipponese government in his trade publications. And as before, the inspiration for this fresh round of anti-Japanese agitation originated in California.

The Gentlemen's Agreement did slow the flow of Japanese to the West Coast considerably. Immigration plummeted from a high of 10,000 workers in 1908 to about 1,700 per year in the years immediately following. But the flow gradually started to rise again, swelled primarily by the ranks of "picture brides" coming to join their new husbands. By 1919, Japanese immigration had grown to 8,000 a year.[15]

Spurred by the continuing campaigns of the Asian Exclusion League—which were strengthened by overt support from such interest groups as the Native Sons of the Golden West and the American Legion—and the demand for further measures to exclude the Japanese in the wake of the Gentlemen's Agreement, the California Legislature in 1913 had passed the first Alien Land Act. Using the familiar "aliens ineligible for citizenship" language, the legislation made it illegal for the Issei to own land. Its passage so angered people in Japan that "a crowd of some 20,000 Japanese in Tokyo cheered wildly as a member of the Diet demanded the sending of the Imperial Fleet to California to protect Japanese subjects and maintain the nation's dignity," and the Japanese government protested angrily to the Wilson Administration, to no avail.[16]

But the notion of a statewide prohibition appealed immensely to Freeman, who founded the Anti-Japanese League of Washington in 1916 and began campaigning for an alien land law in the state. His early attempts at pushing the legislation met with little success, but in 1919, the plight of returning veterans gave him the opening he sought.

Freeman was appointed by Governor Louis F. Hart in early 1919 to the state's Veteran Welfare Commission, which was charged with reemploying returning veterans of the Great War. Though some economists noted at the time that the problem was a complex (but probably short-lived) one caused by slow-acting market forces, for Freeman it became abundantly clear that there was a singular cause: the Japanese, once again.

His opening salvo was a July speech before a group of 170 grocery, laundry, and retail store owners that he titled, "This is a White Man's Country." In it, Freeman decried the steady stream of picture brides into the region since 1907, declaring that Japanese mothers bore five times as many children as white women.[17] If the trend were not forestalled, he warned, the entire Pacific Coast would soon be overrun completely with Japanese.[18] And, he said, they now owned and controlled large amounts of property in the state.

Freeman's speech brought a pointed response from Sumikiyo Arima, publisher of the Japanese *North American Times:* "The opinion of the commission is a great mistake. . . . If there is, as the commission asserts, need to restrict Japanese immigration more severely than it is now, it must mean to restrict Japanese brides who come to America to live with their husbands. But not to allow young Japanese in this country to bring their brides to live with would be inhuman, unjust and un-Christian. Besides, Japanese women are never in competition with returning soldiers."[19]

Arima's response appeared on the front page of the *Seattle Star* on July 25. The next day, Freeman's campaign exploded on the paper's front pages.

Underlying all of the anti-Japanese campaigns of the early 1900s were the bedrock principles of white supremacism. The widespread belief that white people were the consummate creation of nature, and that they were destined to bring the world civilization and light, went essentially unquestioned. It was supported by popular literature and self-proclaimed "scientists" who used the questionable methodology of the day to lend an academic veneer to longstanding racial prejudices.

Among the most popular of the time were Lothrop Stoddard and Madison Grant, who boasted credentials from Harvard and Yale universities, respectively. They approached the matter of race ostensibly from anthropological and biological perspectives, but in fact did little more than clothe white supremacism in pseudoscientific language. Wrote Grant, in his 1916 tome *The Passing of the Great Race:*

> We Americans must realize that the altruistic ideals which have controlled our social development during the past century, and the maudlin sentimentalism that has made America "an asylum for the oppressed," are sweeping the nation toward a racial abyss. If the Melting Pot is allowed to boil without control, and we continue to follow our national motto and deliberately blind ourselves to all "distinctions of race, creed, or color," the type of native American of Colonial descent will become as extinct as the Athenian of the age of Pericles, and the Viking of the days of Rollo.[20]

And as Stoddard would later write in *The Rising Tide of Color Against White World Supremacy*—a 1922 work complete with admiring introduction from Grant—the real threat was not blacks in the South, but Asians: "There is no immediate danger of the world being swamped by black blood. But there is a very imminent danger that the white stocks may be swamped by Asiatic blood."[21]

Both books were national bestsellers that underwent multiple printings. And their core arguments—which became entwined with deeply cherished beliefs about the nature of race—became the heart of the battle to exclude the Japanese. Ultimately the issue was couched, like many racial issues of the preceding century, in the terminology of eugenics, a popular pseudoscience that saw careful racial breeding as the source of social and personal good health.[22] Thus many of the campaigns against nonwhites cast the race in question as not merely subhuman, but as pernicious vermin who posed a serious threat to the "health" of the white race. As James Phelan, arguing for exclusion in California, put it: "The rats are in the granary. They have gotten in under the door and they are breeding with alarming rapidity. We must get rid of them or lose the granary."[23]

Racial intermarriage in particular was commonly depicted as a source of social and personal decay. Only a few weeks before Freeman launched his crusade in its pages, the *Seattle Star* prominently played a story about an apparent suicide, a white Seattle woman married to a Japanese man named Joseph Sugiura. Above a photo of the couple, the headline read: "Seek Body of White Wife of Japanese," while the text beneath explained, "Can't Be 'Somebody' Married to Japanese; She Threatens Suicide." Though cases of suicide by non-public figures typically were then, as now, delicate and painful matters that most newspapers shied away from reporting upon, the clear lesson of this particular morality tale evidently overpowered those concerns:

> Police are searching lake shores and Seattle waterfront Saturday for the body of Mrs. Joseph Sugiura, 19-year-old white wife of a Japanese, who disappeared from her home at 1107 Yesler Way, Friday night, leaving a death note. Temporary derangement caused by sickness and worry over her social position is believed by the authorities to be the reason for the woman's suicide threat.

The story detailed the contents of Mrs. Sugiura's suicide note, which indicated someone dealing with severe depression: "I'm gone. By the time you read this my earthly troubles will be over. 'Life Is Sweet.' Oh, how false! It has always been as bitter as wormwood to me. How I've longed to be something to someone!" Of course, it also explained that she had threatened suicide on three previous occasions in similar fashion, and each time had turned up alive and healthy elsewhere. And since no subsequent stories reporting on whether her body ever was found appeared in the *Star*, it seems entirely likely this case turned out no different.[24]

Amid this milieu, race almost naturally played an explicit role in the crusade launched in July 1919 by the *Seattle Star*. For the month following Miller Freeman's initial outburst, the pages of the paper were headlined with stories relating the dire threat posed by Japanese immigrants. The campaign covered all the bases:

> MORE REVELATIONS MADE IN JAP MENACE
>
> JAPANESE PICTURE BRIDES ARE SWARMING HERE
>
> ASK CIVIC PROBE OF JAP PROBLEM
>
> SHALL WE DODGE JAP ISSUE![25]

The basic tenets of the stories were that neither the Japanese immigrants nor their citizen children could ever become "real Americans"—"There is no hope now or in the future for their assimilation," Freeman declared—and so their growing presence could have no other outcome than to drive off Caucasians.

On the crusade's second day, an editorial beneath the headline asked: "Is This To Remain White Man's Land?":

> Miller Freeman's proposal in *The Star* of Saturday to deport the Japanese from the Pacific Coast and to put up the bars against future immigration from Japan has aroused a storm and it has brought Seattle up-standing—face to face with a problem that cannot be settled secretly and cannot be put off much longer.
>
> The Japs are here. They are rapidly gaining control of the best farming land near Seattle. They are in control of the Seattle markets.
>
> . . . Multiplying five times as rapidly as the whites, the Japs must some day—unless the problem is met now—absolutely control this coast. Just as Hawaii and the Sacramento Valley have been Japanized, so will the state of Washington.[26]

The campaign attracted a congressional hearing in Seattle on the question, chaired by Republican Congressman Albert Johnson, a onetime newspaperman from Hoquiam who had held one of the state's five U.S. House seats since 1913, and had since become chairman of the House Immigration and Naturalization Committee. A parade of local civic leaders spoke, uniformly urging something be done about the tide of Japanese immigrants. "This is the zero hour of Americanism," declared the local leader of the American Legion, "and we should stand for 100 percent Americanism. The republic was founded for Americans, and not for Japanese, who are un-American."[27]

Johnson's committee took no further action on the matter, but by the following summer of 1920—an election year—he wasn't shy about using the issue both on the stump and in Congress. He introduced a bill that year suspending all immigration for one year, with the intent of using the period to investigate the question of Japanese immigration. However, the bill was waylaid by competing legislation that set quotas on immigration for various ethnic groups.[28] So while campaigning in Tacoma, Johnson called for "local agitation" to force the federal government to shut the door on all Asians, and announced that he planned to investigate "the growing menace of

Japanese intrusion into the agricultural and commercial lines of business in the state."[29]

Simultaneously, Freeman and the Anti-Japanese League stepped up their campaign for a Washington version of the alien land laws. Freeman outlined his reasoning in a 1920 speech: "Certainly I did not start out with any prejudice against the Japanese," he said. "And the more I observe of them, the more I admire their perseverance and efficiency.

"They are not inferior to us; in fact, they constantly demonstrate their ability to beat the white man at his own game in farming, fishing and business. They will work harder, deprive themselves of every comfort and luxury, make beasts of burden of their women and stick together, making a combination that Americans cannot defeat."[30]

This was a common refrain among white supremacists, including both Lothrop Stoddard and Madison Grant, regarding the position Asians enjoyed among the races. They uniformly accorded Asians an advanced position in the sciences and arts and acknowledged their intellectual capacities, but considered them as lacking a moral dimension that ultimately rendered them an inferior race. As Grant put it: "These races vary intellectually and morally just as they do physically. Moral, intellectual, and spiritual attributes are as persistent as physical characters, and are transmitted unchanged from generation to generation."[31] This lack of a moral sense inherent in the race made them potentially dangerous as economic or military competitors, according to this assessment, because they lacked the normal restraints that "decent" white folk took for granted as part of the fabric of a healthy society.[32]

Freeman contended that the Japanese already had a leg up on establishing their hold in the Northwest. In an editorial in the *Washington Farmer*, he proclaimed: "Practically all the best farming lands in the vicinity of Seattle are in the hands of the Japanese. . . . The free city market established by the city of Seattle for the benefit of all the people is controlled by the Japanese. They are establishing many commission houses and within a short time will have a virtual monopoly and sell all farm products."[33]

With Freeman leading the charge, veterans' organizations joined forces with various labor groups and grocers' associations, as well as chapters of the American Legion, Veterans of Foreign Wars, and the Native Sons of the Golden West. Soon Freeman's refrain—that the Japanese were outcompeting their white neighbors by accepting conditions that whites would find intolerable—became a common one. (Simultaneously, there was little if any recognition that the "competitiveness" of the Japanese was in many ways a product of conditions forced upon them by whites.) And while the rhetoric revolved around colorful appeals to a racial animus, it is clear that there was a strong economic motive at work among most of these groups, sometimes explicitly so; indeed, the two purposes were often expressed as identical.

Thus, testifying before a Washington legislative committee considering tougher laws for the Japanese, one fruit store owner complained of being offered $5,000 for his business by a Japanese competitor; when he refused, the competitor told him he would spend $10,000 to drive him out, and then engaged in a price-cutting battle that eventually forced the white fruit seller to sell his business for half what he had originally been offered. The legislators were aghast; but none wondered whether the fruit seller's concern would have been germane if his competition had been merely another Caucasian.[34]

Politicians like Albert Johnson in particular were prone to picking up the anti-Japanese cause, since the agitating factions represented several key voting blocs, while the Japanese themselves were excluded from voting and thus had no political clout whatsoever. Various officeholders, especially rural legislators, found that attacking the Japanese threat, and piously talking about saving American civilization, went over well with the voters. But even on a statewide level, the issue received prominent play; Governor Hart, a Republican, campaigned for his ultimately successful re-election on a promise to outlaw the leasing of any property by the Issei, while one of his GOP primary opponents, John Stringer, took it a step further: "It is our duty to take every acre of land on Puget Sound away from the Japs and place it in the hands of our ex-soldiers."[35]

The Japanese and their few allies, which included the produce and agricultural associations that helped distribute their goods, were poorly organized compared to their opponents. They offered token protest of the proposed laws, but found themselves outmanned. When the legislature convened early in 1921, a flood of anti-Japanese bills awaited. The first proposal would have made it mandatory to post American citizens as guards at any Japanese-owned hotel. Another called for an official investigation of the Japanese immigrants. A third prohibited any "aliens and disloyal persons" from teaching in any public or private schools. All these faltered in the legislative process. But the fourth and centerpiece bill—a land law that forbade ownership of land by all "aliens ineligible for citizenship," and making it a criminal offense to sell or lease land to any such alien—flew through both houses nearly unimpeded, passing the House 71–19 and the Senate 36–2. Governor Hart, freshly re-elected, signed the bill in short order.[36]

Flush with political victory, Miller Freeman had the final say on the matter. In an article addressed to the Japanese community, he minced no words: "The people of this country never invited you here. You came into this country of your own responsibility, large numbers after our citizens supposed that Japanese immigration had been suppressed. You came notwithstanding you knew you were not welcome. You have created an abnormal situation in our midst for which you are to blame."[37]

The storm of venom against Japanese immigrants kept raining down for the next three years, often with an official imprimatur. New Mexico passed an alien land law in 1922, and Oregon, Montana, and Idaho all followed suit in 1923.[38] Washington's legislature tightened its own alien land law in 1923 by empowering the attorney general to seize the property of anyone who leased or sold to ineligible aliens.[39]

The United States Supreme Court weighed in as well. Its 1922 ruling in *Ozawa v. United States* officially sanctioned the exclusion of all Asian races. A Japanese immigrant named Takao Ozawa—arguing that he had been almost entirely raised and educated in the United States, was a product of its universities, and was a Christian who spoke English in his home—sought to overturn a district court ruling that denied him the right to seek citizenship. And though the court agreed that he was "well qualified by character and education for citizenship," it denied his appeal on the grounds that immigration laws limited naturalization to "free white persons and aliens of African nativity."[40] Then, in 1923, the court upheld the constitutionality of Washington's alien land law with its *Terrace v. Thompson* ruling (in a case involving a King County landowner named Terrace who openly declared his wish to lease his land to an Issei farmer, and sued the state's attorney general over efforts to enforce the alien land law), which found that an alien ineligible for citizenship did not enjoy equal protection under the law.[41]

The final blow came in 1924, when Albert Johnson, using his offices as chair of the House Immigration and Naturalization Committee, introduced a bill that would limit immigration to a 2 percent quota for each nationality, but further prohibiting the admission of any "aliens ineligible for citizenship."

The bill easily passed the House, but once in the Senate, the provisions were altered to allow for a Japanese quota as well. However, Republican Sen. Henry Cabot Lodge of Massachusetts then stood up in the Senate and denounced a letter from the Japanese ambassador—which had warned of "grave consequences" for relations between the two nations if the measure were to pass—as a "veiled threat" against the United States. Lodge led a stampede of support for the House version of the bill, and the era of the Gentlemen's Agreement was over. Signed shortly afterward by President Calvin Coolidge, complete Japanese exclusion was now the law. Officially called the Immigration Act of 1924, it became known popularly as the Asian Exclusion Act.[42] (Its final clause: "The terms 'wife' and 'husband' do not include a wife husband by reason of a proxy or picture marriage.")

Taken in isolation, these little acts of racial mean-spiritedness may have seemed of little moment. But in fact they had consequences that eventually exploded into the history books. In Japan, the public had been closely watching the passage of the alien land laws with mounting outrage. And when news of the passage of the Asian Exclusion Act was announced, mass riots broke out in Tokyo and other cities. As Pearl Buck would later observe, the then-nascent movement for American-style democracy, which had been slowly gaining momentum in Japan, was effectively wiped out overnight.[43] The military authoritarians who would control the nation for the next 20 years gained complete political mastery, and one of the cornerstones of their rule was a bellicose anti-Americanism that would finally reach fruition in late 1941.

In America, meanwhile, the combination of these laws put Japanese farmers who owned land at the time in a thorny position. Some, like the Takeshita family in Bellevue, got around the law by having the deed to their land placed in the name of a Japanese American adult with citizenship rights. But most of the Issei were forced to place the deeds in the name of their Nisei children, most of whom were not of age, in which case the deed was placed in trust with a local Caucasian lawyer. Those who did not have children or similar means of escaping the law were stripped of their property rights.

The alien land laws also became a handy club for local politicians hoping to raise their profiles. Malcolm Douglas, the King County prosecuting attorney newly elected in 1920, began a series of high-profile prosecutions of supposed violations of Washington's new law, beginning in spring 1922. Led by an aggressive deputy named Ewing D. Colvin, Douglas' office announced it had uncovered some 94 cases of land-law evasion that it would pursue. In short order he filed actions against a couple of farmers on Vashon Island and a White River farming cooperative, enjoyed success in the courts, and began vigorously pursuing even more cases. Douglas claimed in 1923 that he had targeted at least 800 other cases for possible prosecution, including action against whites who ignored the law. Douglas' efforts continued through 1925, but gradually faded after the bloom of the office's early success faded, and several of its high-profile cases ended in defeat.[44]

Ryutan Kurita, who had arrived in Bellevue in 1905 and was probably the first Issei landowner in the town, found himself caught in a Kafkaesque nightmare wrought by another overzealous prosecutor. Strapped for cash in 1915, Kurita had sold title to his Bellevue property along the Sunset Highway (purchased in 1909) in order to meet his final mortgage payment, putting the title in the hands of a Japanese-owned speculation company. The title transferred hands twice more, ultimately leaving possession of Kurita's land to a white-owned investment company. Kurita, meanwhile, had moved away to work in a Snoqualmie sawmill, but returned to Bellevue in 1921, hoping to resume his former farming life. He did so for the next two years—until, apparently out of the blue, the state's attorney general, L. L. Thompson, filed charges against him.

The Bellevue Nisei who remember the case say they suspected someone local put Thompson up to the prosecution because Kurita's land had in the meantime become valuable. Whatever the motivation, the attorney general claimed that the investment companies that held title to Kurita's land were only front companies that allowed Kurita to farm land being held by white title—and thus were in violation of the intent of the Alien Land Law. Facing trial without a jury, Kurita won, surprisingly, when the court dismissed the case as lacking sufficient grounds for prosecution. Thompson appealed to the state Supreme Court, too, and lost. But in the process Thompson had driven Kurita to the poorhouse. Discouraged and broke, he returned to Japan in 1928.[45]

Throughout Washington, as many as 100 cases were prosecuted in the courts removing property from Japanese ownership. Studies later determined that virtually all of the prosecutions resulted from complaints lodged by economic competitors; though, in a few cases, they were instigated by politicians seeking to curry public favor. All told, the number of Japanese farm operators and laborers in Washington state decreased 78 percent between 1920 and 1924.[46] And initially, the anti-Japanese laws had their desired effect. Japanese farms in Washington plummeted from a high in 1920 of 699 farms to less than half that—246—by 1925. The Japanese farmed 25,340 acres in 1920; by 1925, that was reduced to a mere 7,030 acres.[47]

Moreover, there can be little doubt that the passage of the alien land laws and the subsequent prosecutions were an enormous blow to the hopes of Issei farmers who had believed that, by displaying their industriousness, they might eventually win acceptance in American society, and eventually the right to citizenship. Such hopes now looked distant at best, foolishly naïve at worst. In some communities there were discussions about packing up and emigrating elsewhere, possibly to Mexico—though none of them talked about going back to Japan.[48]

However, in the long run, the Issei immigrants' capacity to adapt to circumstances—already thoroughly established in the strawberry fields—won out. Indeed, the exclusionists' hopes of driving down Japanese land ownership backfired. The Japanese farmers who survived, like those in Bellevue, were primarily those who succeeded in buying property by putting it in the names of their Nisei children. Before passage of the anti-Japanese laws, only about 5 percent of the land the immigrants farmed was land they owned; by 1930, that had risen to 25 percent. Thus, despite the initial reversals, the tide gradually shifted back to favor the Issei. 1930 census figures for Washington state showed 523 Japanese farms, totaling some 13,000 acres.[49]

For all of the misery and pain that the alien land laws inflicted, and despite a certain amount of initial dislocation, they ultimately were grotesque failures. As Roger Daniels, who surveyed land tenure in California during the decade succeeding the laws' passage, suggests, the laws were at best "minor irritants" in terms of driving out the Japanese. Other surveys have reached more or less the same conclusions. However, it is likewise clear that the anti-Japanese campaigns did indeed change the character of the Issei farming communities: by driving out the more adventurous immigrants, it made the communities even more conservative, more stolid, more deeply planted in the soil.[50]

As hard as their foes might strive to drive them out, the Japanese had put down their roots in Washington for good.

The Issei truck farmers on the Eastside followed the same pattern as elsewhere: they mostly started in strawberries, then quickly branched out to a cornucopia of other fruits and vegetables. But the strawberries were their real niche, and remained for most of the farmers' tenure their most prominent product, in consumers' minds at least. Indeed, the growers seemed to have a gift for growing big, sweet, and firm berries. Bellevue became renowned for its delicious red fruit.

"People saw Bellevue strawberries," recalled Cano Numoto, whose family farmed a plot near Yarrow Point, "and they always said, 'Oh boy.'"

Bellevue growers initially established their reputation for strawberries at Seattle's Pike Place Market. The large, sweet berries proved so popular that they quickly became the Eastside's signature crop.

The little community was still making incremental steps to becoming a real town. Phones arrived in 1916, and American Pacific Whaling set up its operations in Meydenbauer Bay in 1918, making Bellevue one of the nation's last whaling ports (though the animals themselves were never brought to the Eastside).[51] A small weekly tabloid newspaper, *The Reflector*, started that same year, mostly publishing town gossip and business news. A 20-mile highway connecting Bellevue to Renton from the south was completed in 1920. The town was gradually growing with a white population comprising largely merchants, professionals, tradesmen, and craftsmen. There were some Caucasian agricultural operations: a dairy farm along Kelsey Creek, a couple of chicken ranches, and a handful of apple orchards. Adolph Hennig planted a vineyard on Clyde Hill in 1923, and the grapes that he grew there not only were popular at market, but translated into a booming juice business that at its peak sold 12,000 gallons a year.[52]

The bulk of Bellevue's farming, though, was in the hands of Japanese immigrants and their children. The tracts at Midlakes and Peterson remained the chief centers of the Japanese populace, but their farms were also scattered at various locations around the community as well—in Clyde Hill, at Phantom Lake, and near Wilburton. Truck farming was a labor-intensive and only tenuously profitable way of working the land, since it was based on small acreages that had to be farmed for maximum production, and farmers had to be careful about adjusting their crop sizes to meet demand. Because of that, it was a style of farming that was hardly ever adopted by Caucasian farmers, who were more accustomed to larger tracts that were simpler to tend and did not require intensive oversight.[53]

It's estimated that 95 percent of the famed Bellevue strawberries came from Japanese farms, which still were small plots that relied on hand labor.[54]

The Japanese farmers found they could make in a few weeks with their strawberries what they would make for the rest of the year with their peas, beans, and other vegetables.

Planting and maintaining the crops was a relatively simple operation, albeit labor-intensive. A man and his family could handle most of the chores throughout the growing season. When it came time to harvest the crop, though, many more hands were required.

"During the harvesting season you had to hire a crew," recalled Numoto. "You couldn't do it within the family because you couldn't keep up with the strawberries; they'd always overtake you. They should always be harvested at the proper time.

"We'd go to Seattle and hire these Japanese hourly ladies. They'd come out and stay on the farm there; they'd sleep overnight, you know, for most of the season, and when the season was over you'd pay them out and they'd go back home again. Most of these ladies stayed at the hotels, the Japanese hotels."

So, at harvest time, Bellevue buzzed with a population surging with field workers. Some of the local youngsters also contributed to the picking crews. Soon, tourists added to the commotion.

Bellevue already had something of a reputation as a weekend getaway. From 1906 until the late 1920s, Wildwood Park, an attraction on the shores of Meydenbauer Bay, drew crowds of visitors from Seattle. They typically took the trolley car from Pioneer Square that rode up Yesler Way and dropped over to the shores of Lake Washington at Leschi Park. From there, they took the passenger ferry that landed at Meydenbauer. Among Wildwood Park's attractions were a bandshell and an annual bash called the Big Basket.[55] However, when the ferry from Leschi altered its route and ceased coming to Bellevue—opting instead for a Medina landing several miles away—the tourism trade suddenly dried up. Civic leaders began looking for a new way to boost their little community, and found the needed inspiration on the Japanese farms.

Eastside historian Lucile McDonald described how Mrs. C. W. Bovee, the wife of a local real-estate salesman, came up with the idea for the Bellevue Strawberry Festival:

> One night in 1925 she dreamed of a celebration featuring the strawberry harvest. When she told her husband, who was in the realty business, about her dream he said, "Why not?" and spread the suggestion of a fete among his friends. A committee of five men and five women was formed, $40 was subscribed and the first strawberry festival was staged in June 1925. . . .

Bellevue was becoming synonymous with strawberries, shipping vast quantities of them. With the initial festival a success, another was staged the following June, at which more than 5,000 shortcake servings were consumed, as well as large quantities of strawberries and cream, hundreds of cups of coffee and glasses of milk. The whipping cream bill alone was more than $125. Visitors were entertained with musical programs and exhibits of products. By the third year of the festival, 500 cars from other areas thronged the roads and several large boats of visitors anchored in the bay.[56]

The celebration continued to grow in size, and it became an inseparable part of Bellevue's public image. By the 1930s, it had grown to attract as many as 15,000 visitors—engulfing what by then was still a small town of less than 2,000. A parade opened the festivities, and a Strawberry Queen was elected to lead the parade dignitaries. However, there were never any Japanese included on the festival's organizing committee. And the girls nominated for the honor of Strawberry Queen were always white—though in 1939, a revue of Japanese girls clad in kimonos was added to the festival in honor of the producers.

It was also the most anticipated social event in Bellevue for most of its residents. "We always went to it," says Robert Hennig. "Because you could get a great big, I mean a real big, strawberry shortcake. First it was about 15 cents, and finally the price went up to two bits. There was a lot of strawberries, and gawd, they'd have a whole bunch of women in there hauling strawberries, you know, getting ready. . . . On a Friday, Saturday and Sunday, and they had a group from Kirkland come one night and put on a program, and Renton would come one night and put on a program, and Sunday was for Seattle people—they didn't put on a program, they just came over and ate shortcake."

It was a big event for the Japanese residents, too, though they were often too busy producing the strawberries to actually take part in the festivities. "We enjoyed it," recalls Mitsuko Hashiguchi. "Thousands of people would come from all over, from Seattle and just all over. It was just wonderful. A big crowd. And it was just something I think everybody looked forward to."

Putting down roots in the Bellevue community included the procession of life common to us all: births, weddings, deaths. Tragedy, of course, was not a stranger to the Japanese.

Not far from the Hirotaka family's farm—about a half-mile north on 116th Avenue—was a cemetery for the Japanese families, a section of Pioneer Memorial Park; it was segregated partly by choice, and partly because Buddhist shrines were deemed unacceptable in a Christian cemetery. It gradually filled with headstones and shrines bearing the names of elderly parents of some immigrants, their sickly children, and the victims of fate.

Tokuo Numoto, who had come to Bellevue in 1904 and had put one brother through college and helped another start a neighboring farm, fell victim to the influenza epidemic of 1918 and was buried there.

Kameji Yabuki's first daughter died of influenza in 1920, and then his wife died in childbirth, along with his second daughter. He returned to Japan, remarried through a go-between, and returned in 1921 with a new wife who spoke no English. They raised a new family at the greenhouse in Houghton—four daughters and two sons. Their second daughter, Rose, was born in 1923.

The most striking tragedy befell the family of Teikichi Suda in 1925. After a night of socializing with friends in Seattle, the Sudas drove onto the ferry at Leschi Park for the trip to Medina, and somehow the car failed to come to a stop, driving off the end of the ferry and into the lake. Suda and his wife and two of their children, as well as two children from the Takizaki family of Seattle, drowned in the accident. Two of the Sudas' children survived, and were raised at the Maryknoll Convent in Seattle.[57]

And big, strong Tatsunosuke Hirotaka, one of the first Japanese to farm in Bellevue, suffered a heart attack in 1923 and died, leaving his wife, Nami, to run the farm by herself. Fortunately for the Hirotakas, their sons had grown old enough to perform much of the farm work. And their oldest daughter, Kazue, was now of marrying age, and that in turn brought another young man to their household.

Baseball had become the chief preoccupation of young Tom Matsuoka's life after his arrival in America. Indeed, if anyone had been seeking evidence that, contrary to popular opinion of the time, the Japanese immigrants were likely to blend in well, they need only have gone to the local baseball diamonds to observe the passion with which Issei and Nisei alike adopted the national pastime.

While many immigrants were exposed to baseball for the first time in America, in truth, the game had already spread to Japan. In the 1870s, visiting American missionaries had introduced baseball to the Japanese, and it had quickly gained widespread popularity, even in rural areas. Many Issei arrived in America already familiar with the basics of the game, and they honed their skills further by forming their own leagues. The first Japanese team in Seattle was formed in 1904, and the first Nisei team began playing in 1909. For many Nisei, who were interested in becoming American, baseball was a wonderful bridge between their parents' interests and their new way of life.[58]

Tom Matsuoka had not played baseball in Japan, but cottoned to it quickly while living in Barneston. When he moved to Port Angeles to work at one of the local sawmills, he kept playing. An all-Japanese baseball league sprang up, pitting teams from the sawmills in various towns against each other, and he started playing in it, primarily as a catcher.

"There was a bunch of Japanese boys," Tom says. "They want to play baseball." A friend of his named Nakashima "was in some university in Japan . . . and he was a real good catcher and he was a ball player. And when I started, [there were] quite a few [Nisei] ball players. Yeah, I really learned how to play the ball, by that time at [the] Port Angeles sawmill."[59]

Soon, the game came to dominate his life. He moved back to Seattle and obtained a stall in the Pike Place Market, where he sold his father's farm produce, mostly so that he could spend his evenings and weekends playing ball in the summer. Then he returned to the mill circuit, moving from mill job to mill job, not because of the pay or other reasons, but because he was recruited to come play for baseball teams—which could sometimes translate into cushy jobs. And as the teams became better, the recruiting wars became more intense. He wound up spending most of his time playing for the team from National Sawmill, based at a camp near Mount Rainier.

"Eatonville sawmill, they had a baseball team too. Oh, back and forth we played quite a few times with Eatonville team. . . . They don't like [to] lose a game [to] National so they [would] recruit good players from Seattle, and lots of good players came [from] Seattle. . . . We couldn't beat [them] now. We used to win [against] Eatonville all the time, but we couldn't win. And about [the] next year or so finally we pulled out [of] National because . . . Eatonville get too strong."[60]

Tom moved back to Seattle in 1925 and took a job with Seattle Parlor Furniture Factory, a plant owned by two Japanese men named Maeda and Kanno that churned out low-priced chairs, tables, and couches for middle-class customers. Tom's job was working as a glueman, joining the various pieces together, and he kept playing baseball in his spare time. Like most of the Japanese men at the time, he seemed destined for an extended bachelorhood; there were few single Japanese women in Seattle, and thanks to the Asian Exclusion Act, they had no chance of obtaining even picture brides now. Then fate struck.

"You know, for a glue room, summertime was really hot. No overshirts, just undershirts I was working. The window is right there and I looking in the window one time and, oh, there is a Japanese girl go by.

"I thought, Gee, that's rare. How in the world is [a] Japanese woman going to work? Then I found out that Mrs. Maeda [got] pregnant, and she was making lunch for a few people. . . . And [when] she get pregnant, [it was] hard work for making lunch, so she hired a helper, and that was Kaz. And that's where I met her."

Kazue Hirotaka was one of the most eligible young women in the Bellevue Japanese community, and not merely because she was one of the only single Nisei women of marrying age. Young, beautiful, and popular, she was valedictorian of her 1926 Bellevue High School graduating class and associate editor of the school yearbook.

"She was a forceful character," recalled her oldest daughter, Rae Matsuoka Takekawa. "She was not one to hold back. She was not your typical Japanese lady."

Being one of the first Nisei helped: "She was American born and raised, so she had the advantage of language and she was of course very Americanized."

Unlike some Nisei and all the Issei, Kazue Hirotaka spoke perfect English without a trace of a Japanese accent. "She spoke strictly regular American English," said Rae.

She had a lot of friends in Bellevue of all backgrounds. "She grew up with them, after all," noted Rae, who said her mother moved comfortably among Caucasians, "except for the fact that they were so poor. But I think everybody was sort of poor. There were some well-to-do people, I'm sure, but still, a majority of people were not too well off."

Kazue worked hard not to let the poverty show. "She was very, very clever. She sewed, and of course because they had very little, she sewed her own clothes. And when we were growing up, she sewed clothes for us too, and when my kids were growing up, she sewed clothes for them. I mean, she was just really good.

"She was attractive. I saw a picture of her when she was 17, I think. And yeah, she was a nice-looking gal. She looked pretty stylish, you know. And when I think of the fact that she didn't really have very much, she looked real good."

She was known for "an acerbic tongue," Rae said, but what people remember most was her strength of character: "She always knew what she wanted. She really had a strong sense of what was right, you know, as far as your behavior. I guess a strong sense of morals. She had strong opinions.

"She lived what she believed. She didn't have a sense of ethics for other people than herself and something else for herself. She really behaved the way that she believed."

And unlike her mother or grandmother, or likely any of her ancestors, she wound up marrying for love. Tom stood out, perhaps because he was well educated, handsome, and a Nisei himself. There was no need for a go-between. They hit it off right away, and determined to get married as soon as Kaz was out of school.

"And there was no question that she couldn't go on to school, even though she was certainly capable, but there was just no money," said Rae. "So they got married right away."

"When I met her, she was a high-school junior," Tom said. "Then, after she graduated from high school, oh, her mother was having the hardest time. Her father had died, you know, and she had the four kids: three girls, one boy. And in those days, you know, there was no help, nothing. . . .

"We went together about a year and a half, because she was a junior, and then she graduated from high school, and then she started to work. She worked at the export-import place. She started working for bookkeeping. We talked it over, maybe we should get married; then we can help your mother. That's why we married."

Their wedding in November 1926 was the first Nisei union in Bellevue, and Tom's father helped make it a memorable event. "They had the reception. This was dry, you know," he recalled, referring to the Prohibition Era. "But my dad, he had to have a drink if it's a wedding party. So he made a home brew. I don't know how many gallons he made. But you had to smuggle it into the restaurant. So he puts it in a suitcase and takes it in. Oh, everyone had a hell of a good time."

At first, Tom and Kaz set up home at Tom's place in Seattle. "We decided we would have to help her mother for her. I was making about $100 a month.

She was making $50 a month. So we give $50 to her mother, and we live with my $100. Oh, but that didn't last too long."

Kaz was soon pregnant with their first daughter. "So then the wife can't work, you know. So, there's no sense we live in town, so we went to Bellevue, and stayed with her mom. That would save our expenses. That's why we moved to Bellevue.

"I was still working in this furniture factory. And with the six o'clock boat I'd cross, you know. Our place was at Midlakes. I'd walk to the end of town, and there was a bus that would go to the ferry in Medina. You have to get up about five o'clock in the morning, and then eat breakfast, then walk to Bellevue, then the bus would leave about 15–20 minutes before the boat, and I'd catch the 6 o'clock boat. And you'd go to Leschi Park, then cable car, the Yesler Way cable car. And I'd go to First Avenue. And the streetcars would leave from First Avenue. And the streetcars were the longest ride, because they'd have to go to Denny Hill, and then go through the Interbay area. There was a roundhouse there. We'd cross the bridge and go over to Fort Lawton. It was awful."

Rae was born in 1927, the first Sansei (third-generation) child in Bellevue. Three more followed in short order—two boys, Tats and Tyrus (named by his father for Detroit Tigers star Ty Cobb[61]), and another daughter, Rulee. Rae remembered her mother continued working through it all: "I know that when she was pregnant with my sister, that she was cutting lettuce. You know how strenuous that is? You're bending over all the time. And the night that my sister was born, she was out there in the field. And then she decided, well, she'd better go." Rulee was born that evening.

In addition to his factory job, Tom continued to work evenings and weekends on the family farm. And on top of all that, he and Kazue turned to making Bellevue a better place for raising young Nisei and Sansei boys and girls.

The life of a child on the Japanese farms could be tough, especially if you were the firstborn in the family, as Mitsuko Hashiguchi was.

"Being the oldest is a little bit different," she recalled. "I was the oldest, and there were six of us kids. But I was being the oldest and I had the full responsibility because my mother had to get up and go out and go and work on the farm. Therefore, it was my job to—I had to get up and make breakfast for all the kids, make sure they were all fed, whatever you do with the kids. And then I had to make sure that when we started going to school and make sure all the lunches are all made and all ready to go out too. So we were all ready to go to school and everything. It was a lot of work—and make sure the laundry's done on weekends, and of course, we didn't have water like we do now. We had to pump it out of the well."

Summers, likewise, were sunup-to-sundown affairs, and then some. "I always had to work on the farm," Hashiguchi said. "Because Dad had strawberries, peas, tomatoes, cauliflower, corn and all that type of thing. For that reason there's always work to be done. And like I tell everybody, before I went to school even in the mornings I had to help Dad. After I'd get my brothers and everything all ready to go to school, I'd always have to help Dad with different things. In the evenings, like tomato season, we always had tomatoes in the greenhouse, after we'd picked all the field green, we'd put them in the greenhouse, and then after we'd ripen them, after that we had to sort 'em and pack 'em. And that was a night job all the time for Dad, so I used to help him do that. And my sister didn't like to do farming, so that was a different story.

"So that was the reason that I had to work until late at night. And then I had to do my homework after that. And then I'd go to school in the morning all over again."

The Japanese work ethic did not go unnoticed by their neighbors, who ceased resenting it and started admiring it.

"They were a hard-working bunch of people, that's all there was to it," recalled Robert Hennig, Adolph Hennig's son. "There were, oh, a few people that would make cracks once in awhile about being Japs or something like that. Mostly, there wasn't much conflict, though, between the Japanese and the whites."

"And the whole family worked . . . like all day, late hours, year round," remembered Beatrice Mathewson, a granddaughter of the town's founders who graduated from Bellevue High in 1934. A visit to the Ito residence in Factoria was firm in her memory because her woodworker father had been hired by the family for a small job: "I remember he made a Lazy Susan to put on their dining table . . . and there was all these things they didn't have to take off and clean, and there's room around the table for the plates. I probably was about five years old. I remember that so plain, going down to their place with him."

Later, when her older brother, Russell Whaley, built an auto garage business near Sturtevant Lake in the Midlakes area and her family moved there, she found herself surrounded by a number of Japanese neighbors. Her brother maintained the water rights to the lake, which was the water source for most of the farmers' fields, and he helped sell and repair the pumps. "Well, they had pumps, and they pumped water out of the lake," she recalls. "If somebody had a problem, they'd call him, and it could be middle of the night."

Life on the farms wasn't always hard work. Mitsuko Hashiguchi could remember looking forward to the Strawberry Festival, but she was really most fond of Independence Day, which was her one big break each year.

"What I looked forward to was July the Fourth," she said. "My Dad let us all go to Seattle because we had an Okayama family in Seattle that lived on Jackson Street, that let us come over, because that would be the one day of vacation, a holiday that Dad would give you. . . . We got to see the parade, and they had the Bon Odori [Festival] down there, so we went to see that. There were things like that."

Issei in the Bellevue community maintained close ties with a number of fellow Japanese in Seattle's *Nihonmachi* (or Japan Town); the city residents often were a lifeline of both material supplies and familial support for Japanese living in rural areas. Most often, the connections ran back to the prefectures of their respective origins—families from Okayama, Kumamoto, Fukuoka, and Hiroshima were all common on the Eastside, and many of their friendships in Seattle were derived from those old bonds. More often, the Bellevue Nikkei had familial and cultural connections to the larger White River community to the south, which remained closer to Bellevue in terms of driving time, the availability of a ferry notwithstanding. They also had numerous connections with the Bainbridge Island Nikkei community, partly because both were in the business of growing strawberries, and partly because of familial and prefectural connections. Moreover, a few Bainbridge Issei families had gotten their start in Bellevue between 1905 and 1912 before moving to the island, and maintained their old ties over the years.

Still, the Bellevue community grew to have an identity of its own, if for no other reason than that the life of truck farmers could never resemble that of urban workers. More often than not, the Japanese in Bellevue had more in common with their Caucasian neighbors than with the old friends in Seattle. Certainly, their racial relations were different. Where in Seattle the ethnic

Figure 2.1. A sunny day on the Seguro farm in the Midlakes area. Left to right, front: Sumie and Toshi Seguro. Back: Mae Seguro, Eva Aramaki and Mitsue Seguro. Courtesy of Densho: Japanese American Legacy Project/Akizuki Family Collection.

communities were highly segregated, there was more of a blending effect in rural settings like Bellevue's. Some of it was the forced interdependency of rural life, and some of it was the simple mutual respect that came from working and living in close proximity. All of the Nisei today can recollect neighbors and friends who treated them kindly and as full equals.

"I remember, we had one neighbor, Mr. Clancy Lewis, who was very, very good to us," says Mitsi Shiraishi, who grew up in the Newport Hills area. "He always helped us out. I remember when I was young, he told me, 'Mitsi, you'll always find people who are for you, and people who are against you.'"

In between the hard work and school, the Nisei children of course found time to play—and at times, the life of a child in Bellevue could be downright idyllic. "No one was playing around when somebody else was working," recalled Tosh Ito, whose family worked a farm among the Peterson Hill tracts. "I think we all pretty much worked and then we played together.

"When I was at Peterson, though, I do remember this one thing, is this First Creek. Like many other streams and creeks around Bellevue, they were just loaded with sockeye, and chum salmon, and sometimes cohos, and kings. And you could stab a pitchfork into a small pool, and most of the times you come up with two or three sockeye. Almost every time."

Joe Matsuzawa remembered the salmon, too, even running up into ditches dug for farming. "Why, the fish would come right up those ditches even, and spawn. Then, summertime, all year round we used to go fishing down there, but all we'd catch is little baby salmon. They weren't very big, but they had hatched up somewheres, and we'd fish for 'em. Once in awhile we'd catch something that's probably six, eight inches long, a rainbow, but most of it was little salmon. But that was the source of our fun, for us to go down there and fish. . . . And another [thing] down there was crawfish. There used to be a lot of freshwater eels in the streams too. It was unbelievable."[62]

Chizuko Norton, the second daughter of Enji Tamaye, had something of a magical experience with a fish. "Our well was very special because we had a trout living in there. It was a good-sized one, and someone—I think the family's name was Koura who moved to Bainbridge Island, but I was told that their son had caught this fish and put it in the well. But it was fascinating.

"We used to spend what seemed like hours—I'm sure it wasn't hours—leaning over the well, with everyone saying, 'Get away. You'll be falling in!' And we were watching this fish swim around. Those wells were not all that large, for all I know . . . but he lived to be a ripe old age."[63]

Children being the innocents they are, it was common for Japanese youngsters to play with their Caucasian neighbors. However, the amount that the children mixed tended to depend on how well their parents had acclimated to life in the United States. The parents who spoke only Japanese in their homes tended to lead more insular lives, associating only with other Japanese, while those fluent in English, particularly Nisei parents, tended to be more comfortable with their neighbors, and their children were more likely to feel integrated.

It wasn't until later, when she was a teenager, that Rae Matsuoka realized that there was something setting her apart from her classmates. "See, I don't think I realized I was different. . . . When we went to school, we just considered ourselves American. And, we didn't differentiate between [oneself] and a Caucasian classmate. I guess I realized fairly soon that I wasn't exactly Caucasian, and of course, we found out for sure when the war broke out. But before that I am sure that someplace along the way you get exposed to attitudes and, of course, prejudices. And you learn from that. So we absorbed that, but on the whole, I was more friendly, more close, to some of the Caucasian kids."[64]

Conversely, the youngsters whose parents spoke little or no English often remained cocooned in the Japanese community until they reached school age. Mitsuko Hashiguchi recalled that when she first enrolled, she was acutely aware of her difference from other children: "Like when I first went to school at first grade, I couldn't talk English. I couldn't even write my own name, to tell you the truth. Of course, then, after that, I became an American.

"But we were Japanese until a certain age, and then after that, maybe about second grade, I began to Americanize right away. Because I had my American friends. Oh, there were Japanese girls to play with, but that would be your neighbor friends. As far as activities in schools, I was involved with American friends."

Barriers tended to fall away once the children picked up the language and acclimated to their schoolmates. In school at least, the Nisei in Bellevue felt they were largely accepted as equals.

"Oh, yeah, I was part of the school," said Hashiguchi. "And my neighbor was a German family, over the fence—it went that way, north of me, were

German people, and so we went over there and grew up with Mary all the time. Everything we did was with Mary there. So I think I became Americanized quicker than my other Japanese friends for some reason, I don't know. I really don't know. Our family was that way, I guess."

And in truth, many of their Caucasian neighbors thought highly of their Japanese neighbors. "I think most people admired them because they were so industrious, and they were so honest, and the children—apparently the parents put a lot of value on education, so the children were very good students," said Patricia Sandbo, who returned to Bellevue after she graduated from high school and taught in the Bellevue schools. "I think we admired them. . . . They were just as American as the next kid."

However, not all their neighbors were so congenial, nor were all the usual social barriers cast off entirely. "Like our friends, we were friends at school," said Mitsi Shiraishi. "But after school, there was no more of that friendly relation. When I was little, about six or seven, I had a very good friend, Sylvia Schultz, and I really loved that girl. She used to come over and play with me, and all that. But the people we went to school with, we never continued our friendship after school. We graduated, and that was all."

The Japanese have their own word for the silent kind of racial prejudice they encountered from their Caucasian neighbors. They called it *haiseki,* a Japanese word meaning to exclude or to ostracize. In Japan, the word referred to situations in which someone of standing, through loss of face, was made a social outcast, and as such, it always carried connotations of shame. In the United States, it took on a new dimension: It became part of everyday life.

Mitsi Shiraishi recalled a school outing as a young girl. "When I was about in fifth or sixth grade, our schoolteacher was taking about seven or eight of us on an outing," she said. "And she had to wait on the side of the road for the bus to come. And I remember, she put all the Japanese kids—I think there were three—we would be in the back, and she'd have all the Caucasian children in the front.

"I knew then that the reason why was that if we were in the front, the bus driver might not pick us up there. It wasn't a bus stop. We stayed in the back so that the bus driver would see the Caucasian children in the front."

Sometimes the teachers weren't quite so generous. Rose Matsushita, who grew up in the Houghton area of Kirkland, recalled one teacher's backhanded compliment. "I was the best speller, I remember, a couple of years in class. And she admonished the rest of the class for not being able to spell better than me, since I was Japanese."

The white adults evidently passed the same attitudes on to their children. Akira Aramaki recalled a swimming hole along Kelsey Creek he and his friends frequented in their free time in the summers.

"I remember we went swimming in the creek," he said. "There were some kids, part of a German family living near there. These German kids started throwing rocks at us, yelling, 'War on the Japs! War on the Japs!' Yeah, they were throwing rocks at us. We had to run, naked, you know. Then, after they went, and we came back to find our clothes, we couldn't find them. We found them in a beaver hole; they had buried them there."

The silent barrier only reinforced the Japanese community's insularity. "I think we were kind of sticking together quite a bit," recalled Tosh Ito, a Bellevue native. "I think a lot of us felt there was a need for that. It was hard to mingle in.

"I remember one time I went to a school skating party outing at Vasa Park [on Lake Sammamish]; there was a roller rink there. And they wouldn't sell me skates, so I couldn't skate. And that was a school outing. I very clearly recall that."

Despite being told at every turn—sometimes even inadvertently, amid acts of kindness—that they could never hope to really fit in, the young Nisei children wanted desperately to be considered normal Americans like everyone else. They worshipped Gary Cooper and Mary Pickford, Sonja Henie and Babe Ruth, just like their classmates, and wore clothes and hairstyles like them, too. And secretly, they wished they weren't Japanese.

"I am very dark compared to most Japanese, and so I was teased about that," said Chizuko Norton. "Well, I have to admit that I did a lot of complaining about being different and also having that called to my attention by my Nisei friends as well. Because to be dark was . . . I still think it's not all that much appreciated among the Japanese. And I remember sticking adhesive tape all over my hands. You know, when you tear off the tape, your skin is light. Well, I thought that that would keep light for longer than just a few seconds. And the other thing is . . . praying to be white for just one day."[65]

"Ah, I wished I were white" recalled Kiyo Yabuki, who was born in 1923 in Yarrow Point. "I put the white on a pedestal. Even though I would criticize or condemn, maybe, I still had that mentality where I wished I were white. It may have been that I was ashamed of my own features."

above and right Figure 2.2. The dedication of the Bellevue Japanese Association clubhouse in 1930 brought hundreds of people out, including leading figures in Bellevue Society. Courtesy of the Eastside Heritage Center/Cano Numoto Collection.

A dinner at the home of a favorite teacher drove home the point to Michi Nishimura, the daughter of Asaichi Tsushima. When she sat down at the dinner table, she was confronted for the first time in her life with a steak—and eating such a thing with a new kind of utensil.

"I had never had a steak before," she recalled. "And I had the hardest time cutting it. The kids—they had children—they would sit there and snicker at me. Mrs. Cash said something; I remember her talking to them, saying, 'That's not polite.'

"There were so many things like that which—it's not things that we would think of now as what our children would go through. It was something foreign to us, to eat with knives and forks, because we ate with chopsticks all the time. Things that ordinarily you wouldn't think about, and yet they made us different from our Caucasian friends.

"I think a lot of us were ashamed of our parentage at times. There were times when I must have thought: I wish I weren't Japanese."

The Nisei children were caught in a limbo between two worlds—the unfamiliar traditional Japanese culture of their parents and the unaccepting world of the whites in which they lived. Most spoke English almost solely, but used a smattering of Japanese at home, just to communicate with their parents.

In many cases, the children became the parents' bridge to American society, and often wound up giving them English lessons. And because the chil-

dren were often isolated socially and forced to develop relationships largely at home, a striking symbiotic relationship between Issei and Nisei evolved. In many ways, even as the Issei came increasingly to depend on their children, the Nisei grew more determined to create identities of their own, meaning their familial bonds were often colored by an unbridgeable cultural chasm.

"It's my mother who taught me how to jump rope and also juggle beanbags and play some of the Japanese games, and, of course, songs," recalled Chizuko Norton. "I taught her the American songs and oh, even taught her the Pledge of Allegiance."

But because their parents were so ignorant of American ways, many of the Nisei children found themselves acutely embarrassed by them. "My mother became interested in PTA, though I would come home and tell her that—you see, some of me had this discomfort being different—that I would tell her that the PTA wasn't meeting this month and that she didn't have to go, because her English was not very good," Norton said.

"I almost died when I found that one of my teachers had visited my parents to let them know how well I was doing in school. In those years, if you made honor roll or got a special recognition . . . , instead of writing a letter, they would visit the home to bring the good news. Well, I just about died, I mean, of mortification, when I found out that this one teacher [had visited].

"I said, 'You didn't feed her anything,' and she says, 'Yes,' yes she did. She served sembei and these dried cherries and, oh my God—and tea, not coffee!"[66]

Many of the elders, and some of the older Nisei like Tom and Kazue Matsuoka, were concerned about raising a generation of children in that kind of alienated environment. Even though their own kids were too young to participate, in 1927 the Matsuokas organized the Bellevue Seinenkai, an organization for youth activities. It was the first attempt to provide Nisei children a social life outside of school or the farm.

But the Issei were also concerned about the growing gap between them and their children. Since many of the immigrants themselves had little formal education and were nearly helpless when it came to learning English, their first solution was to educate their children in Japanese language and culture as a way of strengthening communication as well as ties to their heritage. A Japanese language school had been started in Bellevue in 1921, but was shut down amid the Alien Land Law agitation. Though the main intent of the Issei was simply to close the language and cultural gap between themselves and their children, the schools consistently were a source of suspicion in Caucasian communities along the Pacific Coast, in no small part due to anti-Japanese propaganda claiming that the Nisei children were being indoctrinated into emperor worship and forced to swear loyalty to Japan. Those suspicions, at least in Bellevue, were utterly groundless; none of the Nisei can recall any lessons even remotely approaching such topics, other than geography and history lessons about Japan incidental to learning the language.

A second language school opened in 1925 and held classes at an Issei home in the Downey Hill area until 1929, when community leaders organized the first Japanese language school at a building in Medina. Asaichi Tsushima was the first teacher.

Around the same time, leaders of the Japanese community began making plans to build their own center for gatherings. By 1930, they had built the Japanese Community Clubhouse at 101st Avenue Northeast and Northeast 11th Street and dedicated it in late July of 1930. It had 16-foot-high ceilings to accommodate the basketball court the builders installed as its main floor. Some 500 people, including the leading citizens of Bellevue, attended.

The language schools were consolidated at the clubhouse, which soon became the hub for the community. The Seinenkai meetings were held there, as were practices for the various sports teams. The language lessons at the schoolhouse, which initially were held only on Saturdays, were expanded to daily hour-long sessions after school.[67]

The sessions weren't always popular with the young Nisei. Many of them, the boys especially, hated trudging the extra mile or so to the schoolhouse while all their classmates got to have Saturdays or after-school hours off. And they weren't really interested in learning Japanese. They, after all, wanted to be Americans. Most of them recalled being good students at regular school, but poor students in Japanese.

"I used to pack my lunch, go over there, get in fights, learn how to throw a baseball," remembered Alan Yabuki, whose parents operated a greenhouse in the Yarrow Point area. "That's what I used to do."

Mitsuko Hashiguchi, however, reveled in the cultural growth the school offered: "I loved the Japanese school. And I went 12 years, and I went to night classes."

Tom Matsuoka did not make his children attend the Japanese school. "He says, 'I want you guys to be able to learn English, speak it well, because this is where you are going to live. Don't want to get muddled up in this'—a lot of these people speak in mixed idioms once in awhile," recalled Ty Matsuoka.

"Oh, but those kids just go for eating lunch, that's all," was how Tom described it. "They don't learn nothing. They talk the English all the time back and forth, you know."

Still, Matsuoka chipped in and helped drive the teachers, who usually came from Seattle, from the ferry dock to the school, since by 1932 he had a car, which was frequently pressed into service chauffering youngsters and their mentors to and from activities of all kinds. Tom recalled that he was happy to help, "[But] I never sent the kids, and had nothing to do with the Japanese school."[68]

Sports, on the other hand, were popular with the Nisei, and also provided them with a great deal more social acceptance than the Japanese school. Several Nisei already had built reputations as standouts on the Bellevue High School football teams. Farm life had made them tough, durable athletes, and some of them even used their farms as training grounds.

"Takeshi Sakaguchi was a good football player," recalled Tom Matsuoka. "A good fullback. Then, when we would string up the tomato wires, he'd practice; he'd try to go under the tomato wires. That was how he would practice so that he could go low to the ground. Our homes were next to each other, you know. We used to laugh, we would look, and say, there goes Takeshi, gonna try again."

Robert Hennig remembers the impact the Japanese athletes had on Bellevue High's football teams, too. "One thing I'll always remember, we were playing a game with, I think it was North Bend, and Bellevue was kind of pushing the North Bend guys around, and the fact is we were probably ahead by 20 points or something. And they were getting kind of ticked off at us, because there were a lot of Japanese on our team. And this one guy hollered over from North Bend team, he hollered over to our side, 'Ah, you guys wouldn't have any football team at all if it wasn't for these damned Japs!'

"He shouldn't have said that. Because, I think they had the ball, and the next play, they threw a pass, and the guy was running for the goal line, and there wasn't anybody in the way, it was all an open path in his way. And all of a sudden out of nowhere comes two Japanese boys from the Bellevue team, and they hit him like a ton of bricks. He never made the touchdown. I remember that."

The Matsuokas helped organize the first all-Japanese sports teams in 1931. Tom ran the baseball teams, which played in the enormously popular Courier League, organized by the editor of the *Japanese-American Courier*, James Sakamoto.[69] Kazue, who had played high school basketball herself, coached the girls' basketball team. Both of them drove their teams to out-of-town games and tournaments and shepherded their young charges into adulthood. The kids looked up to them as modern, fully American Nisei.

"They were community leaders," recalled Mitsi Shiraishi, who played center for the girls' team. "Always working for the young people, trying to make us become somebody, you know. They were very helpful. Very kind."

"He was a leader," said Joe Matsuzawa, describing Tom's prominence in the community. "Everyone went to him if they had a problem. Of course, he was educated in Japan, and he talked English real well, and he understood. He was a real understanding person, you know?"

Tom's baseball teams were a favorite. They drew crowds, and the Issei, many of whom couldn't understand English but could understand baseball, came out to watch and root fanatically. Indeed, the Sunday baseball games were social events; everyone would get into their Sunday best to come watch.

"Every Sunday, I always played baseball, at least two games," said Tom. "Sometimes three games. There weren't too many public playing fields. So Garfield, the high school, had two fields we played on, but we would have to drive around from field to field if they were taken up.

"In those days, Sundays were the one day of vacation the Japanese young people had. So we had these all-Japanese teams; the whole league was Japanese players. From Seattle and Bellevue, some from White River. . . . And I remember Tats would sit behind home plate, while I played catcher, and yell for me: 'Da-a-a-d!' He had a high-pitched voice that everyone could hear. It was funny."

The girls' basketball team, however, was a slightly different story. Most Issei had very firm ideas about the model of Japanese femininity; after all, it was still considered important then, if possible, to send one's daughters back to Japan to receive full training in proper behavior for a Japanese lady until

Figure 2.3. The Bellevue Seinenkai girls' basketball team in 1930. Back row: Suyeko Yamaguchi, Mitsi Shiraishi, Mary Aramaki. Front: Tomoko Inatsu, Kikue Hirotaka, Nobuko Inatsu. This team was coached by Kazue Matsuoka. Courtesy of the Eastside Heritage Center/Cano Numoto Collection.

Figure 2.4. Tom Matsuoka with his two son, Tyrus and Tats, in front of the Bellevue Vegetable Growers Association warehouse in 1932. The building still stands as part of a glass operation. Courtesy of Densho: Japanese American Legacy Project/Matsuoka Family Collection.

they came of marrying age. Watching these young girls leaping around in gym shorts left many elders aghast.

"My dad, he saw the girls' basketball team playing," recalled Cano Numoto. "He went, 'Gee, they're wild, you know.' Without knowing that basketball was played that way, well, it's no wonder they sent girls back to Japan to be better ladies."

Not that the style of play was particularly wild, nor was the dress, by today's standards. They played Iowa rules basketball, which restricted players within three zones. And Mitsi Shiraishi, a star for the Bellevue team, recalled that while they wore shorts, they also covered their legs with rayon stockings: "We were that old-fashioned."

Still, the sports were just about the only fun the youngsters were able to squeeze in. The rest of the time they spent either in school or working on their families' farms. The farmwork, they all recall, was grueling, especially in the summer, when it required steady labor from sunrise to sunset. But most of the Issei couldn't have operated their truck farms without the ready work provided by their children.

While Tom Matsuoka was trying to build a sense of self-worth among the younger Nisei, he was simultaneously helping build the economic power of the Japanese community. In 1932, he helped found the Bellevue Vegetable Growers Association, a cooperative venture under which the Japanese hoped to gain some economic clout through their crops.

Japanese farmers in Sumner, in the White River Valley area, had already organized in a similar fashion, and the Bellevue farmers modeled their association on that one. All the 50 or so members who wanted to join pitched in $25, and then the leaders went to work. They bought a rail car for shipping out produce from their friends in Sumner and for the first year of operation, relied on them as well to coordinate the sales of the produce back East. By the second year, the Bellevue growers were more organized and were eager, having made decent profits the first time around.

"We done real good," remembered Tom. "And the funny thing, we had Northern Pacific, they had the railroad that goes through Midlakes. And we have the place to load the car, so we asked Northern Pacific for a sideline. And build a warehouse so that we can load up there and ship it out in the car, you know. So they did that."

A financial disaster nearly wiped out the association in the second year, though. When trying to buy supplies for the next go-around—twine and stakes for growing peas, mostly—Tom Matsuoka discovered that the association had no cash in its account. When he investigated, he found that the group's first secretary had no records of any money in the bank, and neither did the bank. The secretary was fired, and Tom was placed in charge. He and Tok Hirotaka traveled to Seattle the next day and persuaded another banker to lend them the money to get through the next few months. The association survived, and in short order was flourishing, largely because Matsuoka began expanding the reach of their market through the rail line, adding even more cars to their repertoire.

Soon, Bellevue produce was being shipped out regularly across the country, primarily to states along the Eastern Seaboard, their trademark navy blue "Belle-View" brand ("Fresh! From the Pacific Northwest") slapped onto all the crates. The venture turned out to be very profitable for the Japanese farmers on the Eastside, the first real success they had seen since arriving in the United States.

The warehouse soon became one of the most bustling operations in Bellevue. Robert Hennig spent a couple of summers working there. "There were no Japanese working in there," he explained. "They were all busy farming and bringing produce in. They had a white man managing it, and I think there was one or two Japanese in the office working, but the rest of it was all white kids working.

"They'd bring these peas in and pack them in these hampers, they call 'em, about [five feet] high, and the girls would stand there and when they topped them off they put the peas all in there just so, you know. Then they'd pack them in these refrigerator cars, and I was on the ice gang. They'd bring these 300-pound cakes of ice in, and they'd bring them in on a truck and slide them down a slight ramp, and then we'd grab them with the tongs and put them in a pile. Then we'd chop these 300-pound cakes into six pieces and there was a chipper, oh about [four feet] off the ground, you had to pick the cake up and throw it in there and grind it up and blow it in the boxcar."

Both Hennig and Ty Matsuoka have sharp memories of the big Irishman named Russ Gallagher who headed up the warehouse crew. "He weighed about—he was a little bigger than I am, but I think he stood about 6 foot 1, and weighed over 200 pounds—he was pretty big," Hennig said. "He'd do that for about half the shift, and then he'd be in blowing ice in the car and it'd be up to me to shovel the rest of it in. One night he wasn't there and I had to do the whole damn work by myself. That was something else.

"And then when the boxcar was loaded, they'd have another one, an empty one, standing on the track, and Gallagher would—what was the call he'd holler out? 'Boxcar' or something like that. And he had a long-handled tool, [about eight inches] around, wooden handle, about that long [arm's length], and he'd get out there and get that under the wheel of the freight train and pry up on it, and they'd have everybody in the plant out there pushing on that boxcar at the same time, and then with this thing that he had there, it'd kind of get it moving a little bit, and they'd move that boxcar, well, the length of the car, plus the one behind it, in position. Because they didn't always wait for the freight train to come along and pick it up."

It was not long before the operation became more independent and financially solvent. "In 1934, '35, things were pretty bad for farmers," said Tom Matsuoka. "A farmer would have to spend three cents to grow a pound of peas, and they sold them at the warehouses for a half-cent a pound. So we decided to take charge.

"The Northern Pacific people had this shed next to the railroad track that they didn't use. It was costing them money to keep it up. They approached us, asked us if we wanted to buy it. We voted on it, and we decided to buy it. We paid $350 for it. We thought it was a lot of money at the time.

"We had vegetables from a lot of big acreages coming to us, from Fife to Bellevue. Our biggest market was in New York, but we shipped all over the country. When we were in full season [at harvest], we shipped out 40 to 50 cars at a time."

Even as the Bellevue Japanese began enjoying greater prosperity in the late 1930s, so too were fortunes improving for their white neighbors. The economic stimulus provided by the Japanese farmers enhanced the mercantile wealth of the Bellevue area. Further, many wealthy Seattleites were moving to the Eastside to take up scenic property along Lake Washington's eastern shores and building expansive mansions. They usually commuted to their urban workplaces by boat (which often were expensive yachts).

Among the new residents was Miller Freeman, devout advocate of the "Yellow Peril" conspiracy theory and still president of the Anti-Japanese League. Freeman not only took up residence in Medina in 1925; he began buying parcels of land around the Eastside—though, true to form, he evidently never leased them to Japanese farmers. He had bigger plans.

Among the early visitors to his new property in Medina was Dr. Henry M. Suzzallo, president of the University of Washington and a longtime friend of Freeman's. He asked the publisher and longtime public figure why he would choose to remove himself from the bustle of Seattle.

"I wanted to get away from the pressure of the city during the home hours," Freeman responded. "I wanted a place for the boys to grow up off the city's streets. I wanted a place where I would not be involved in many affairs. I want a home where there will be no outside demands upon my time and attention and interest. In short, I want to go rural, to put affairs of everything but family behind me when I leave the office."

"Don't kid me," replied Suzzallo. "You will soon be sparking ideas all over Medina. You will be involved in a water project. You will be building. You will be getting new roads and better roads built. You will be involved in community affairs and you can't help it. You won't even want to help it. You are coming over here to get away from something when actually you will be getting into something, a lot more than you actually realize. You will be into all kinds of projects. Why, I wouldn't be surprised if you got involved in a scheme to bridge the lake."[70]

Suzzallo was either prophetic or just knew his man too well. Indeed, Freeman envisioned a future for the Eastside built around a metropolitan Bellevue. He was not alone in this vision; James S. Ditty, one of the largest landholders in the Bellevue area, likewise foresaw a time when Bellevue could become an Oakland to Seattle's San Francisco. Ditty even drew up a map in 1928 for a modern city of Bellevue that bears a striking resemblance to the city as it exists today.

The waters of Lake Washington were the chief obstacle to realizing this vision. Because the lake is some 30 miles long, and Bellevue and Seattle both situated almost directly at the center of opposite shores, transportation to and from the Eastside required considerable travel. Bellevue was far out of the way of any direct transportation lines except by boat.

Then, in 1937, a state transportation engineer named Homer Hadley suggested a radical idea: building a floating bridge from the western shores of Seattle's Central District across the lake to Mercer Island, which already was linked to land near Mercer Slough, on Bellevue's southern end. Because this stretch of water forms the narrowest neck in the lake, such an idea had been suggested before, but had been quickly discarded by engineers when confronted with the realities of the harsh windstorms that often turned the lake into a churning maelstrom. A typical floating wooden structure, which the lake's considerable depth would have necessitated, would be chopped into driftwood by the first of those storms to come along.

But Hadley proposed something that sounded laughable on the face of it: a bridge made of concrete. Hadley, however, understood that floating pontoons could be constructed of concrete that were capable of remaining stable in fierce waves. Joined together and lashed to the lake bottom by cables, the pontoons could form a perfectly stable bridge. But when local newspapermen caught wind of Hadley's idea, they practically laughed him out of town. The *Seattle Times* ran derisive editorials. The *Times'* cartoonist depicted Hadley's concrete pontoons washing up on shore with the first stiff Lake Washington winds.

But Miller Freeman, who may have had other interests in mind, came to Hadley's defense. In the pages of his Seattle newspaper holdings, including the *Town Crier*, Freeman called Hadley a visionary. Freeman also used his pull with Republican legislators in Olympia to obtain funding for Hadley's proposal.[71] Other newspapers joined in, including the *Post-Intelligencer* and the *Seattle Star*. And the *Bellevue American*, to no one's great surprise, pronounced Hadley's plan a capital idea.

The primary motives, of course, for many of the bridge's proponents were more than simply providing a boost to Bellevue's fortunes. Naturally, a bridge meant improved access to the Eastside's expanding agricultural wealth. More important, it offered shorter, more direct access to the Sunset Highway and Snoqualmie Pass, which provided Seattle's vital land link to the east. Building the bridge simply made good sense.

Soon, no one in Seattle was laughing. Final plans were drawn up, and construction of the Mercer Island Floating Bridge began in 1938. It opened to great fanfare—and a widely despised 25-cent toll—in 1940. It was promptly hailed as a major feat of modern engineering, especially after several Lake Washington windstorms came and went to little apparent effect on the bridge. Drivers marveled at the bridge's stability, and it quickly transformed the Eastside from a sleepy farming community to a significant residential and commercial center. Now, instead of an hour away, Bellevue was within 15 minutes' drive of downtown Seattle.

"I was married in 1940," recalls Cano Numoto. "The Mercer Island Floating Bridge was opened in June of that year. I was married in the springtime. My dad, he said, 'Well, you're a family man now, so I'll retire and go back to Japan.' And he left me and my wife on the farm."

Before his father left, though, he got a ride over the new span.

"I remember, it was sometime within the first weekend after the dedication of the bridge, I said [to his father], 'Well, I'll have to take you up on the bridge.'

"Well, I didn't say anything [after that]. I just drove and took him over, and he said, 'When are you gonna take me over the bridge?' 'You just crossed it,' I said. 'Turn around and look. The lake is back there.'

"He thought that when you crossed a bridge, you'd feel this way, you know, with everything rocking. So when we got turned around and came back, I said, 'Now the bridge is down there. Now we're gonna go over the bridge.'

"And he said, 'This is no bridge. This is a four-lane highway!'"

Life in Bellevue would never be the same.

The mounting years and hardships continued taking their toll among the Issei. Hichiro Matsuzawa, sickly from the day he had been gored by the bull on the dairy farm, finally succumbed in 1932, leaving his wife, two daughters, and four sons.

Hikotara Aramaki, one of the first Bellevue Japanese, fell ill in 1936 and died. His two sons, with 23-year-old Akira in charge, took over the Midlakes farm operation that already was in their names.

And Tom Matsuoka's father, Kanju, died. "Dad went back to Japan," Tom explained. "He got kicked in the head by a horse. He was incapacitated. We got a specialist, and he said you can't do nothing; if we operate on him, he'll probably die. So he thought he'd go to Japan and go to the hot springs; he thought that would help him with the pain. He went there around '38. He stayed there, and he died in '39." Tom's younger brother John, attending the University of Washington at the time, was forced to move back to Auburn and resume farming after the passing of their father, whose pension provided his tuition.

However, even as the first generation was reaching its end, the second generation was beginning to flourish. By the late 1930s and early 1940s, the Japanese began to see their farms producing actual profits, thanks largely to the rapid rise of the Bellevue Vegetable Growers Association.

When the bridge arrived in 1940, their financial security was assured. Or so it seemed.

Japanese families began to be able to afford a few creature comforts—perhaps a car, some appliances like refrigerators and washing machines, even a few tractors. And they were slowly being accepted by their neighbors.

"That seemed like it was more of a time when there was not too much agitation, and everything seemed like it was going good," recalled Joe Matsuzawa. They even had more leisure time: "We were all playing ball."

"It was really getting good before the war," said Mitsi Shiraishi. "It was just beginning to get that the children are growing bigger, and all the families are able to maybe buy a passenger car, whereas before they just had a truck. Things were really getting a little nicer."

But there were storm clouds on the horizon. Tensions were growing between the United States and Japan because of the Sino–Japanese War, particularly since the Americans had sided with the Chinese in that conflict, and Japan's territorial aggressiveness elsewhere in the Pacific. Moreover, the Japanese had entered into an alliance with Hitler. In 1940, the United States imposed economic sanctions.

In Bellevue, those events seemed far away. But Tom Matsuoka said he remembered signs of the gathering storm. From 1939 on, he said, "it was beginning to smell fishy." The Japanese consul paid a visit to the Bellevue clubhouse and told the community that the situation looked grim between the two nations.

"In 1940, I took some kids, around 10, 12 kids, to Japan," Matsuoka recalled. "In Japan that year, they had the 2,600th-year anniversary of the country. . . .

"I took those kids, I traveled around, and oh, always the secret service is behind me. They're always concerned with what train you're on. It was really terrible."

Matsuoka said suspicious Japanese policemen questioned him at length, "because they say I'm the leader. They asked me all kinds of questions: 'Why is this boy's color different?' [I said] it isn't.

"Then they said, 'Look, it's really [a] different [color]—American boys and Japanese people, [there] is a color difference.' . . . Funny kind of question, but that's what they want to know."[72]

Matsuoka returned from that trip with a sense of foreboding. Still, Bellevue seemed far removed and a safe place. Then his world fell apart.

It all ended suddenly, with hardly any warning, on a sunny Sunday morning. It was a clear cold day, the kind of morning when the sun and the crispness made it feel like nothing could go wrong.

Rae Matsuoka Takekawa, like her father, clearly remembered that day. The sky was cloudless, and it was quiet in the way it can only be out in the country. Tom was outside working in his garden, readying it for the coming winter chill, while Rae was tending to chores inside.

"It was around noon, and I did have the radio on, and it dawned on me what was being broadcast on the radio because of course, they interrupted regular programming," Rae recalled. "Dad was working outside. He was covering up this Japanese plant—it's called *udo,* I remember that—and I went running out to tell him. I don't know where my mother was. She was probably visiting someplace because this was Sunday; and I went out to tell him, and he wasn't overly surprised that this had happened."[73]

Six decades later, Matsuoka himself could manage a gentle smile as he remembered the day. "The kids came running out," he recalled. "They heard it on the radio. 'It's a war started!' 'What!' 'Yeah! The Japanese planes have bombed Pearl Harbor!' Oh, God. . . ."[74]

Rae says his reaction was typically Japanese. He was quiet for a moment, contemplative. Then, after awhile, he turned back to his work without a word. The rest of the day was quiet, too. No one talked a lot.

It was only a report on the radio of events that seemed so distant they would take forever to reach their lives in a little backwater farm town like Bellevue. But that night, all hell broke loose.

Chapter 3

"A Jap is a Jap"

THE FBI CAME POUNDING ON TOM MATSUOKA'S DOOR AT 3 A.M. THE morning after the bombing of Pearl Harbor.

"We were sleeping," Matsuoka would recall a half-century later. "There were three guys, three FBI guys. And I thought it was the local police or something. They had two cars without license plates."

Rae, their 15-year-old daughter, had been sleeping in her main-floor bedroom, and hid there, frightened. "So they came in," she recalled. "My mother, I told you she was feisty. She was mad. She was really yelling at those FBI guys.

"Now that I think about it, she was screaming about her rights. She knew. She said, 'You have no right! I have my *rights!* I'm a *citizen!*' This incensed her. She didn't care. She was just yelling at them."

The agents searched the house and confiscated letters and diaries, to see if they could link the owners to Japanese espionage. They made a move to check the loft upstairs, where the family's two boys were in bed, but Kazue Matsuoka barred the way. Perhaps sensing a lost cause, the agents remained on the main floor.

"Then I asked them, 'What you gonna do with me?'" recalled Matsuoka.

"'Well, we'd like to have you questioned in Seattle.'

"'Well, do I need a change of clothes?'

"'Yeah, maybe. You have to take your shaving kit, your toothbrush.'

"Oh boy, that's when I knew I'm not gonna come home right away."

When the FBI drove Tom Matsuoka away in their unmarked cars, he did not know that he would not return to Bellevue. But then, probably no one among the Japanese Americans, in Bellevue and everywhere else on the Pacific Coast, had even an inkling of what the future had in store for them: barbed wire, sagebrush, and the utter destruction of life as they knew it.

Three people were taken away from their homes in Bellevue that night by the FBI. All three were Japanese community leaders—Matsuoka, who was business manager of the Bellevue Vegetable Growers Association; Asaichi Tsushima, who had become a popular public speaker and was the man behind the community's first Japanese language school; and Terumatsu Yabuki, a Yarrow Point greenhouse owner who had the misfortune of having been elected secretary of the Bellevue *Nihonjinkai*, or Japanese Community Association, that year.

If it was the Justice Department's intent to arrest Japanese community leaders, then in the cases of Matsuoka and Tsushima, they had targeted the right men. But Yabuki lived at Hunts Point, away from most of the rest of the community, and had only become active in the *Nihonjinkai* relatively recently. His arrest was mystifying.

"I don't think he was expecting it," recalled his son, Kiyo Yabuki. "He wasn't really a community leader. I was really flabbergasted when they came and took him."

Asaichi Tsushima may have suspected that he would be singled out. His daughter, Michi Nishimura, recalled that when she brought home the news of the attack on Pearl Harbor, "I remember things just got real still. It was quite a traumatic experience. The bottom just fell out of our world.

"That night, some man called and asked if my dad would be home that evening. I said yes. And then a couple of FBI men came over. I didn't know they were FBI until quite a bit later.

"They came over and said, 'We've got to take your father with us.'

"And they wanted him to get some of his clothes together. They wanted to know if we had any guns or anything. Of course, we didn't. I think they went in the bedroom with my dad for him to pack a few things, and they took him off, and that was it."

For all three of the families, the arrests brought home their vulnerability, especially since the remaining households were primarily women. An incident that night underscored their fears. "My mom and I were left there alone," said

Michi Nishimura. "We didn't know what to do. Later that night, it was raining real hard that evening. I slept upstairs by myself. There was just a couple of rooms up there, and I was upstairs, and I had this funny feeling. Just kind of a creepy feeling. And I turned off the light and looked outside, and there was somebody crouched under my window. I ran down the stairs.

"Well, what happened, next day we found this ladder up against the front of the house. My dad had put it there; he had been working on the roof or something. But there was a ladder there, and somebody had crept up there, and was looking in my window. We never did find out who it was."

Matsuoka, Tsushima, and Yabuki held some of the few positions of prominence in the Japanese community, and that seemed to be the main reason they had been arrested. The FBI, working from information that had been compiled from several years' surveillance, had deemed them potentially dangerous under the sudden circumstances of war with Japan.

In fact, the wheels of the nation's intelligence-gathering agencies (initially the Office of Naval Intelligence and later the FBI) had been set into action in 1936, when President Franklin D. Roosevelt, apprised of contacts between Japanese living in Hawaii and Japanese merchant ships that docked at Oahu, ordered that any immigrants who had such contacts "should be secretly but definitely identified and his or her name placed on a special list of those who would be first to be placed in a concentration camp in the event of trouble."[1]

Roosevelt, in fact, had long been a subscriber to the hoary mythology of white supremacy regarding Asians. He was largely skeptical of "Yellow Peril" conspiracy theories regarding Japanese imperial plans for invading America, but he otherwise had fairly conventional views about race, particularly regarding racial attributes and the "Oriental mind." He fervently believed notions that the Japanese comprised an "unassimilable" race that would never be accepted in the American melting pot.[2] In a 1925 editorial column, he laid out these views:

> Let us first examine that nightmare to many Americans, especially our friends in California, the growing population of Japanese on the Pacific slope. It is undoubtedly true that in the past many thousands of Japanese

> have legally or otherwise got into the United States, settled here and raised up children who became American citizens. Californians have properly objected on the sound basic ground that Japanese immigrants are not capable of assimilation into the American population. If this had throughout the discussion been made the sole ground for the American attitude all would have been well, and the people of Japan would today understand and accept our decision.
>
> Anyone who has traveled in the Far East knows that the mingling of Asiatic blood with European or American blood produces, in nine cases out of ten, the most unfortunate results. There are throughout the East many thousands of so-called Eurasians—men and women and children partly of Asiatic blood and partly of European or American blood. These Eurasians are, as a common thing, looked down on and despised, both by the European and American who reside there, and by the pure Asiatic who lives there.
>
> The argument works both ways. I know a great many cultivated, highly educated and delightful Japanese. They have all told me that they would feel the same repugnance and objection to having thousands of Americans settle in Japan and intermarry with the Japanese as I would feel in having large numbers of Japanese come over here and intermarry with the American population.
>
> In this question, then, of Japanese exclusion from the United States, it is necessary only to advance the true reason—the undesirability of mixing the blood of the two peoples. This attitude would be fully understood in Japan, as they would have the same objection to Americans migrating to Japan in large numbers.[3]

FDR's 1936 order for surveillance of Japanese in Hawaii indicated he also subscribed to the widespread doubts about the loyalty of Japanese Americans, some of which had been inflamed by a 1933 report from Army Intelligence in Hawaii charging that a majority of the Japanese in Hawaii, both Issei and Nisei, were actively disloyal and would side with Japan in the event of a war. Moreover, its particular wording—calling for placing "every Japanese citizen or non-citizen" linked to suspicious activity in Hawaii in a "concentration camp"—made clear that Roosevelt, like a majority of Americans, made little distinction between Japanese nationals and Japanese American citizens.[4]

Roosevelt expanded this surveillance to the mainland in 1938, when the War Department began gathering information on Japanese living along the Pacific Coast, again with no differentiation between citizens and Issei. An experienced investigator for the Office of Naval Intelligence, a lieutenant named Kenneth Ringle, was assigned in July 1940 to look into "the Japanese situation" in Southern California; his report concluded that the Nikkei living on the West Coast were "increasingly Americanized" and "believed intensely in the United States and its vision of a better life," and that the number of potentially disloyal Japanese was very small and identifiable. Ringle was directly involved in breaking up the notorious Tachibana spy ring operated by Japan in Los Angeles in 1941, and the evidence he gathered during that investigation indicated, in fact, that officials in Japan viewed American Japanese with great distrust as cultural traitors.[5]

Data the ONI collected through other means suggested a similar assessment. Among these were the ultra-secret "MAGIC" cables, encrypted high-level communications among Japanese diplomats and their home offices that were intercepted and successfully decoded beginning in fall 1940. There were over five thousand of these cables, and the data they revealed was truly vital. In particular, they exposed the existence of a highly active espionage ring operating out of the various Japanese consulates, including the one in Seattle, employing primarily nationals who were agents of the Japanese government. A few of these cables discussed plans to organize a broader espionage network by recruiting civilian spies, including immigrants and their Nisei children. These same cables, however, clearly prioritized targeting disaffected blacks and anti-Semitic neo-Nazis (notably William Dudley Pelley's Silver Shirts organization) for recruitment into such a spy ring, and discussed Japanese Americans only as a kind of final resort, since (the cable noted) they were more likely to arouse suspicion and possible detection, and any detection using such spies would likely bring harsh retribution upon the larger Nikkei communities in the United States. Notably, none of the cables indicated whether any such contacts were ever established, nor did they ever identify any citizen spies.[6]

Roosevelt obtained external analysis of the threat posed by Japanese Americans as well. Some months before the war arrived, President Roosevelt had secured the services of Chicago businessman Curtis Munson in coordinating an intelligence report on Japanese in the United States. Munson's report, delivered on November 7, 1941, couldn't have been more clear: "There will be no armed uprising of Japanese [in the United States]. . . . For the most part the Japanese are loyal to the United States or, at worst, hope that by remaining quiet they can avoid concentration camps or irresponsible mobs. We do not believe that they would be at least any more disloyal than any other racial group in the United States with whom we went to war."[7]

The Justice Department in May 1940, with war clouds forming on the horizon, established a special investigative unit focused on espionage and sabotage, eventually called the Special Defense Unit. It combined information from sources as diverse as the Naval Intelligence intercepts to local FBI informants to build dossiers on more than 2,000 potential suspects.[8] These men were identified by three categories:

- A: "Known dangerous" suspects, people who were influential within their respective communities or who, because of their work, were considered likely members of a "fifth column" of enemy spies.
- B: "Potentially dangerous" people who were suspected of disloyalty but who had not been investigated yet.
- C: Suspects who had demonstrated pro-Japanese leanings or engaged in pro-Japanese propaganda. Under this category, mere participation in local community associations could land a person in the FBI's dossiers.[9]

Armed with this array of intelligence, law enforcement officials believed they were prepared to disarm any kind of serious threat from within by any active spies or fifth columnists in the event of an outbreak of war. When it finally came on December 7, they acted.

None of the three men arrested in Bellevue had any inkling of the surveillance that had resulted in their arrest. Tom Matsuoka always wondered who might have fingered him for suspicion, but said it was clear that his leadership role in the community was responsible. Along with 1,265 other Japanese along the West Coast (103 of them in Seattle the first night; ultimately the Seattle FBI would arrest 413 "enemy aliens"),[10] the three of them were rounded up and taken to holding cells. Since the arrests affected only three Bellevue families, and since the authorities had hinted darkly that these three, like the others being held, might have participated in Japan-sponsored sabotage and espionage, their imprisonment made only a ripple in Bellevue, at least among the community at large. But among the Japanese, it cast a black pall over their future.

"Yes, they got picked up right away, and then everything got even more panicky," recalled Mitsuko Hashiguchi, who by then had gotten married to a Seattle fellow named Mutsuo Hashiguchi, and the two of them had taken the reins of her parents' farm in 1940. She said the arrests had everyone in the community looking over their shoulders, or waiting for a knock at the door to come at night: "Who's gonna be picked up next?"

Other Nisei found unmistakable signs that their world had changed because Japan, a nation they knew little about, had attacked the United States at Pearl Harbor.

Tosh Ito remembered being in Seattle that Sunday when he heard the news. He had taken his mother to visit some of her friends and heard the announcements on the radio. "We spent the day there," he recalled. "Towards evening, I started driving back. Just as I approached the entrance to the tunnel [leading to the Interstate 90 floating bridge], a police officer stopped me. He asked me what I was doing, and I said I was going home to Bellevue. He proceeded to inspect the car, and he looked in the trunk, to see what I had, if anything.

"I guess he couldn't find anything, so he said, 'OK, I'll let you go.' That's the type of things that were going on at that time. There were a lot of unnecessary, uncalled-for excuses to search us to see if we were doing something subversive, or spying."

The next morning, the Japanese children at the local schools received the first harsh lesson in what was in store. "I remember very much, of course, the next day in school," said Rae Takekawa. "And they broadcast President Roosevelt's 'day of infamy' speech. And that, I know, I thought: 'Oh, I'm Japanese.' You felt that. You sort of felt that this was something that really concerned you. Because the whole school listened to this speech. And I felt a little self-conscious about the fact that I was Japanese and not completely American."

Before then, she said, "I went along my way, and I felt I was just as American as anybody else. But from that event, I think I realized more that, in fact, I was not the same as my friends."[11]

The same morning, a school bus driver for the Medina School refused to allow five Japanese children to board his bus, citing an FBI directive against transporting any Japanese. The school's principal, Einar Fretheim, drove to their stop in his own car, picked them up, drove them to school, and then drove them home that afternoon.

He complained to the young school district's youthful board chairman: Kemper Freeman, Miller Freeman's well-educated second son. Freeman asked the FBI for a clarification, and was told the order was not meant to include children. The Nisei students resumed their usual seats on the bus the next day, wondering what was going to happen next.[12]

It was only the beginning.

In the wake of the surprise attack on Pearl Harbor, an immense wave of fear swept the entire Pacific Coast. Expecting the next attack to come on these shores, Americans took to practicing blackouts, watching the skies, and keeping a close eye on their neighbors.

The caution in short order escalated to outright hysteria. On the night of December 8, shortly after 11 o'clock, a mob in downtown Seattle went on a rampage against any business that dared violate the city's suddenly imposed blackout order. Led by a 19-year-old firebrand of a sailor's wife named Ethel Chelsvig, some 2,000 people thronged Seattle's streets and began shattering the plate-glass windows of businesses where lights were showing, including a jewelry store and a sign shop. Police moved in and made a few arrests and the crowd dispersed.[13]

The same night, a false alarm of an air incursion was sounded in San Francisco. Military trackers reported a group of enemy aircraft flying in over the Bay area and later said that the aircraft had turned back to sea without attacking. Headlines along the coast sounded the alarm: "30 ENEMY PLANES FLY OVER S.F.," read the story in the *Seattle Times*, reporting that the planes' presence meant a carrier was in the vicinity, and that "Army Interceptor planes followed the first of the enemy squadrons, but were unable to determine where they finally went."[14] As it turned out, they went nowhere—since there had been no such incursion.[15] (The *Post-Intelligencer*, meanwhile, reported that the "mystery planes" had been "routed."[16])

The next morning, Lt. Gen. John L. DeWitt, the commanding officer of the Fourth Army and Western Defense Command, stormed to the forefront of the scene. The response in San Francisco to the air raid sirens that had sounded the night before had been somewhat less than spectacular: the city had remained lit up as though nothing had happened. DeWitt was furious.

"You people," he told Mayor Angelo Rossi and a gathering of 200 civic and business leaders, "do not seem to realize that we are at war. So get this: Last night there were planes over this community. They were enemy planes. I mean Japanese planes. And they were tracked out to sea. You think it was a hoax? It is damned nonsense for sensible people to think that the Army and Navy would practice such a hoax on San Francisco." However, a dropped bomb or two could have been a good thing, DeWitt opined: "It might have awakened some of the fools in this community who refuse to realize that this is a war."[17]

The next day, a "reliable source" informed DeWitt's staff that an armed uprising of 20,000 Nisei was planned, and the general and his aides spent that night preparing a plan to put all of them in military custody. DeWitt's plan was halted before it could get off the ground by the chief of the local FBI station, Nat Pieper. The "reliable source," it turned out, had been previously employed and fired by the FBI because of his "wild imaginings." Indeed, the number of reputed revolutionaries slightly exceeded the total number of Japanese men, women, and children who resided in the Bay Area.[18]

Acting on similarly "reliable information," DeWitt two weeks later drafted a general alarm for the city of Los Angeles, advising all civilians to leave the city because an attack was imminent. It was, fortunately, never broadcast. By this time, Maj. Gen. Joseph Stillwell—later to gain fame as "Vinegar Joe" of the Burma Campaign, but then still a staff general under DeWitt—had grown impatient with the string of false alarms and noted in his diary that the Presidio staff were behaving like amateurs, and described DeWitt as a "jackass."[19]

Given the benefit of hindsight, it is clear that DeWitt's jitters were largely unfounded. While sporadic raids or attacks along the coast in fact were planned and executed by the Japanese military, a serious invasion—particularly of the scale envisioned by a populace long conditioned to "Yellow Peril" military fantasies—was never seriously contemplated, nor was it logistically feasible at any time.

Though there was very little Japanese naval activity off the Pacific Coast, there was in fact a fleet of nine Japanese supersubs—each carrying tiny one-seat airplanes, midget subs, and state-of-the-art torpedoes—patrolling the coastline in the months immediately after Pearl Harbor. And according to one account, the subs' commanders were prepared to launch a Christmas Eve attack on San Francisco, but were called back at the last minute out of fear of harming Japanese Americans.[20] The fleet, however, was more striking for its ineffectiveness. Compared to its German counterparts in the Atlantic, who sank more than 200 vessels off the American coast, the Japanese subs patrolling American waters sank only 14 merchant ships, never attacked a military vessel, and wound up their abbreviated career with a couple of half-hearted bomb attacks.

The first of these attacks occurred the evening of February 23, 1942, when a sub surfaced and lobbed 13 shells at an oil storage facility on the coast of Santa Barbara, California, only lightly damaging one tank. (The attack inspired the "Battle of Los Angeles" the next night, when the city was blacked out and antiaircraft guns blazed away because of a false report that Japanese fighters were flying overhead.) The second occurred June 21, when Fort Stevens, Oregon—a lightly manned fort on a heavily wooded peninsula near Astoria that provided the defenses for the Columbia River—received similar treatment. The sub fired 17 shells in the vicinity of the fort, causing only damage to a handful of trees. The midget planes carried by the same sub were responsible for releasing a set of incendiary bombs in June and September that landed in the Oregon woods near Mount Emily and Brookings, sparking a forest fire. The bombs also sparked a flurry of headlines in regional newspapers, which in turn inspired federal officials to boost funding for firefighting efforts in Northwest forests.[21] (These bombs at first were described in press accounts as "balloon bombs," though in fact they had been dropped from planes; but a little over two years later, Japanese balloon bombs in fact began arriving in the Northwest. Beginning in November 1944, a Japanese Navy program launched an estimated 9,000 balloons with incendiary and antipersonnel bombs attached into the jet stream that would carry them to North America, though only a few hundred made it, to locales as disparate as Hawaii and Wyoming; the only casualties were a minister's wife and five children who stumbled upon one of the bombs in the woods in Oregon in 1945 and were killed when they tampered with it.)[22]

General DeWitt did not have the luxury of hindsight and had to have the defense of the West Coast as his first priority. Certainly the presence of the Japanese submarines underscored the vulnerability of the numerous defense installations along the coast, as well as various key infrastructure facilities like oil storage tanks and dams. And the news from the battle front was relentlessly bleak: Japanese conquests—of Guam, Wake Island, Malaya, and the Philippines, then Hong Kong and Singapore—came steadily, and news of atrocities like the Bataan Death March inflamed Americans' anger.

DeWitt's concern was reasonable; but as history has shown, his response was not. Erring on the side of caution is one thing, but DeWitt displayed a talent for erring on the side of hysteria and overreaction. When he should have been attempting to calm the populace he instead inflamed it; and rather than assess the threat to the West Coast realistically (as others at the War Department already had), he leapt to assume the bleakest of all possible scenarios, based often on dubious information. He especially assumed the worst regarding Japanese Americans, and here his racial prejudices clearly affected his judgment. Though he initially scoffed at suggestions that all Japanese, immigrant and citizen alike, should be incarcerated, he came to believe that American citizens of Japanese descent posed a significant threat to the security of the coast in general. And the steps by which he did so indicate the nature of his mistake.

DeWitt, as many historians have observed trenchantly, could not have been more poorly suited to the position into which fate had thrust him. The ideal commander of the Western Command would have been a vigorous man with a steady demeanor and a keen understanding of strategic defense. DeWitt, by contrast, was an elderly man with an unremarkable military career who had risen to his position by virtue of steady bureaucratic climbing. He had been a veteran of the Spanish–American War and spent a number of years assigned to duty in the Philippines, where it is clear he was exposed to theories—of the kind popularized in Homer Lea's *The Valor of Ignorance*—regarding an expected invasion of Luzon by Japan. (He later told a reporter he kept a copy of Lea's book handy.) He almost certainly was familiar with the "Yellow Peril" theories and clearly had a disposition toward believing the widespread tales of Japanese treachery common at the time, including the notion that language schools were centers of pro-Japanese propaganda and indoctrination. He repeated as self-evident truths various false stereotypes about the Japanese immigrants, including the old trope that they were highly insular and had no intention of remaining in the United States. Moreover, he was rather credulous, and entertained a paranoia about radio transmitters that underscored his tendency toward hysterics.[23]

The reality might have inspired prudence in a man more inclined toward it. The FBI and other authorities, for instance, seized a total of 2,592 guns,

199,000 rounds of ammunition, 1,652 sticks of dynamite, 1,458 radio receivers, 2,914 cameras, and 37 motion-picture cameras from the Issei whose homes and businesses they raided in the early hours after Pearl Harbor. But there was nothing indicating that any of these items were for anything other than personal use. As the Justice Department explained in its report: "We have not, however, uncovered through these searches any dangerous persons that we could not otherwise know about. We have not found among all the sticks of dynamite and gun powder any evidence that any of it was to be used in bombs. . . . We have not found a camera which we have reason to believe was for use in espionage." After the war, an army historian declared: "In fact, no proved instances of sabotage or of espionage after Pearl Harbor among the west coast Japanese population were ever uncovered."[24] Indeed, as we have seen, the intelligence available to federal authorities already had made the assessment that Japanese Americans generally posed no threat to the security of the nation.

Likewise, military strategists at the War Department were well aware that the Pacific Coast was under no serious threat of being invaded or under any kind of sustained attack. General Mark Clark, then the deputy chief of staff of Army Ground Forces, and Admiral Harold Stark, chief of naval operations, both ridiculed the notion of any kind of serious Japanese attack on the Pacific Coast when they testified that spring before a Senate committee,[25] though Clark (who had spent several years as an officer at Fort Lewis, Washington) did admit that the possibility of an occasional air raid or a sustained attack on the Aleutian Islands "was not a fantastic idea."[26] Secondarily, DeWitt's clamorous appeals for devoting badly needed troops for the defense of the West Coast were dismissed by War Department officials who knew better; to the planners there, preparing an offensive army for operations in Europe and the Pacific, such requests were self-indulgent wastes of their time.[27]

Still, the circumstances surrounding DeWitt's earlier preparations to arrest and evacuate civilians raised for some War Department officials a certain legal difficulty they already were thinking about: there was no precedent for establishing military control of the civilian population, including potential enemy aliens, in non-battlefield situations. Provost Marshal General Allen Gullion, the army's top law enforcement officer, had been concerning himself with the question since 1940. At the request of Army Intelligence, he had prepared a memorandum answering two key questions in anticipation of a possible war: Could the military take police action against "enemy aliens" in a time of war? And what about civilians who aren't aliens? The first question Gullion answered affirmatively, with the stipulation that the aliens be 14 or older; and to the second, rather chilling question, he replied no.[28]

When DeWitt, an old acquaintance, began calling him—well outside the chain of command—to discuss his views about the Japanese American population on the West Coast, Gullion was receptive. DeWitt had, on December 19, 1941, urged the War Department "that action be initiated at the earliest practicable date to collect all alien subjects 14 years of age and over, of enemy nations and remove them" to some location inland, where they would be kept under guard. This action would have affected not only Japanese nationals but Germans and Italians as well.[29]

Gullion began pushing the idea in the War Department. The chief of his Aliens Division, then-Maj. Karl R. Bendetsen, soon drafted a memorandum proposing that the president "place in the hands of the Secretary of War the right to take over aliens when he thought it was necessary." By the turn of the year, Bendetsen (who was shortly promoted to the rank of colonel) and DeWitt were conferring on how to devise plans for the surveillance and control of the Nisei on the West Coast.[30]

DeWitt was hardly alone in fanning the flames of hysteria that ran rampant on the Pacific Coast in the months following Pearl Harbor. In many respects, the record suggests he also was responding to public pressure from a broad array of federal and local officials who began chiming in on the "Japanese question," often trumpeting unfounded rumors to the press as stated fact. Secretary of the Navy Frank Knox, for instance, had declared to reporters that the Pearl Harbor disaster had been a direct result of "fifth column" activity by Japanese-American spies in Hawaii (a report that later proved to be completely groundless).[31] Not surprisingly, politicians of nearly every stripe joined in the headline-grabbing spree. The old anti-Japanese legends of the 1920s surfaced for a fresh retelling: the immigrants were insular mercenaries who intended to return to Japan anyway. Their children were all thoroughly indoctrinated subjects of Tojo. They could never be "American." And they secretly hated us.

A popular consensus had already been reached, confirming suspicions many had held for years: the "Japs" in their midst were spying for Japan. And it was openly encouraged by military and civic leaders.

"People in positions where they could influence the population, they sure did," recalled Tosh Ito. "I think people listened a lot more to them. There was a lot of hysteria because of the media, too."

For a war-happy press anxious for a local angle on the conflict, the prospect of a West Coast invasion made great-selling copy. The *Los Angeles Times* ran headlines like "Jap Boat Flashes Message Ashore" and "Caps on Japanese Tomato Plants Point to Air Base."[32] Pretty soon, everyone was getting into the act. Reports of "signals" being sent to unknown, mysterious Japanese boats offshore began flowing in. One report, widely believed at the time, came from someone who heard a dog barking somewhere along the shore of Oahu, and believed that it was barking in Morse code to an offshore spy ship.[33]

In the Seattle area, the stories were almost as ridiculous. "Arrows of Fire Aim at Seattle" shouted the *Seattle Times*' front-page headline of December 10. It told of fields in the Port Angeles area, between Seattle and the Pacific Ocean on the Olympic Peninsula, that had been set afire by Japanese farmers in a shape resembling an arrow when viewed from the air; ostensibly, the arrow pointed to the Seattle shipyards and airplane-manufacturing plants, a likely target for incoming bombers. The *Seattle Post-Intelligencer* blared a similar front-page story the next morning.[34] Neither paper carried any subsequent stories about the fires—which investigators soon determined had been set by white men who were clearing land.

"Then I heard stories about these guys at Midlakes," remembered Joe Matsuzawa. "They had these wires, and cloth hanging on the wire, out in their crops to scare the birds away. And they said that was pointed to help guide the planes in." The tomato-cap story first circulated in Los Angeles was bandied about in Seattle, too.

Despite having his father locked away, Ty Matsuoka found that his family came under suspicion just for being Japanese. "Our house was on top of the hill there on Bel-Red [Road], and we had a yard light," he recalled. "And you know, you're supposed to shut the yard light off. All lights are supposed to be off at sundown. Ah, you know, kids will be kids, and sometimes you forget to shut the darn yard light off because you'd be out there. I guess 8 or 9 o'clock it'd get dark. And this woman lived on 116th, which would be down the hill and across. And she would call the sheriff's office whenever we didn't shut the light off by 9 o'clock. So he'd have to come. And the thing is, I was in the same grade as her son. Those kinds of things you tend to remember."

Self-appointed protectors of the community also forced Japanese Americans out of their jobs. In Seattle, 26 young Nisei women were forced to resign their positions as clerks in the Seattle School District after a group of mothers in the Gatewood PTA protested their employment.[35]

Miller Freeman—still recovering from a stroke he had suffered in November—believed fully that his warnings against the Japanese had been proved prophetic by Pearl Harbor, and sprang into action on the Eastside. He spearheaded a "special committee" of Bellevue citizens intended to ensure that none of their Japanese neighbors engaged in treasonous activity. He convened a series of meetings, the first held December 13 at the Camp Fire House with a delegation of white community leaders, including A. J. Whitney, editor of the local weekly, the *Bellevue American*—which dutifully reported on the sessions—and five representatives from the Japanese community: three Nisei, including Tok Hirotaka, Akira Aramaki, and Masami Inatsu; and two Issei, Kanji Hayashi and Komaji Takano.[36]

Freeman opened the proceedings with a speech that outlined his intentions: "Our job is to see what can be done to face the practical problems before us. Naturally we are interested in the defense of this nation. Some of you are aliens and some are citizens. We want to deal with the problem with you people in an orderly way; in one that is considerate and thoughtful, but not through prejudice or emotion. We don't want things happening in this district. We want to deal with you frankly; don't want anybody's feelings hurt, but we are at war and we can't pussy-foot about it.

"There are some things that are going to be required of the Japanese in this district; some of which has already been imposed upon you, such as restrictions on finance and on travel, etc. War just having broke out, there are still a lot of details to be worked out. My own feeling is that it is possible to undertake in every way possible a joint consideration of these problems rather than to have something done that is a hardship on you people.

"If there is any injustice, we want to see that that is controlled. We want to protect you people, but do not want to let the situation drift."

Freeman added that he would like to make a model in this district "of our relations with the Japanese who are here in justice and fairness, and which may be a model for the rest of the country wherever there are Japanese who are colonized."

Akira Aramaki responded first. "American citizens and nationals are willing to do their part 100 percent," he said, "but at the present time the young people, a lot of them are afraid to venture out on account of the hysteria at the present time. Last night we went to a JACL meeting, and they are 100 percent—in all National Defense, Red Cross, etc. The older people were telling me to do everything we can for National Defense, and so I just go around now and start whatever we can locally. We would have enough to do here. We have been a little slow at it for fear of going out. We are told to stay in as much as possible."

Another committeeman suggested that a good place for the Japanese to start showing their loyalty would be by turning in any "Fifth Column" spies in their midst or reporting on any "un-American activities." Freeman pursued the point further.

"I am coming now to certain recommendations I want to suggest to you for consideration, which in view of your own background and training you may at first find it difficult to accept or even clearly understand, but I think we should face these things frankly," he said. "These are not suggestions of the committee, but of myself.

"One: You should sever all connections with the Japanese Government—that includes disbanding any pro-Japanese organizations designed to promote the Imperial Japanese government interests. There can't be any half-and-half business—must be 100 percent.

"Two: Stop all relationships with Japanese consular representatives.

"Three: Stop using the Japanese language."

Kanji Hayashi, one of the only Issei at the meeting, interrupted, trying to explain to Freeman that he misunderstood the position of the Nisei. In halting English, he told the gathering that "some people have the idea some of them are under obligation to the Japanese government, but that has never existed—they have no relations with the Japanese Consul. The first generation cannot become citizens of this country and their country (government) must look after the welfare of those people. What they did was just to take care of them."

"Let us put an end to all that," declared Freeman.

Freeman was repeating a tenet of "Yellow Peril" mythology: the notion that Japanese children born in the United States were automatically given dual citizenship in Japan, and that the emperor considered all the Nisei to be his subjects. There was only a grain of truth to this; dual citizenship was indeed granted automatically until 1924, at which time the Japanese government altered its policy, allowing Nisei to gain such status only if their parents registered their names at a Japanese consulate within two weeks of their birth.)

Freeman then continued with the remainder of his points: "Now, I think that all Japanese language school should be stopped."

"Already stopped," Kanji Hayashi volunteered.

"You have had it up to now?"

"Yes."

"May I ask now," Freeman queried, "what was the purpose of running those schools and the older people requiring that the younger people go to the Japanese schools?"

"Just teach them the Japanese language, that is all," Hayashi explained. "No other purpose, I think."

"Our feeling is that they were propaganda schools to teach loyalty to the Japanese empire," Freeman said. "I think we should stop all Japanese-language newspapers and publication in this United States of America. English is the language of this country. Use English and English papers."

Tok Hirotaka piped up: "Because our parents couldn't speak English, so they had to teach children something about Japanese."

"I am going to suggest it was the business of older people to talk English rather than Japanese," Freeman replied.

"I wish someone could have told them before, we couldn't," said an exasperated Hirotaka. "People like Mr. Hayashi—his children never did go to Japanese school, but they (the old folks) don't all understand English like he does; or Mr. Takano. My mother is 65—here 40 years, longer than she was in Japan, but she can't talk English very well. Rest of us all talk English at home, but to her I still talk Japanese."

"I suggest that in the future no longer should older Japanese insist that these young students be raised and trained in the ways of the Japanese and their language," Freeman said.

Hayashi tried to explain why the Issei found the language so hard: "Japanese language is entirely different from other nations' and it is awfully hard for people to get mastery of it."

"The English language is not hard to learn," replied Freeman.

"Italian or Swedish understand English better than Japanese," said Hayashi.

Freeman moved on. "We have in this country a situation, not merely with the Japanese, but with Germans and Italians, of what we call dual citizenship. I think one of the ways young Japanese can show loyalty to us is to make a demonstration—show that they have obtained release of citizenship from Japan, in other words, apply to the Japanese government to be expatriated. To what degree has that been done? How about you young fellows?"

Tok Hirotaka was firm: "I am an American citizen. I have never had dual citizenship."

Freeman proceeded to lecture them: "Your standing would be so much better and I would like to see you young fellows get together and make a study of that, and reflect, and see what legal ways there are to get on record that you are free from any thoughtless conditions that are allowed to come up," he said. "It is not going to be easy, it is complicated. You can do your share by applying for it in the proper legal way.

"You fellows think you are Americans, you are loyal. Unless you try to get expatriation from Japan, they claim you are citizens regardless of whether you are or not."

The Nisei were astonished: "I never knew that," Aramaki said.

"Oh, no," demurred Hayashi. All of them shook their heads.

"We might investigate further," said Freeman, not so sure of himself now.

"Do you mean if we are American citizens, born here, we still have connection with Japanese government, regardless of whether we were born here?" asked Tok Hirotaka.

"That is correct, unless you could show positive proof of definite release," Freeman said. "Every one of you fellows are subject to draft of Japan."

"No," said Aramaki.

"Oh, no," said Hirotaka.

"Unless you get that release," Freeman kept saying.

"As American citizens they don't take you in the army," Aramaki said. "I am positive." And he would have been; he had just accompanied Tom Matsuoka to Japan the year before and had observed the military's behavior firsthand.[37]

"If they registered at the Japanese consulate then they become Japanese citizens," explained Hayashi. "If they did not register, he or she, born in this country—Japan has never claimed their citizenship."

"Are your children registered with Japanese consulate?" queried Freeman.

"No," answered Hayashi. Komaji Takano, the other Issei at the meeting, also answered negatively.

"Is it desirable or practical to have a census taken in this community? Does your association have a census?" asked Freeman.

"Not all the children," Takano replied. "Just old folks. . . . It was about April or March I tried to see Japanese, if there are any dual citizens, and I found out there are no dual citizens."

"Who did you ask?" Freeman said.

"All of the Japanese around here, so I don't think [there are any]."

"It may be in spirit," Freeman said. "Question is, I am asking you about the legal status."

"You mean, you want action," Aramaki said.

"I would like to suggest that you get rid of Japanese language newspapers. Instead of there being a lot of mystery and secrecy, let us all lay the cards on the table in good American fashion."

"There is no Japanese paper published in Bellevue," said Hayashi. "All cannot read or speak English so their news is just through Japanese papers."

"I tell you you fellows can read these papers," replied Freeman. "Japanese papers are like German papers—carry propaganda, et cetera, threats."

"The FBI stopped that right away," Aramaki replied. "Japanese papers now come out with [the] same thing as United States papers translated in Japanese."

Speaking of the FBI, the Nisei inquired as to the whereabouts of Tom Matsuoka and Asaichi Tsushima. Freeman said the committee would look into it—and on that note, called it a night.

Tosh Ito was also at the meeting, and he recalled the implied threat of Freeman's message: that the Japanese were now at the mercy of their neighbors and had better not step out of line. "The thing that stuck in my mind was that he said, 'You guys are going to have to learn to live with the shitty end of the stick,'" Ito said.

At its next meeting two weeks later at Freeman's home, the only topic of discussion was a letter Freeman had received from R. P. Bonham, director of the Seattle District of the U.S. Immigration and Naturalization Service. Bonham's explanation corroborated Kanji Hayashi's explanation in every detail and shattered Freeman's premise: "In connection with the Japanese laws on the subject, it appears that prior to 1916 all children of Japanese parentage, wherever born, were considered the subjects of Japan, regardless of whether the birth was recorded at the Japanese consulate or otherwise. . . . On December 1, 1924, the Japanese congress enacted a statute which provided in effect that children born outside of Japan to Japanese subjects would not be considered citizens of Japan unless the subjects' births were reported to the nearest Japanese consulate within two weeks after the date of the birth."[38]

Freeman's committee nonetheless "recommended that the extent to which the children of Japanese parentage have been so registered with the nearest Japanese consulate be determined." The committee also recommended an investigation of Japanese schools, saying it "believes the real purpose of conducting these schools was as propaganda agencies to assure the loyalty of American-born Japanese to the Japanese government."

Eight days later, on New Year's Eve, Freeman called the members of the committee for yet another session. Not all the Caucasian board members were present—Whitney was absent, though Freeman's son Kemper was along—but neither were all the Japanese who had been "invited." Only Kanji Hayashi, Komaji Takano, and Akira Aramaki showed. And that was a problem.

"Why are two other men of your committee not here?" demanded Freeman. "I want to make perfectly clear that when you are called to meeting here it is the United States Government!

"Now, as I told you before—the aim of this committee is to try to be cooperative with you Japanese in understanding your difficulties and to try to have an exchange of views and what may be done. The objects: first of all—protecting you Japanese; but more than that, assuring your cooperation with this country in the war. We don't want any misunderstanding about it. Regarding the failure of these two men to appear immediately does this—it puts you all, as a community, under suspicion."

No one had a reply.

"You had notice yesterday—why are they not here? We all here left our work to sit down and talk with you about your problems. The feeling is becoming much more serious all the time in this country. If it is going to be your disposition to cooperate with this Government, we want to know it and we don't want any fooling.

"There were two other men at the last meeting. Hirotaka—did he go to Kent [in south King County]?"

"I told him but he didn't come," Akira Aramaki answered. "Inatsu—he has no telephone. I asked Hirotaka to tell him. I asked him to last meeting, and he did. I didn't go myself."

"I want to be fair with you people," Freeman said. "I don't like the business of calling a meeting with everybody notified and not all being here."

There was nothing further to be said. Freeman, disgusted, called the meeting off in short order, saying the committee could reconvene when better Japanese representation could be had.

There is no evidence the committee ever met again.[39] Nor did it ever answer the question of Tom Matsuoka's whereabouts.

When Tom Matsuoka got out of the car with the FBI agents who had arrested him, he recognized right away where he was: the Immigration and Naturalization Service building in Seattle. "That's where the first they—all the ones they picked up they bring out to the Immigration building. They picked them up, then went in. They don't even say name: '99!' My number was 99. Oh, that's it. They knew, 99, who it is. So they must have been already prepared."

Matsuoka found himself in familiar company. "And now I went in, in the one room—'Holy smoke! You come too, Tom? Aw, doggone it!' And that was, the . . . export-import company people was in [the] room where I went in. There must have been 40 or so.

"Then next morning, [we went to] breakfast, and . . . a whole bunch of Japanese was in the hall already! 'Oh, there you are! You in the house too!' That's all we know. But we know that the leaders in Seattle, all those [were] picked up first, I think. Those people were already there eating breakfast.

"Oh, they got to talking and it's back and forth, back and forth," he recalled with a laugh. "'Is Freddie here? Is Freddie coming?'"

Arrangements had already been made to house the detainees at the army base in Missoula, Montana, some 500 miles inland, after they had cleared their initial processing. Most Nisei citizens caught up in the sweep by accident were released, since the target was "enemy aliens." Likewise, most "Kibei"—the Nisei with American citizenship who were educated in Japan and returned to the United States as young adults, like Tom Matsuoka—were released, though they were considered potential sympathizers with the Japanese cause. Matsuoka remembers other Kibei being released within a few days.

Matsuoka, however, was something of a special case. He was unable to produce proof of his citizenship; he had no birth certificate, and the county records in Maui, where he was born, were unavailable, so he was ordered to remain in custody.

His family came to see him before he was to be shipped out. "Now, my mother, I don't know how she arranged it, or whether she did have to arrange it," said Rae Takekawa. "All I know is that she took us, all of us, she took us to see my dad. And we went to this . . . well, I understand now that it's the immigration office. It was actually a jail, where they held them. It was like that.

"And we all filed into a room, and they brought him in so that we could talk. And I was, let me see, 14. . . . And you just don't know what to say. So you sit there in a row, all of us kids, my mother, and you say the most insane things; I know I said some really stupid things. But you just can't believe how it felt to be in this room with your father, who you hadn't seen, and realize that it was ... a rather precarious situation, 'cause you just didn't know what was going to happen. . . . It was a situation that was sad."[40]

On December 18, some 364 of the remaining detainees were shipped out by rail car to Fort Missoula in Montana, and arrived in the little college town the next day. Tom Matsuoka was among them.

Most of his fellow detainees were shocked to arrive at their new quarters in the middle of winter. "Missoula, you know, they think that was a hell of a cold place," laughed Tom Matsuoka, who eventually would wind up spending the next 48 years as a Montanan. "But it's not—Missoula is not that cold. People in Montana, they call it the Banana Belt."

Already interned at Fort Missoula was a contingent of about 900 Italian nationals arrested shortly after Pearl Harbor, seamen who'd had the misfortune to be docked in American ports when war broke out. The two factions were largely kept separate, sharing only dining facilities that were used in segregated rotations. By April 1, 1942, the detainee population totaled 2,003 at Fort Missoula, roughly half of them Japanese and half Italian. The Italians were housed in old wooden Army barracks, while the Japanese were placed in hastily constructed tarpaper barracks whose appearance would become familiar to all of the coastal Japanese within the year.[41]

Despite the region's reputation for vigilantism, the residents of Missoula were admirably restrained in their treatment of the internees. The local paper, the *Missoulian*, counseled local residents: "There is no excuse for anti-Japanese hysteria in this part of the United States." The fort's supervisor of alien detentions, Nick Collaer, reported that the Japanese had expected harsh treatment upon their arrival at the fort, but were "very much surprised at the kind treatment afforded them."[42]

The detention centers, though, were not designed for activity. With stifling boredom their chief prospect for the coming months, the detainees settled in for the winter and awaited spring's arrival, whatever it might bring.

Some of the Nisei made bold public efforts to reassure their white neighbors that they were loyal citizens. Even before Pearl Harbor, 46 of the Japanese in Bellevue—including Tom Matsuoka, Michi Tsushima, and Kameji Yabuki—gained public notice in setting a local record by purchasing some $1,875 worth of U.S. Defense Bonds. The deed garnered a front-page story in the *Bellevue American* of November 21.[43]

After Pearl Harbor, the public relations efforts became more pronounced. Leaders of the Japanese American Citizens League held press conferences announcing their intent to cooperate fully with the war effort and to prove their loyalty to the nation. To that end, they even proudly described their cooperation in the arrests of the community's Issei leaders. James Sakamoto, editor of the *Japanese-American Courier*, averred that the Nisei "will remain unswervingly loyal to the United States" and that they would be the "first to uncover any saboteurs" among pro-Japanese elements. "There may be a little hysteria, an occasional outburst up and down the Coast. But I have a lot of confidence in American fair play. Americans are fair to the underdog. And the American-born Japanese are in that spot right now."[44]

These rather abject pleas fell on deaf ears, particularly where it counted. In private conversations, Gen. DeWitt and Karl Bendetsen, discussing the loyalty of Japanese Americans, remarked to each other that the very Nisei proclaiming their loyalty were actually more suspicious: "The ones giving you only lip service are always the ones to suspect," Bendetsen said.[45]

Nor was the public any more sympathetic. By late February the removal of all Japanese from the West Coast had become a favorite topic from Los Angeles to Seattle, led particularly by politicians. One of these was Rep. Andrew Jackson Hinshaw, an Orange County Republican, who demanded in early March that the Roosevelt administration "stop fiddling around" and begin removing all Japanese from the coast. According to the Associated Press, Hinshaw "said he had word that Japanese plans call for a major attack on Hawaii and West Coast sabotage next month. His information, he added, came 'from a source which has been heretofore reliable, though unheeded by our government.'"[46]

The removal would not be without problems, warned some. "Approximately 95 percent of the vegetables grown here are raised by the Japanese," noted J. R. Davidson, market master for the Pike Place Public Market in Seattle, where Eastside Japanese sold many of their goods. "About 35 percent of the sellers in the market are Japanese. Many white persons are leaving the produce business to take defense jobs, which are not open to the Japanese."[47] Letter writers to the local newspapers raised the same concern.

Their fears were quickly derided. Wrote Charlotte Drysdale of Seattle in a letter to the *Post-Intelligencer:*

> It has been interesting to note how many contributors have been afraid we would have no garden truck if the Japs are sent to concentration areas. We had gardens long before the Japs were imported about the turn of the century, to work for a very low wage (a move for which we are still paying dearly) and we can still have them after we have no Japs.
>
> Isn't that discounting American ability just a little too low?
>
> And by Americans I mean not the children of the races ineligible to naturalization. The mere fact that a child is born in this country should not give him the rights and privileges of citizenship.
>
> The fourteenth amendment, granting automatic citizenship to American born, was placed there for the protection of the Negro and at that time the great infiltration of Japs was not even thought of. In recent years there has been so much fear of hurting the feelings of these people that no one has had the courage to try to rectify the situation. Now it would seem that the time is ripe to put things right, for once and for all time.[48]

She was not alone in this sentiment. Senator Tom Stewart of Tennessee proposed stripping citizenship from anyone of Japanese descent: "A Jap's a Jap anywhere," he said.[49]

The press became the chief cheerleaders for removing the Japanese. The *Seattle Times* ran a news story alerting its readers: "Hundreds of alien and American-born Japanese are living near strategic defense units, a police survey showed today. . . . There are Japanese in the neighborhood of every reservoir, bridge and defense project."[50]

The *Times* also ran columns by noted conservative Henry McLemore, who frequently attacked the presence of Japanese descendants on the West

Coast. In one column, headlined, "This Is War! Stop Worrying About Hurting Jap Feelings," McLemore fulminated: "I am for the immediate removal of every Japanese on the West Coast to a point deep in the interior. I don't mean a nice part of the interior, either. Herd 'em up, pack 'em off and give 'em the inside room of the badlands. Let 'em be pinched, hurt, hungry and dead up against it. . . . Personally, I hate the Japanese. And that goes for all of them."[51]

His sentiments were shared by many of the locals. Wrote W. M. Mason of Seattle, in a letter to the editor of the *Post-Intelligencer:* "If there be those who would say we can't do this to citizens, let them remember that we took this country from the Indians, killed thousands of them, arbitrarily moved other thousands from their homes to far distant lands, and to this day have denied them the rights, duties and privileges of citizenship.

"If we could do that to the Indians, we can do something about the Japs.

"Let's do it now!"[52]

At the outset, General DeWitt was opposed to a chorus calling for the expulsion of all "persons of Japanese ancestry," calling it "damned nonsense" and asserting in mid-December: "An American citizen is, after all, an American citizen. And while they all may not be loyal, I think we can weed the disloyal out of the loyal and lock them up if necessary." This seemingly remained his position for the next month or so, during which time he gradually shifted to the opposite view.[53]

This metamorphosis occurred under a combination of circumstances, the most notable of which was the apparent influence of Provost Marshal General Gullion and his lawyer protégé, Karl Bendetsen, a native of Aberdeen, Washington, and a Stanford graduate. At first, DeWitt and Bendetsen devoted themselves to mapping out militarily sensitive areas that would be designated "exclusionary zones." The first iterations of these zones included cities with large Japanese populations, including Seattle and Portland (though the order would have affected Germans and Italians as well). The logistical difficulties of evacuating thousands of people from these areas raised an immediate red flag from Attorney General Francis Biddle, who scotched the proposal. Biddle also refused DeWitt's requests for conducting mass raids on the Japanese communities in hopes of turning up evidence of espionage, citing the rights of citizens against that kind of search and seizure.[54]

It also became readily apparent that separating out the loyal from the disloyal would be more difficult than first imagined. For starters, the Kibei—widely suspected, after the Issei, of staying loyal to the emperor, due to their ostensible "indoctrination" in Japanese schools—were in fact American citizens, so using citizenship as a criterion was rendered more complex. Further, thousands of the Nisei were still children fully dependent on their Issei parents; evacuating the Issei would wind up tearing many families apart, an outcome the planners sought to avoid. These difficulties no doubt began to nudge the planners toward a "clean" solution, like blanket evacuation.[55]

However, DeWitt's credulous inclination toward "Yellow Peril" conspiracy theories and preconceptions about "Orientals" also played a significant role. Intelligence reports rolled in that he found highly alarming, including one suggesting that there was an "espionage net containing Japanese aliens, first and second generation Japanese and other nationals . . . thoroughly organized and working underground."[56] DeWitt reported to Guillion that an FBI raid on Bainbridge Island had turned up "guns, ammunition, explosives, radio, short-wave, and other contraband. . . . I wouldn't have you repeat that, but it shows the situation up here."[57] Of course, most of these items would have shown up in a search of any Japanese farmer's belongings—or any Caucasian farmer, for that matter—but the ethnicity of their owners was the difference in DeWitt's mind. By this time, he seems to have concluded that none of the Nisei could be trusted, either. In a January 21 phone call with General Mark Clark, DeWitt proclaimed that he expected "a violent outburst of coordinated and controlled sabotage" among the Japanese population.[58]

DeWitt also had a predilection for believing false or grossly distorted information. He repeated in high-level meetings the charge that every ship departing from the mouth of the Columbia River encountered an enemy submarine, even though his own intelligence reports made clear that this was not the case (in fact, there had been only sporadic submarine sightings along the Pacific Coast in the weeks immediately following the outbreak of war, after which they tapered off dramatically). And even though the FCC repeatedly informed him it had no evidence of shore-to-ship radio communications, he repeated in various written reports and meetings regarding enemy aliens the claim that these were occurring with great frequency.[59]

DeWitt's credulousness made him, in the estimation of many who knew him, highly susceptible to strong personalities. In this respect, Allen Gullion and (particularly) Karl Bendetsen played critical roles. DeWitt readily followed their leads, and in the end became a kind of front man for their agenda: namely, to transfer authority over a civilian population in wartime to the War Department. Bendetsen, in fact, authored nearly all of the policies regarding control of "enemy aliens" and citizens adopted by DeWitt during the aftermath of Pearl Harbor. If there were any true architects of the subsequent internment of Japanese Americans, Bendetsen comes closest to the description, and Gullion the authority behind him. Incrementally, in some cases almost imperceptibly, they proposed a series of policies that eventually resulted in the mass evacuation and internment of Japanese Americans under military authority.

There is no indication that the initiative for the evacuation came from above, as some have theorized. Both Secretary of War Henry Stimson and Assistant Secretary John McCloy, their immediate superiors, remained skeptical about the constitutionality of (as well as the need for) removing the Japanese from the coast. Both pressed DeWitt for more information regarding his claim for the "military necessity" of evacuation. In the meantime, however, Stimson agreed to DeWitt's request to establish "prohibited zones" in the western states, limited tracts from which enemy aliens might forcibly be removed to ensure the safety of military and key industrial sites in those regions. On January 25, Stimson recommended to Attorney General Biddle that the zones be established.[60]

However, it is also clear that among the people responsible for establishing these policies, from President Roosevelt down to General DeWitt, the belief that Japanese American citizens were untrustworthy and likely to engage in spying and sabotage was considered almost conventional wisdom; likewise, the subsequent perception that there was little point in attempting to differentiate between Japanese nationals and Japanese American citizens. In the case of Roosevelt, it's clear that this worldview was established well before the outbreak of war and was predicated on the kind of false stereotypes that were the legacy of the anti-Japanese campaigns of a generation before.

The same was probably true of the other participants as well. By February 9, it became apparent that Bendetsen, Gullion, and DeWitt had persuaded Stimson and McCloy to agree to the thrust of their proposals. Stimson remarked in his diary that he now favored mass evacuation, since it was clear that Nisei citizens' loyalty was questionable, observing that "their racial characteristics are such that we cannot understand or even trust the citizen Japanese." McCloy, on February 11, urged Stimson to persuade FDR to evacuate both citizens and enemy aliens from the West Coast.[61]

Biddle was the only high-level official in the administration who opposed the proposed evacuation. From the outset, he "was determined to avoid mass internment, and the persecution of aliens that had characterized World War I." He was skeptical that Nisei citizens posed a threat to either general security or the military, and suspected that the "military necessity" that DeWitt claimed was a figment of his imagination and prejudices. Further, he had grave reservations about the constitutionality of evacuation.[62]

But Biddle had few allies on this front, other than J. Edgar Hoover, who scoffed at the military's insistence on pressing for mass evacuation. In particular, Stimson had swallowed DeWitt's claims whole, and he had the president's ear on all things military. Just as important, the rising tide of popular sentiment against Japanese Americans among whites on the West Coast, stoked by the hysterical press accounts, brought congressmen and senators out of the woodwork to pressure both Biddle and Roosevelt.

Helping lead the charge in Congress was Washington's own Senator Mon Wallgren, a New Deal Democrat from Everett who was chairman of the Committee on Alien Nationality and Sabotage.[63] Though military authorities transmitted information to his panel that the West Coast was not under any invasion threat, the advice was rejected insultingly, with "hotheads" on the committee calling military leaders "jackasses" and declaring they were not going to wait for another Pearl Harbor in Los Angeles.

From its first meetings on February 5, it was clear that the focus of the sessions would be taking control of all persons of Japanese ancestry on the Pacific Coast, citizen and alien alike. Attorney General Biddle testified against tampering with the rights of citizens. However, Colonel Bendetsen testified that it was the military's view that mass evacuation should occur. Ultimately, Wallgren's committee and a combined delegation of West Coast congressmen issued a unanimous resolution recommending "the immediate evacuation of all persons of Japanese lineage and all others, aliens and citizens alike, whose presence shall be deemed dangerous or inimical to the safety of the defense of the United States from all strategic areas."[64]

Congressman Leland Ford of Los Angeles demanded on the House floor that all Japanese, citizen and alien alike, be evacuated. Growing impatient, he reported that he called Biddle's office "and told them to stop fucking around. I gave them twenty-four hours' notice that unless they would issue a mass evacuation notice I would drag the whole matter out on the floor of the House and of the Senate and give the bastards everything we could with both barrels. I told them they had given us the runaround long enough . . . and that if they would not take immediate action, we would clean the goddamned office in one sweep. I cussed the Attorney General himself and his staff just like I'm cussing you now and he knew damn well I meant business."[65]

With Pearl Harbor as a pretext, the voices of white supremacism rose to assert themselves in the fore. "This is a race war," proclaimed Mississippi Congressman John Rankin on the House floor. "The white man's civilization has come into conflict with Japanese barbarism. . . . Once a Jap always a Jap. You cannot change him. You cannot make a silk purse out of a sow's ear. . . . I say it is of vital importance that we get rid of every Japanese, whether in Hawaii or on the mainland. . . . I'm for catching every Japanese in America, Alaska, and Hawaii now and putting them in concentration camps. . . . Damn them! Let's get rid of them now!"[66]

The Japanese, charged Tennessee's Tom Stewart on the Senate floor, "are among our worst enemies. They are cowardly and immoral. They are different from Americans in every conceivable way, and no Japanese who ever lived anywhere should have a right to claim American citizenship. A Jap is a Jap anywhere you find him, and his taking an oath of allegiance to this country would not help, even if he should be permitted to do so. They do not believe in God and have no respect for an oath. They have been plotting for years against the Americas and their democracies."[67]

DeWitt echoed that sentiment when later asked to justify the army's plans for mass deportations. "A Jap is a Jap," was his famous response at a congressional subcommittee hearing (though the catchphrase had been around since the heyday of James Phelan). "They are a dangerous element. There is no way to determine their loyalty. It makes no difference whether he is an American citizen; theoretically he is still a Japanese, and you can't change him. You can't change him by giving him a piece of paper."[68]

Initially, Biddle agreed to establish DeWitt's exclusion zones along the Pacific Coast, but only for the purpose of excluding enemy aliens—not citizens. That, however, fell far short of satisfying DeWitt. In early February, he asked Stimson to seek approval to expand the size and scope of the exclusion zones. Stimson went over Biddle's head and, on February 11, talked directly to the president, saying the Justice Department was dragging its feet, and that he wanted to make plans to evacuate all people of Japanese descent from the military zones. Roosevelt gave him the green light, telling Stimson "there will probably be repercussions but it has got to be dictated by military necessity," adding: "Be as reasonable as you can." This telephone conversation eventually proved to be the decisive point at which the internment became inevitable.[69]

In the meantime, the FBI stayed busy investigating each of the reports of radio signals, numerous "arrows of fire," lights flashing in Morse code, and all the other reports of potential spy activity, both in Hawaii and along the West Coast. Investigators found not a single case where any actual spying activity had taken place.

FBI director J. Edgar Hoover personally discounted the reports after viewing the evidence. In a memorandum to President Roosevelt, he reported that Knox's assertion about "fifth column" activity in Hawaii was simply false, and in other memos he derided DeWitt's "hysteria and lack of judgment." He referred to the Seattle "arrows of fire" report as a specific instance where normal, innocent activity was mistakenly cast as something sinister; white landowners had been clearing land and burning slash, with winds blowing from the west pushing the fire eastward, and a nervous neighbor had reported them. In every case, Hoover found, supposed Japanese espionage activity was nothing other than hysteria.[70]

Yet in the Kafkaesque logic that became DeWitt's hallmark, this very lack of evidence became proof itself of the Japanese plans for sabotage. On February 14, he issued a detailed memorandum at Stimson's request (authored by Bendetsen) outlining his assessment of the situation facing the Western Command. It foresaw not just military attacks on the coast, but active sabotage by a fifth column: "The Japanese race is an enemy race and while many second and third generation Japanese born on United States soil, possessed of United States citizenship, have become Americanized, the racial strains are undiluted. To conclude otherwise is to expect that children born of white parents on Japanese soil sever all racial affinity and become loyal Japanese subjects, ready to fight, and if necessary, to die for Japan in a war against the nation of their parents. . . . It therefore follows that along the vital Pacific Coast over 112,000 potential enemies, of Japanese extraction, are at large today. There are indications that these are organized and ready for concerted action at a favorable opportunity. The very fact that no sabotage has taken place to date is a disturbing and confirming indication that such action will be taken."

DeWitt's memorandum, which included all Japanese American citizens among the categories of people to be excluded from "sensitive areas," called for their mass evacuation, which would necessitate establishing "initial concentration points, reception centers, registration, rationing, guarding, transportation to internment points and the selection and establishment of internment facilities." The memorandum, with Stimson's seal of approval, essentially made mass evacuation all but a *fait accompli*.[71]

Stimson shortly convened a meeting of War Department aides to plan a presidential order enabling the evacuation under the auspices of the U.S. Army. A few days later, on February 19, 1942, Roosevelt signed Executive Order 9066, "Authorizing the Secretary of War to Prescribe Military Areas."

The fate of the Japanese on the West Coast had been sealed.

In Bellevue and other Japanese communities, uncertainty mingled with fear for both Issei and Nisei. Rumors ran rampant; some wondered aloud if they were going to be lined up against a wall and shot. But a massive relocation of their population was the one constant in all the discussions.

"The Japanese who were citizens assumed that the ones who were going to have to go away were the Japanese who were not citizens," recalled Rae Takekawa. "They never really dreamed, at the beginning, that it would happen to them too."

With all the community leaders arrested, there was hardly anyone left to speak up on behalf of the Japanese—except, perhaps, for the Japanese American Citizens League, and its national leaders (as well as those in Seattle) were announcing their intention to cooperate with evacuation, on the condition that the "military necessity" be made clear.[72] By the time DeWitt issued his final recommendations, political pressure overwhelmed any quibbling, even though his reasoning was suspect at best. Moreover, popular sentiment shouted down any whites who might defend their Japanese neighbors. Those who did were labeled "Jap lovers."

When Roosevelt signed Executive Order 9066, Congress went to work as well. A House Select Committee headed by Democratic Rep. John Tolan of California held hearings at various cities along the coast with the ostensible purpose of deciding what to do about the "Jap problem." Actually, that had already been decided; army officials were drawing up the plans for the evacuation of the 120,000 Issei and Nisei who lived in DeWitt's "military exclusion zones."

Though this was not public knowledge, the Japanese sensed the matter indeed was settled, and watched the Tolan hearings with some degree of skepticism. Many now call the hearings "a farce." The general tone of the hearings, said one Nisei, was "to give us a fair trial before they hung us."

When the hearings came to Seattle the first week of March, some of the region's leading Japanese bashers came to voice support for a course of action that had already been decided. Miller Freeman, who had a long and colorful history of making denunciations against the Japanese, leapt front and center. His testimony in favor of immediate evacuation of all Japanese to the interior, where they could be kept under guard, led the *Post-Intelligencer*'s coverage of the Seattle hearing.

"Freeman Calls Japan Society 'Fifth Column,'" read the headline. The story revolved around a recapitulation of Freeman's oft-stated views regarding Japanese Americans, which were portrayed as keen foresight:

> Prominent officials of the United States government, lawyers, educators, ministers, peace advocates, and members of the Japan Society of Seattle are 'being played for suckers' by the Japanese government, Miller Freeman, publisher and former member of the Washington State Planning Commission, told the Tolan committee yesterday.
>
> Freeman, whose views were given the committee yesterday both orally and in writing, told the committee the Japan Society of Seattle is a "fifth column organization" and should be disbanded, even though the majority of its members are not disloyal to America.
>
> "They are simply being played for suckers," Freeman said, explaining that the society is made up of agents and others employed by Japanese interests, and lawyers, educators, ministers and peace advocates.
>
> Prominent officials of the United States government are directors and members, he said.
>
> "Japanese are in America through fraud, deception and collusion," he added. "The Japanese government, ignoring the Gentlemen's Agreement, has accomplished the miraculous feat of permanently planting 300,000 of her people in this country, quadrupling the original number since the agreement was entered into in 1907, limiting the Japanese influx.
>
> "Compounding this 300,000 population's birth rate over the next fifty years, it becomes clear that we are handing on to future generations a problem of an insoluble race that will continue to become increasingly grave.

"This could only have been accomplished by the weakness of our national government in failing to resist Japan's colonization efforts and enforce the principles and spirit of exclusion measures that had been adopted.

"Japan's designs for colonizing the Pacific Coast states and Hawaii were abetted by pro-Japanese elements in this country such as the Japan Society, which is national in scope, with local chapters."

Freeman urged that all Japanese, alien and native-born, be evacuated from Pacific Coast states and military areas to interior points and there kept under strict surveillance.

"We are to blame for having permitted Japanese language schools to operate without supervision," he continued. "There the native-born Japanese have been taught loyalty to Japan by teachers assigned to that purpose.

"If Japanese Americans are as loyal as they say they are, why didn't they raise any protest against Japan's aggression in China? They didn't raise any objection, though such a stand would have carried a lot of weight."[73]

Many others sounded similar if not identical notes at the hearing. Seattle Mayor Earl Millikin noted that a number of Japanese merchants in his city would lose their livelihoods, but he offered no sympathy for their losses. "That's their tough luck," he said.

Governor Arthur Langlie, Attorney General Smith Troy, and dozens of other key civic leaders all paraded before the committee to testify in favor of the evacuation. Some said the evacuation was for the good of the Japanese, since they had heard rumors already of planned vigilante action against local Japanese. Others offered variations on Miller Freeman's suggestion that Japanese Americans were part of a vast conspiracy to overrun the coast, and could never be trusted because of blood ties to Japan.

What few voices spoke out in protest were treated derisively. Two Wapato residents, Dan McDonald and Esther Boyd, told the committee they believed the clamor for evacuation "is coming from economic rather than patriotic sources."

"We've heard some of the whites say, 'Get rid of the Japs and we can have more land,'" said Boyd. "But I have found and believe that the Japanese in our area are loyal Americans."

Floyd Oles, a spokesman for the Washington Produce Shippers' Association, warned the committee that the state's vegetable and fruit production would suffer if the Japanese were evacuated and urged the members to reconsider. He was told that plans were already being formed for replacement farmers to take over the operation of the Japanese farms. And he was questioned about his business connections with Japanese produce cooperatives, including Bellevue's.

A University of Washington sociology professor, J. F. Steiner, urged caution. Congressman Lawrence Arnold of Illinois, one of the committee members, interjected: "No need for haste! Suppose a Japanese aircraft carrier should approach within 200 miles of the Pacific Coast today and send bombers in to destroy Seattle plants? Do you think that would affect the civilian population?"

"It could only be a sporadic raid—" Steiner began, but was interrupted by Arnold: "Do you mean sporadic like Pearl Harbor?"

"I would hope we would be better prepared than that," Steiner replied.

"We can't afford to take chances," Arnold said.

Local church authorities spoke out against the internment. The Rev. Harold Jensen testified as a representative of the Seattle Council of Churches against the transparent discrimination against Japanese the evacuation represented. His testimony provoked the most revealing exchange of the hearing's two days.

"This (discrimination) is due partly to prejudice and partly to fear and hysteria augmented by unfortunate events in the Pacific," he said. "But I see no reason to question the loyalty of Japanese-American citizens more than any other second-generation citizens.

"In America we're famous for our humanity and internationality. I'm definitely opposed to mass evacuation unless it is a military necessity."

"You must realize we're at war with an enemy who does not share our views," retorted Arnold.

"Many people there do share them," Jensen said.

"But they're not running this show," snarled Congressman George Bender of Ohio.

"I believe that's true," was Jensen's only reply.

At the end of the hearings, Tolan expressed satisfaction that the issue had been explored fairly. "I might say, it won't be long now," he surmised.[75]

It wasn't. The next day—March 2—General DeWitt told reporters that everyone of Japanese descent, alien and citizen alike, was to be evacuated from the Pacific Coast. In announcing that he had created a series of "military

Figure 3.1. Fumiko Hayashida (whose family farmed in Bellevue between 1903 and 1910) and her 11-month-old daughter Natalie await the ferry at Bainbridge Island that will begin their odyssey to the Manzanar concentration camp. Mrs. Hayashida had just found out a few days before the evacuation that she was pregnant. Courtesy of Seattle Post-Intelligencer Collection, Museum of History and Industry.

zones" in the coastal states, he added that this included a classification for people affected by the order—Class 2 were Japanese aliens; Class 3 were citizens of Japanese descent; Class 4 were German aliens, and Class 5 Italian aliens. "Persons in Classes 2 and 3 will be required by future orders to leave certain critical points within the military areas first," DeWitt said.[75]

At that point, government officials hoped that a program of "voluntary evacuation" would handle the lion's share of the work, and DeWitt urged all Japanese to leave the coast on their own volition. But racial hatred of the Japanese had spread well beyond the coast and into the interior, and the government's program brought an outpouring of protest from officials from the interior counties and states to which the evacuees were supposed to go—in rural California, southern Oregon, and eastern Washington, efforts to move Japanese farmworkers into the area were met with angry resistance. Governors of the nearby states told federal officials that the only way they would accept the influx were if the evacuees were placed in concentration camps and kept there for the war's duration.[76] Idaho's governor, Chase A. Clark, told a gathering of state and federal officials: "I want to admit right on the start that I am so prejudiced that my reasoning might be a little off, because I don't trust any of them. I don't know which ones to trust and so I don't trust any of them."[77] Less than three weeks after it began, the voluntary relocation program came to a screeching halt.

On March 24, the hammer came down. DeWitt held a press conference announcing a series of edicts that made the evacuation a sudden reality. The most immediately significant was one announcing the imminent evacuation of Japanese residents from Bainbridge Island; and indeed, notices were posted by Army officials that same day, announcing the forced removal of anyone of Japanese descent on March 30.[78] On the appointed day, Army personnel—under the direction of Colonel Karl Bendetsen, who had been placed in charge of DeWitt's new Wartime Civil Control Administration[79]—showed up on the island and escorted 276 Nisei and Issei from their homes, loaded them onto the ferry, and took them to Seattle, where they boarded a train that took them directly to Manzanar, California, where the first of the internment camps had been erected.

Bainbridge Islanders officially were chosen because of their proximity to lanes used by Navy ships and the presence of sensitive radio installations on the island; Admiral C. S. Freeman had been badgering DeWitt for their removal since January, citing an intelligence report focusing on "contraband" found among Bainbridge farmers, which also apparently alarmed DeWitt.[80] As a result, they were the first Japanese on the West Coast to be evacuated by the military and transported to a relocation center.

"That's when we knew what was going to happen," recalled Mitsi Shiraishi. "After that—'Oh, I guess they really are going to send us away,' is the way we felt."

Another of DeWitt's March 24 edicts, however, had a much wider impact, because it placed the conduct of citizens under military control—specifically, it ordered an 8 P.M. curfew for all persons of Japanese descent, and it forbade them from possessing any firearms, explosives, or weaponry of any kind, as well as any kind of radio transmitter or camera.[81] "We couldn't cross the bridge, after certain hours," Mitsi Shiraishi recalled. "We couldn't go any more than eight miles. We had to get permission to go to funerals, permits. And we had to be home by a certain hour."

The curfew was generally received with a mixture of resignation and obedience, though a young Bellevue Nisei man, Hideo Sakai, was one of the only people arrested in Seattle on curfew violations charges and was later sentenced to 15 days in jail.[82] Mutsuo Hashiguchi's reaction was more typical. He told a reporter that the curfew wouldn't much affect Bellevue's farmers until the crops started coming in May, and joked: "There's no law that says you can't stay home and play pinochle. But maybe we going to have to play it over the telephone," then pretended to pick up a phone and said: "I play the ace of spades."[83]

Their radios, the dynamite they used for clearing stumps, and any other items that authorities feared might be used for sabotage were all confiscated. In the case of the dynamite, the confiscations often were treated as proof of the threat posed by the Japanese. A few days later, on March 27, DeWitt ordered all Japanese persons within the evacuation zone to remain there; and later commanded them to register with authorities in anticipation of the coming roundup.

In all events, the Japanese complied, like good citizens. This was particularly true of the Nisei leaders of the Japanese American Citizens League, whose advocacy of cooperation had turned into abject capitulation in the face of an aggressive campaign to displace their constituency. Soon they became the government's chief channel of information about the looming exodus for the community. "It seemed to me, the JACL was far more efficient in administering the process of evacuation than in organizing against it," observed

Seattle JACL official Frank Miyamoto, who later compiled a report detailing the extensive cooperation with authorities:

> The weakness of the JACL in organizing against evacuation, however, may have had its basis in the general political stand which it took from December 7 on. . . . If the JACL was weak in organizing against evacuation, it seems that this weakness arose from the stand the organization took. . . . The Nisei were not in a position to condemn powerful governments in their action against weaker minorities. Out of this paradox, it seems, grew the attitude of cooperation with the Army that prevailed among the JACL leader[s] in Seattle throughout this period.[84]

If the JACL was overly prostrate, it was not much emboldened by the Japanese community at large, which was singularly stoic in the face of the onslaught. In addition to the Buddhism that many Japanese practiced, there was also a culturally based inclination to keep a low profile when threatened. "The nail that sticks up is the one that gets hammered down" is a favorite Japanese proverb, readily recalled by the Nisei years later.

There was, however, also strength in that stoicism.

Kazue Matsuoka, determined as ever, hardly broke stride after her husband's arrest. "I think, unlike a lot of Japanese families—maybe partly because they were so American—but she had a lot of say, like in the running of the farm," remembered her daughter Rae. "Once my dad took that job with the packing house, she really did run the farm. And that's why when he got picked up, she just kept on running the farm until of course we evacuated."

Her mother, Rae said, never cried or let the kids see her fear, if she had any: "She was very, very tough. She never complained about it. I'm sure she was worried. And I'm sure she was very anxious after all. I was the oldest, and what was I—thirteen, fourteen? And she didn't know when she was ever going to see him again. I remember though that she did take my little sister, she did go to Missoula once, just to see him."

Finally, even pets had to go. "I had a dog, a real cute dog that there was no one in the world I could leave with; I loved her too much," remembered Mitsi Shiraishi. "Well, I couldn't take her. So I wrote General DeWitt a letter.

"Busy as DeWitt was, I wrote him a letter asking him, 'My dog is an exception; I can carry her in a shopping bag and take her with me; could I take her?'

"The general's office wrote me a letter telling me, 'At this time, you cannot take your pets with you. But at a later date, you may be able to send for it.'

"That was my biggest problem. That poor little thing, we'd lay our blankets on the floor, and we'd be wrapping up our baggage to go, and the poor little thing stands right in the middle of the carpet looking at me so sad, you know. And so, I'd have to sit down and cry.

"So we finally found a place with the (Charles W.) Bovees; they had real estate in Bellevue. They were wonderful friends, really wonderful. It was fine with Mrs. Bovee, because the dog was a cute little thing, long-haired and plume-tailed, and I couldn't find anybody else to leave her with that I felt like she would be safe. Anyway, I took the dog over, and I had to be home by eight, so all we could do was hurry over, leave the dog, the blanket and the foods, and hurry home.

"Oh, that was a real sad thing. It was only a dog, but it was part of the family."

Despite the likelihood they would soon be banished from the land they had cultivated, government officials warned the Japanese that any act hampering war operations could be interpreted as sabotage. And that clearly included failure to plant and maintain their crops.

"The funny part of it is, the law was, you had to keep on working or you would be fined or arrested," Mitsi Shiraishi recalled. "So we had to fertilize the plants. The peas were growing so pretty, you know. We'd have to put twine on it. We'd put fertilizer on it. No, they kept saying we had to keep the farm up. The lettuce was growing nicely, just about ready for the harvest."

It was rhubarb time on the Matsuoka farm, and Kazue had to run the show with only the help of her children. Sometimes Tok and other relatives would show up when they were able to break away from their own farms.

"I had my farm all ready to harvest," remembered Akira Aramaki. "And then we had to go in and sign up and everything. If I didn't get someone in there, the government called us saboteurs, we were sabotaging. So I had to get somebody, and I got this good friend of mine, an Italian boy, put him in there.

"And gosh, the minute they took over—I wanted to stay in the house until I went into camp. And he even charged me rent. Yeah, and he's going to take over all my vegetables free of charge, and harvest the vegetables, and then he charged me rent."

The Bainbridge Island evacuation sparked a massive selloff of Japanese crops. Those that were ready for harvest could hardly be sold, partly because the market was suddenly flooded with lettuce and peas, and partly because merchants were refusing to buy from the Japanese. Aramaki remembered selling lettuce for a penny a head in Everett. "You couldn't even give them away," he recalled.

"We had five acres of peas, too," Tok Hirotaka recalled. "The harvesting would start in two weeks."

The curfew hampered production, too. Produce markets ran dry when Japanese farmers, required to stay at home from 8 P.M. to 6 A.M., were unable to deliver their goods on time. Market schedules, especially at Seattle's Pike Place Public Market, were in chaos. Similar shortages were reported along the rest of the West Coast.

The press ran stories about the problems posed by the abandonment of the Japanese farms. *Post-Intelligencer* financial editor Fred Niendorff wrote a series of columns warning that the evacuation of Japanese farmers posed a serious threat to the region's supply of fresh vegetables. Already, federal farm authorities were scrambling to harvest the large strawberry crop left in the wake of the evacuation on Bainbridge Island. The likelihood of the same happening at Bellevue and in the White River area, where the communities were larger and their combined output of produce considerably greater, made the problem more than a headache.

Despite the looming crisis, though, the evacuation's popularity induced a general dismissal of these concerns. There was widespread confidence that a little American ingenuity would eventually handle the situation. Remarked Laurence I. Hewes, Jr., the regional administrator for the Farm Security Administration, in an interview with Niendorff: "Since increased production under the Food for Freedom program is of vital importance to our military effort—affecting not only supplies for our army but supplies being sent to Britain and Russia—keeping the Japanese lands in production is a basic war measure."

"There can be no question about the validity of this line of reasoning," wrote Niendorff. "Yet keeping the Japanese-controlled farm lands in continued production in Western Washington and, most likely, elsewhere, is a problem of considerably greater magnitude than might appear to some of the arm-chair strategists and superficial critics who have been raising their voices for 'action.'

"The cold, sad fact—as any government official who has been dealing with the problem will tell you—is that the white American farmer is not interested in taking over on the Jap lands where the Japs leave off, simply because truck gardening is not his business, and the average Japanese truck garden is not large enough to accommodate his type of farm operation."[85] Indeed, this was the situation along the entire coast, where those truck farms held a virtual monopoly in such crops as snap beans, spring and winter celery, cucumbers, and strawberries, and dominated a wide variety of other crops as well.[86]

Soon, it became a patriotic duty to ensure that the Japanese farms were kept in production. FSA administrators offered loans, and other wartime officials tried lining up outside companies to take over the chores.

Perhaps sensing that there could be profit as well as patriotism from pursuing the farm problem, Seattle attorney H. C. Van Valkenburgh set up a company intended to rescue the Japanese crops in Bellevue once the evacuation took place and to keep the farmlands in production for the war's duration. The company, called Western Farm and Produce, began showing up on the Eastside, passing out forms to the farmers, asking them to list crops they might be interested in selling, as well as tools, equipment, and vehicles. They offered in return to pay the farmers for the 1942 crops, and then to provide them with enough to pay their leases in subsequent farming years, until they were able to return. Western Farm also negotiated with the Bellevue Vegetable Growers to take over their warehouse facilities in the Midlakes area.

It all appeared to be a square deal, until Western Farm began offering prices. Dealing from a considerable advantage—they were the only ones offering—the company's proposed payment for the equipment and crops was usually less than half their worth. A half-acre of strawberries, for instance, brought an offer of about $70, which was nearly $100 less than what the crops would fetch at the market. To accept the offer for most of the farmers meant to take a serious financial bath.[87]

The dearth of offers from wholesalers became cause for alarm. Federal officials said they were "disappointed over the few offers from white Americans for farm lands to be evacuated by the Japanese."[88] The concern had spread to other halls of the administration, and soon relocation officials were even considering allowing a delay of 60 to 90 days for evacuation from the time the orders were posted. That would give the Japanese, they reasoned, at least enough time to harvest their berry crops.

Lettuce already had been harvested, and the strawberries were nearly ripe and ready. Tomatoes were due to go in soon. Peas and cucumbers were in the ground, scheduled for later harvests. All the while, the families maintained their lands. Besides the crops, all the equipment needed to grow and harvest them also had to be sold: tomato stakes, irrigation pipe and pumps, pea stakes and vines, lettuce crates. Tractors and trucks were put on the block, and classified ads were filled with urgent low-cost farm sales.

At least the Eastside farmers who owned land were in a position to rebuff the gouging. Most of the 12 or so Bellevue families who were property owners through their Nisei children managed to arrange with neighbors for their care while they were away. But the farmers who leased their acreage—some 48 families—had little choice. There were no other serious offers.

Western Farm, at least, promised that the lands would stay in production, and would be there for the Japanese when the war was over. So most of the leaseholders signed the papers turning over their farms to Western Farm and Produce for the war's duration. Some of the farmers, in disgust, simply packed it in. Kameji Yabuki, who owned and operated a greenhouse in Kirkland, decided to put it up for sale. It went for a pittance.

But the farm equipment was only a portion of the Japanese families' goods. Most found places to store their goods, but washing machines, cars, refrigerators—these all had to be sold. And there were plenty of people ready to take advantage of it. Some of the Nisei referred to them as "vultures."

"People came to buy things for nothing," recalled Mitsi Shiraishi. "We would have people come to the door, they'd want to buy the washing machine, the sewing machine, and they knew that we had to sell. And they would offer you a measly five dollars or something for something that we could still use."

Tosh Ito remembered selling his family's car and the truck and tractor from their farm for next to nothing. "We had to take cash for everything," he said, "so there was no fair way to dicker or try to get a fair market value for the goods. The same with the crops. There were no buyers bidding for prices. They came along and took a look at what you had, and they offered you so much, and you pretty much took it."

Kazue Matsuoka continued running the family farm as though nothing had changed, and then arranged with Johnny De Los Angeles, a Filipino man Tom had hired to help on the farm, to take over and harvest the produce and continue operating things in their absence. "We stored all of our personal belongings in the . . . attic of the house," Rae Takekawa recalled. "And I think they probably put everything, including all of our memorabilia, our pictures, and our souvenirs, and probably she had some nice dishes and the lacquer boxes for picnics—she had wonderful sets, the *jubako* sets—and all of these things went into the attic to be stored."[89]

On April 21, notices were posted in Seattle on bulletin boards and telephone poles telling Japanese residents they were to be evacuated the following week. When it came time to depart the evacuees were transported by train to Puyallup, where "Camp Harmony," a temporary processing center, had been built around the state fair stables to house the evacuees.

The White River Japanese from the southern part of the county followed. The Bellevue Japanese expected perhaps to follow in the footsteps of their Seattle neighbors. But since no one would tell them where they were to be transported, it remained a mystery.

The signs—Civilian Exclusion Order No. 80—appeared suddenly on Friday, May 15, announcing that the Japanese in Bellevue would be evacuated the following Wednesday, May 20. Though the announcement had been long expected, the short period of time left to prepare created fresh ripples of panic.

Always the organizer, even Mitsuko Hashiguchi was caught off guard: "Well, when they said, 'Now you guys all gotta pack and get out of here,' that's right, then you think, 'God, now what do we do with all the stuff we got out in the farm and all the things that had to be taken care of and all the things you've got and all the household supplies and everything else that goes with it?'

"Well, like our place, we didn't have anybody really to tell us to keep all our stuff, so we just stored it there and closed it up and hoping it would be there when we got home."

Her husband, Mutsuo, wrote an open letter to the community that he submitted to the *Bellevue American*, and which published it the day after their departure:

> Dear lifetime buddies, pals, and friends: With the greatest of regrets, we leave you for the duration, knowing deep in our hearts that when we return, we would be welcomed back, not as pariah but as neighbors. Although mere words cannot adequately express what or how we feel, those of you who have gone to schools with us, those who have grown up with us, know how

> we feel about the whole evacuation matter. There will be no trace of bitterness within our group, or any show of disrespect toward our government, (I say "our" because many of us are American citizens.)
>
> We accept the military order with good grace. We write this letter to thank the community for its past favors shown to us, the spirit of sportsmanship showered upon us, and the wholesome companionship afforded us. This is not a letter of good-bye, but a note saying—au revoir.
>
> Respectfully yours, Mutsuo Hashiguchi

Patricia Sandbo, who had grown up with Bellevue Japanese children as classmates, was by then a teacher at the elementary school. Three of her students were among those scheduled to be exiled, but the suddenness of it left her shaken: "One day in May, these children were gone," she recalled. "It was just very upsetting. It seemed at the time that it was very sudden.

"I just thought it was so unfair. We really could hardly believe it, that it was going to happen."[90]

Families finished up business. Farmers wrapped up the sales of their crops. Some families stored their most prized possessions with trusted Caucasian neighbors, leaving other items in storage at their homes. Last flowers were laid on graves, and friends said farewell.

"We were allowed a suitcase apiece and one duffel bag per family for bedding," remembered Seichi Hayashida, who farmed next door to the Hashiguchis. "They said to have your bedding, blankets and pillows, but a family of five, four or five, you couldn't get it all in one duffel bag, but that's what we were limited to. But I remember carrying a small, what would be today an overnight case. And that's all we left home with."

So it was that on a sunny Wednesday—May 20, 1942—they assembled at the small way station in Kirkland. There, they boarded a collection of old passenger cars pulled by an old coal-driven locomotive, and began their odyssey to an American purgatory.

Chapter 4

Exile

WHEN THE TRAIN PULLED OUT OF KIRKLAND ON MAY 20, IT CARRIED Bellevue's entire Japanese population—some 60 families, over 300 people in all, more than two-thirds of them American citizens. Not one knew where they were being taken.

Some thought they would be transported to the "Camp Harmony" processing center at the state fairgrounds in Puyallup, like the Seattle and White River groups evacuated before them. Instead, the train chugged past Puyallup and continued south. Summer had arrived early, and the days were hot. The 300 passengers had been crowded into a string of decrepit passenger cars pulled by an old-fashioned, coal-burning locomotive that spewed black smoke.

"That," recalled Tok Hirotaka, "was a slow boat to China."

The cars were poorly suited for the trip, he said: "I think they were all old World War I passenger coaches. They were all rusty and dirty, and they had MPs on every car, at both ends."[1]

The trip took four days, largely because the train traveled mostly by night, stopping during the day on sidetracks. "During the day we're out, side-tracked where the main line, [while] passenger lines, freight lines [ran daily, and we] traveled during the night most of the time," remembered Seichi Hayashida.[2]

The old train's thick black smoke wafted directly back in to the rail cars. In a few days' time, everything the exiles owned was covered by soot. Most remember tasting grit and soot and baking in the heat throughout the ride.

Each family was given a number. Children were tagged, like the luggage, in case they were separated from their parents. The numbers became a token of the evacuees' objectification. They had replaced their identities. To this day, virtually all of the Nisei can remember their numbers.

"Everything was Family Number 17123," recalled Mitsi Shiraishi. "I've still got a box there with that number on it. I won't forget. That was all we went by."

The army rules had been designed to force the evacuees to travel light, but not everyone did. "We were told to bring no more than what we could carry," said Cano Numoto. "We could make only one trip. I know some people in Bellevue, oh my gosh, they must have had 600 pounds of stuff that they took.

"There was a carpenter, he had one of those great big carpenter boxes, besides his duffel bag and anything else he must have had there. Gee whiz, I know that box was a heavy wooden box."

For some of the passengers, the trip wasn't all bad. Ed Suguro was six years old turning seven, and it was his first train ride. He viewed it as a big thrill.

"This was a completely new experience," he recalled. "It was like going to summer camp. It was all a new experience, new scenery, new place, you took a trip. Of course, that's not the kind of trip most people think of going on."

But for the older Nisei, especially those in their teens and early twenties, the evacuation was the worst of all possible outcomes. Instead of starting out their lives, they were being herded off to what amounted to a prison camp. Most of them were numb with shock over what was happening to them.

"The younger ones didn't feel the pain like us older Nisei," recalled Rose Matsushita, who was 19 at the time. "For us, it was humiliating, so painful."

"For people who were teenagers and above, it was a much different experience," said Tosh Ito. "It was very hard. They didn't really know . . . at least in my case, I didn't really know what I was gonna do or what was gonna happen. So it was just day-to-day. I don't know about outrage, but I certainly felt it was unfair to uproot American citizens and treat them as aliens, or even worse, traitors."

As the days progressed and authorities continued to refuse telling them their destination, the evacuees' imaginations began getting the better of them. "We kept wondering where we were gonna go," said Seichi Hayashida. "There were rumors flying right and left, where we gonna go, what they were gonna do to us. Lot of people, especially the Issei, couldn't understand. And their children couldn't tell them. They got some wild ideas, what's gonna happen to us. . . . They said they were gonna put us in a prison. Put us away and separate the families."[3]

"We thought, 'Oh my gosh, where are we going?'" recalled Mitsuko Hashiguchi. "Because nobody will say anything and they said we can't look out the windows, got to keep the shades down because the enemy might attack us and so we just went along. And every night or every day it seemed like we were all stopping at a station or stopping someplace on the siding, they call it—was always stopping someplace somewhere.

"And it seemed like we'll never get to California or wherever they were taking us. We are going south, we knew that at least, but they never told us where we were going until we got closer to the area is what it was. Then they told us Pinedale, and we never even heard of Pinedale. But we knew it was hot when we got out of the train, I'll tell you that."[4]

The Fresno area is renowned for its baking heat. It is no accident that it calls itself the raisin capital of the world. And the families from the Northwest shriveled, too, behind the fences at Pinedale, a little town just to the north of Fresno.

"We came from a moderate climate, you know," recalled Joe Matsuzawa. "You go down to Pinedale, and boy, that was hot. It was over a hundred all the time. And you were in those tarpaper shacks."

At Pinedale—which was an interim "assembly center," a way station for holding the evacuees while the internment camps, or "relocation centers," were finished being built—the evacuees got their first taste of what their living quarters for the next few years would be like. These were barracks arranged in blocks designed to hold 250 people, with army cots set out for sleeping. Hastily erected atop asphalt pads, the tarpaper buildings were hot and porous; when the wind blew, dust seeped into every crevice of the dwelling. Families were assigned to single rooms, sometimes as many as seven to a room. An argument at one end of the block could be heard at the far end. The oven-like boxes would grow so hot in the daytime that everyone stayed outdoors. And the bedposts would sink through the softening asphalt.

"You had to go around and pick up blocks of wood and put them under the legs so they would stay up," said Al Yabuki.

"You didn't have privacy," said Ed Suguro. "That was the one big drawback. You had neighbors too close to you. It was that way from the first day we went to camp until the last."

The shacks were not designed to keep out the elements, either. "If the wind blew at night, you'd get up, you'd look on your pillow to see where your head was," said Ty Matsuoka. "Everything [on the pillow] was grey or black around white. That's how much dust blew in."

"The mess hall, they had the waste water going into these open pits," added Matsuzawa. "The thing looked like it was boiling and bubbling up a stink."

The privacy-conscious Japanese were especially unsettled by the very public arrangements of the camps wrought by the sheer numbers crowded into a limited space. "The outhouses, the buildings for . . . they had about ten people going into one bathroom, I guess it was, or something like that," Mitsuko Hashiguchi said. "It's public, is the way they built [the camps] for us. And the bathrooms are the same, showers all built for community showers."[5]

And the truth was, compared to many of the other internees, those at Pinedale were fortunate. "We were luckier than a lot of the evacuees, in that Camp Pinedale was built from the ground up, new," said Seichi Hayashida. "They didn't take over a racetrack like some in Southern California. Santa Anita was used as a collection point. . . . I heard of cases where evacuees were put in horse stalls and they hadn't even whitewashed them, or washed them down or anything—smelly, dirty. But we had a brand new camp."[6]

The Pinedale center, in fact, had been built on the site of an abandoned sawmill. Most of the assembly centers were located at fairgrounds and racetracks, which had been selected because it was believed they would have essential facilities on hand already and space enough for further housing. The hastily prepared assembly centers were designed to be temporary arrangements strictly until the relocation centers—mostly sites selected inland from the "exclusion zones" on the Pacific Coast—were completed and ready to be occupied.[7]

The overcrowded and chaotic conditions at the assembly centers like Pinedale and Puyallup were a product of the herculean task that faced the War Relocation Authority (WRA), the independent civilian agency which had been created on March 18 by another Roosevelt executive order—No. 9102—to take charge of all facets of the evacuation. Forced to prepare and facilitate the massive relocation of more than a hundred thousand people in just a few weeks' time, a certain amount of chaos was inevitable. All things considered, the WRA actually executed the move with surprising smoothness.[8] By agreement with the WRA, the army was charged with handling the actual evacuation from people's homes to the assembly centers, while the Wartime Civil Control Administration was given the job of organizing the evacuees and then running the assembly centers, until the WRA could build the relocation centers.

Between March 2 and October 31, 1942, there were a total of 114,490 persons evacuated from the "exclusion zones" of the Pacific Coast. 18,026 of them were sent immediately to the two relocation centers that had already been built—namely, Manzanar in Southern California, and Poston in Arizona. While construction began on eight more such centers at a variety of remote locations, mostly in the West, the WRA moved the remaining 91,401 into 15 assembly centers, most of them located near the evacuees' communities; the 4,048 from Washington and Oregon who were sent to Pinedale were removed the farthest from home of any group (except, of course, for the 276 Bainbridge Islanders interned at Manzanar). At peak population, Santa Anita, which contained 18,719 evacuees, was the largest of the centers, while 7,390 (mostly from the Seattle area) were housed at Puyallup's "Camp Harmony."[9]

Of the 117,000 evacuees, some 72,000 were American citizens, though only 22,400 of these were over 21 years of age. The Issei numbered 38,500. Removal of all aliens from Area 1—largely comprising the Pacific coastal communities—was accomplished by June 1942, and Area 2—areas of the coastal states for another 100 miles or so inland—was evacuated by August 7.[10]

The evacuees awaited word of their next destination. They had been told they would be moved to a point inland, at a camp that was being constructed to house them. No one knew, however, where it would be.

In the meantime, War Relocation Authority officials began the process of trying to instill democratic values in their charges. The basic purpose of the centers, according to a general policy statement, lay in "the training of residents of the community in the democratic principles of civic participation and community." So the necessary functions of the centers—schools, police, fire, hospitals, recreation, and maintenance—were to be run by the evacuees themselves. One of the WRA's first memos to center administrators outlined a system of self-government to make those ideals a reality.[11]

"I ended up in a fire department," recalled Joe Matsuzawa. "So did Tok [Hirotaka] . . . and several other people I know."

He said the department never fought any fires. "We had a practice, or whatever you call 'em. And we had to make the rounds every nights, or during the day. You had different crews. And we got acquainted with people who we didn't know."

Tok Hirotaka remembered how the department was organized: "There was 21 members in that fire department, and we divided into three groups of seven each. And then it would rotate, this seven would take an eight-hour shift. . . . We had quite a few Bellevue boys in there, though."

"Those people who took the night shift, well, [they] had the best shift because, sometimes why, they could sleep," added Joe Matsuzawa with a laugh. "You could catch 'em sleeping, see. . . . Some people got a reputation of sleeping all the time."[12]

Outside of their official duties, the internees found various kinds of recreation to occupy themselves. There were fly fishermen's clubs, enthusiasts of *goh* (a popular Japanese board game) held tournaments, dances were held for teenagers, and crafts shows displayed evacuees' handiwork. Schools were organized and the young students took an array of the usual classes, and Issei elders were free to take English classes. And of course there was baseball, in one form or another. Seichi Hayashida's wife started playing softball on a team, so he kept busy by picking up a job coaching their team.

"We just tried to make the best of the situation," he said. "Tried to keep busy. They had classes, art, stuff like that. I was surprised by many of the Issei, the talents they had. . . . There were a lot of hidden talents that, when they were busy, life, coming over here and trying to make a living for the family, [they] didn't have time. The Issei enjoyed it, which they deserved. They worked so hard. I can remember my mother and my dad would work from daylight to dark, even after dark, seven days a week. And now, when they went to camp they didn't have to worry about working hard to keep the family going, just so they were together. . . . It was a change for them."[13]

It was a change for the youngsters, too, and not always a good one. Rae Matsuooka, who had just turned 15, remembered that having a lot of idle time on her hands provided a devil's playground. "When we went down there, we got into trouble, hanging out with a bunch of kids—of course, I guess you'd call them gangs now," she said. "Of course, he [her father] wasn't there. I guess you could just about imagine. And my brother found friends. Mom—there were always calls for volunteers and she was always busy with that. And then he came back."

Tom Matsuoka remained at Fort Missoula for more than six months while awaiting his chance to gain release through the Alien Enemy Hearing Board set up to handle the men's cases. Also holding him up was his birth certificate—officials in Hawaii were having difficulty locating it, since the town in Maui where he had been born had at one time had its records destroyed.

Like the evacuees at the assembly centers, the mostly Issei men who were held in detention were largely preoccupied with staving off sheer boredom during their confinement. They developed programs aimed at various kinds of recreation, particularly crafts during the winter months, and a library that eventually grew to some 5,000 Japanese- and English-language works was begun. Twice a week, Hollywood films were shown to both Italian and Japanese prisoners.

In the spring, when the snows began to recede, the prisoners began getting outside, where they found the wild Montana landscape more inviting than they expected. The weather became pleasant and mild. Camp officials provided equipment for softball, tennis, volleyball, horseshoes, fishing and hiking. Some of the boatwrights among the crew took up their craft and built a little rowboat—dubbed the "Minnehaha"—that the men used for fishing expeditions on the Bitterroot River, a crystalline stream with a bounty of trout bordering the camp. Some of the men even developed a crude nine-hole golf course on the fort's abundant grass grounds, and camp officials provided them with a couple of sets of clubs to play on it.[14]

While walking the fields at the fort's compound, prisoners began discovering what seemed like a mother lode of agate and soft stones, sometimes garnets. This set off one of the camp's biggest fads. "Around March the snows stopped and the thaw began," said Tom Matsuoka. "You could get outside now. All around the camp rocks had worked to the surface. Rocks with real pretty lines and designs. Pretty soon everybody's out digging up rocks.

"So we'd take the rocks back to our shower room, which had a cement floor, and we'd polish 'em by rubbing them across the floor. Beautiful now.

Really beautiful! Then we'd take our government issue blankets and get a really high polish.

"We made all sorts of things with them—jewelry, ash trays, vases. One guy picked up a milk bottle and put cement on the outside. I don't know where he got the cement; maybe where they were building new barracks for the people who arrived later. Anyway he put cement on the outside of the milk bottle then put a rock in the middle. That was something. Two or three times we had exhibitions of people's work in the mess hall. Really popular.

"Someone must have written to his wife at another camp about our 'stone fever'. Pretty soon a letter comes back from the worried wife, wondering about the epidemic at our camp and if everybody was sick. Ha!"[15]

Matsuoka kept his favorite polished rock, perhaps a memento of dark days. It is a smooth, irregularly shaped stone with a flat bottom and stratified colors of rust, green, and purple. It remained tucked away in a nook of his home until 1992, when it became part of an exhibit at the Wing Luke Asian Museum in Seattle.

Finally, after six months' wait, Matsuoka had his hearing in June. "In this hearing, the hearing board was one FBI, and some well-known people of the neighborhood, you know. . . . Anyway, what they asked, not too much about the Bellevue stuff, you know. Only thing they ask about is when I took the boys to Japan. . . . Main thing, 'Why [are] you a second-generation American and you [are also] lots of Japanese groups' officer?' I did religion stuff and *Nihonjinkai*, you know.

"I said, I'm not Japanese. I said, 'Even [though] I'm an American citizen, still I am in Japanese [groups]. Because the American government did not support the Japanese.' They didn't do nothing for the Japanese, you know."

Though the hearing board may have had suspicions of his intent, his biggest problem was that he still did not have proof of his citizenship. Nonetheless, Matsuoka appears to have convinced the board that he was in fact a citizen, because it eventually recommended his release. However, the Department of Justice declined to concur with their ruling, and instead ordered Matsuoka placed on parole—meaning he could rejoin his family at Pinedale, but he would be required to remain in WRA custody.[16]

He was fortunate in that regard; many of the other detainees encountered much harsher treatment during the hearing process. Fort Missoula nearly became the focus of an international incident when word began emerging that internees were complaining of mistreatment at the hands of

INS interrogators. Records later revealed that the sessions in question involved the INS's efforts to determine when a number of the Issei entered the country; if they had arrived after 1924—when the Asian Exclusion Act was passed—then they were in the country illegally and could be deported. The inspectors didn't believe many of the Issei accounts and, according to numerous witnesses both inside and outside the chambers, resorted to violence to wring "the truth" out of them. Several witnesses said the inspectors verbally and physically abused the internees, calling them "yellow-bellied cowards" and "liars," shoving them against the wall, yanking their hair, and punching them in the stomach. After the Justice Department investigated the charges, two Korean interpreters were fired, and the three inspectors responsible for most of the abuse were suspended for 90 days, and one was demoted.[17]

Even men in positions somewhat similar to Tom Matsuoka's encountered difficulties with the hearing board. Possibly the most striking case involved Masuo Yasui, an Issei businessman from Hood River, Oregon, who had been prominent in town, too—co-owner of a thousand acres of farm and orchard land, member of the Rotary Club and the Apple Growers Association, and a leader of the local Methodist Church. Yet when he went before the board, only his past associations with Japanese civic organizations, including the award he received from the emperor for promoting American-Japanese relations, were considered relevant.

"The proceedings were a complete farce," recalled his son, Minoru, himself a Nisei activist who had challenged the curfew laws in Portland and attended his father's hearings. "The most incredible thing was when they produced childlike drawings of the Panama Canal showing . . . drawings of how the locks worked. The hearing officer took these out and asked, 'Mr. Yasui, what are these?' Dad looked at the drawings and diagrams and said, 'They look like drawings of the Panama Canal.' They were so labeled, with names of the children. Then the officer asked my father to explain why they were in our home. 'If they were in my home,' my father replied, 'it seems to me that they were drawings done by my children for their schoolwork.'

"The officer then asked, 'Didn't you have these maps and diagrams so you could direct the blowing up of the canal locks?' My father said, 'Oh no! These are just the schoolwork of my children.' The officer said, 'No, we think you've cleverly disguised your nefarious intent and are using your children merely as a cover. We believe you had intent to damage the Panama Canal.' To which my father vehemently replied, 'No, no, no!' And then the officer said pointedly, 'Prove that you didn't intend to blow up the Panama Canal!'" Masuo Yasui was remanded to the custody of federal authorities and kept in army prison camps until the spring of 1946.[18]

A similar fate befell Tom Matsuoka's two friends from Bellevue, Terumatsu Yabuki and Asaichi Tsushima. Both were declared security threats because of their *Nihonjinkai* and language-school associations and spent the bulk of the war years at a prison camp in Albuquerque, New Mexico.

Tom showed up at Pinedale in late June. Since he had gone to Missoula in the dead of winter, all he had with him were his woolen winter clothes. And Pinedale was in the middle of a heat wave.

"Oh, the temperature was up around a hundred degrees," he recalled, wincing. "Oh! It was really hot!"

He didn't like what he found. His children were getting into trouble, there was no family life to speak of, and the living conditions were horrendous.

Rae remembered that her father had seemed mostly unchanged by his ordeal. "He did not say much of anything about what he had gone through," she said, but "I think he was the same as far as his basic character. . . . And I think he was just a little appalled at the kind of existence we had in the camp. . . . He saw what was going on, and the fact that we no longer really were a family unit . . . like [at] meals, we ate with our friends. We wouldn't sit down as a family really."[19]

Tom decided to get the family out of there at any cost: "Oh, but you think about that, the camp life, oh, that's hard," he said. "That was no place to raise a family." Evidently unaware that his status as a parolee might keep him behind barbed wire, he began making plans.

Before he could make a move, though, the WRA made its own. In late July, the evacuees at Pinedale were transferred by army transport to the just-finished internment camp—officially known as a "relocation center"—at Tule Lake, California, just south of the Oregon border near Klamath Falls.

The train ride, once again, took an unusual length of time because it traveled only at night and remained on sidetracks during the day. "So it seemed like forever it was taking us to get there, and we said, 'God, I thought that was right there in Oregon, but it sure is far for something that's in Oregon,'" recalled Mitsuko Hashiguchi. "They said that we're the last on the tracks, that's supposed to be on the track. . . . So it seemed like we were always stopped someplace in the dark, and we weren't supposed to look outside. We don't know where we're at."[20] Finally, after two days, they arrived at their new home.

The camp at Tule Lake had been built on an emptied lake bottom in northern California. They were still located in the desert, but it was on a high plateau surrounded by mountain ranges. The nights were cooler and the living conditions were better.

"You had a lot of sagebrush out there," said Ed Suguro, "and you had rattlesnakes and scorpions—not inside the camp, but near the mountains—which we had never been accustomed to here. People would go out and capture the snakes and show them to us. Or they'd put a scorpion in a bottle and say, 'This is poisonous.'"

Suguro had the usual seven-year-old's delight at such things. "But you know, it was all a new experience. So it was like an exciting new experience, and you didn't mind it at all. You just thought it was normal, because everyone else was in the same boat.

"Everyone else is doing this, and everyone else is in these kinds of quarters, and everyone else has to go eat all together, everyone else is using the same latrines, everyone else has to use the laundry and take turns. It seemed a normal life, because everyone else was doing it."

Ty Matsuoka enjoyed the life in the camps, too: "I had a good time. Kids my age, they had no responsibilities, all they had to do was be sure they were around the mess hall when chow time came."

Each family now was assigned to its own apartment, usually a designated area within a multifamily living space. The Nisei described apartments designed ostensibly for a family of five that typically held two families of four or a single family of up to eleven people.

Eating, bathing, laundering, and using the toilets all took place communally. This was too much for many of the older Issei, for whom privacy in all these functions was deeply ingrained. Much of their suddenly acquired free time was spent grumbling about the conditions.

Tom Matsuoka didn't wait. When he heard of an opportunity to leave the camp and ship out to Montana to work on a sugar beet farm, he leapt at it. A group of Montana farmers from along the state's northern Hi-Line region were in dire straits with a labor shortage and a healthy crop of beets ready to be harvested, so they came to the internment camps to recruit potential laborers.

One farmer, a German named Gottlieb Blatter, hired Tom Matsuoka and Tok Hirotaka and their families.

Of course, Matsuoka officially speaking was still a parolee, requiring him to remain in the camp. But WRA officials had not yet received or processed the paperwork from Fort Missoula indicating he was to be placed in their "stop" file, so the officials at Tule Lake signed his work release papers and let the family depart.

Thus, in late September, the Matsuokas and the Hirotakas and a few others who took up the farmers' offers boarded a train headed for the Big Sky plains of northern Montana. They remained under armed guard, at bayonet point, by young army recruits itching to be sent overseas.

Tom Matsuoka remembered, with a laugh, sitting in a latrine and overhearing a couple of the young guards: "And behind the door, they're talking to each other: 'I wish someone would run and try to get away—so I could shoot 'em!'"

Arriving in the little farming town of Chinook, a town with no electricity, was a little disconcerting—especially the change in climate. "You know, we got off that train, and it was snowing," remembered Rae. "I thought I would die! September, and it was snowing!"

When they got a look at their living conditions on the farm, they wondered to themselves if they had been smart to leave the camp: "I know that when we went out there, and we went up where the farm was, and he took us to where we were going to live, I wonder what my mother, she must have thought," said Rae. "There were two rooms and seven of us. One room was the bedroom. We had three little beds and a little crib-like thing. We got no heat with that room. And the other room was where Ma did the cooking.

"And she would try to mop that floor, because she was so fussy, she would try to mop that floor and it would freeze."

Rae particularly admired the way her mother—who was now pregnant with the Matsuokas' fifth child, a boy who would be born in May 1943—held up during the ordeal: "You know, she never, never complained, or let us know how she really felt about it. It must have been very, very devastating to go out to this place and see where we were gonna live."

Work on a sugar beet farm was more in the line of hard labor than the careful cultivation they had known before, too. "Well, a typical day, we get up at dawn and we would go out to the fields," recalled Rae, "and it would be chilly and cold, not uncomfortably cold; but nevertheless, it was cool, and we

Figure 4.1. The Matsuoka, Hirotaka, and Ito families at the end of a workday on a Montana beet farm. From left to right: Rulee Matsuoka (child on far left); an unidentified worker; Itaro Ito (holding sugar beet); Chiye Ito; Rae Matsuoka; Tom Matsuoka; Kazue Matsuoka; Kiku Hirotaka; Mits Hirotaka; Sumi Hirotaka; Hiroshi Ito; Tom Matsuzawa; Tokio Hirotaka; Tats Matsuoka (boy on car hood); Roy Matsuzawa; Tosh Ito. Seated in front: Ray Marks, Gus Lundeen, John Matsuzawa. Courtesy of Alice Ito.

would start the topping of beets [which had already been dug up by farm machinery]. We used a machete-like knife, and on the end of a knife is a hook, a steel hook, and you stab the beet with the hook and then you chop it off with the machete knife. And then we would pile the beets. . . . And then the truck would come through, in between the rows of beets, and three people on a side would throw beets into the truck. And we did it from early morning until, because of the days being shorter, yeah, from the time that you could see, and finish when it started getting dusk."[21]

Still, they toughed it out. When harvest was over, Tom got a job working for Blatter, earning $70 a month by feeding his sheep daily. When spring came around, they helped with the plowing and planting, and worked at harvest time again. The next year Tom and Tok Hirotaka went to work sharecropping with another Chinook farmer, Gus Lundeen, whose tract was on the other side of town.

Kazue's personality was the kind that helped the family fit in well. "She made friends easily," said Rae. "I know that when we moved out to the wildlands of Montana there, she made friends. People knew immediately. You know how that is? But the minute you open your mouth, and people expect you to be something else maybe, but then the minute you open your mouth and start talking, they reassess.

"And she fit in very well, because among farmers, it's the wives that get together. You know, the wives in the kitchen and the men all sitting around outside or something. She became kind of a leader among the wives after while. She was that way."

Even out in Montana, though, the shadow of the internment camps haunted the family. WRA officials realized that Tom was not eligible for release, and informed the WRA officer in Havre that he needed to return to WRA custody. The officer intervened, though, by pleading the family's case to his superiors: "This family would like to get permanently located and rent a farm, and start making a home for the family. But they explained to me that this is very difficult to do due to the status of Mr. Matsuoka," wrote the officer, a fellow named Murray E. Stebbins. "This is a good, hard working, honest family, and I am very anxious to do all that can be done to help them along. Your kind consideration of this case will be deeply appreciated." Stebbins' plea was initially refused, but he persisted, and eventually Tom was granted "indefinite leave" status by December 1944.[22]

Thus it was that the combination of Tom's personal initiative—particularly his aggressiveness in getting his family out of the camps—a slow bureaucracy, a little bit of luck, and a healthy dose of human compassion from outsiders made the difference between incarceration and freedom for his family. And somewhere along the way, Chinook, Montana, became their home, permanently.

The day after Bellevue's Japanese residents were loaded aboard the train for evacuation, the May 21 edition of the local weekly, the *Bellevue American*, noted their departure with a front-page story headlined, "Bellevue Japanese are Evacuated Wednesday—Sent to California."

On the same page was a smaller item headlined, "No Strawberry Festival This Year." The story put a wartime face on the reasons presented for ending the city's main summer attraction, a 16-year tradition: "With the rationing of gasoline, all agreed that the Festival would have to be abandoned this year. Other reasons given were: the shortage of sugar, conservation of tires, avoidance of large crowds and the war effort that is keeping so many busy."

A simpler explanation, of course, was that 90 percent of Bellevue's agricultural workforce—the people who provided the Strawberry Festival with strawberries—was riding a train to Pinedale, California. That loss became painfully obvious in the next week's paper. A front-page headline read: "200 Workers Needed Now to Care for Crops in Overlake Area."

The Japanese farmers, under threat of law, had maintained their crops through the spring. At the time they were evacuated, the lettuce crop was ready for harvest, peas were a week or two away, and strawberries were red and ready for plucking. Tomatoes and the second crop of lettuce were due for harvest by the end of July.

Western Farm and Produce Inc., which had stepped in as the wartime substitute for the Japanese, received a Farm Service Administration loan the day of the evacuation for $32,107, mostly to cover the costs it incurred in purchasing the remaining crops and equipment to grow and harvest them, from the 33 lease farmers who had signed agreements. The company also set up operations at the Midlakes warehouse the Japanese growers owned.

But it quickly became apparent that the company was going to have trouble raising enough labor to work the fields. H. C. Van Valkenburgh, the lawyer who formed the company and managed it, pleaded for help through the story in the *American:*

> Labor is the biggest immediate problem because of the highly perishable nature of these crops, which are maturing rapidly. The pay is much higher than in normal times, and many of the good people who are helping with such fine spirit, consider the money as secondary to the national need of preserving these foods.
>
> Most of these foods are going to the armed forces, according to Van Valkenburgh, who pointed out that a carload of cauliflower has just been shipped to men in Alaska, and another carload of lettuce has just been shipped to Chicago for the armed forces.[23]

Van Valkenburgh told the reporter he needed 100 workers immediately for picking strawberries and another 100 to care for other crops. A week later, Van Valkenburgh still needed 100 workers for the strawberry harvest. The following week's story in the *American* made no mention of the other crops, but simply appealed for labor:

> "We much prefer to employ local help," said Mr. Van Valkenburgh Wednesday night. "Local help proves more reliable, transportation difficulties are avoided, the number of workers can be regulated, there is more interest aiding a local industry, workers can be trained into steady year-around jobs—and, of course, we would much prefer to keep the money here."
>
> "Consequently, we are making an urgent appeal to all who want to aid in harvesting and caring for these crops to notify us at once, so that we can organize our labor. If insufficient local labor is available, we can get the workers from Seattle, but we want to know how many to send for."[24]

Actually, the ready labor pool in Seattle was not merely short; it was practically nonexistent. Local Filipinos were already in place on Bainbridge Island farms, and the larger White River land tracts were also sapping the usual workforce. Few white farmers would touch the small Japanese tracts, and other laborers were signing up to join the war effort, which had the advantages of better pay and considerably greater glory.

Berry pickers were paid by the carry—a wooden tray that held a large number of smaller berry crates, which meant that the fastest pickers were paid the most. The company also hired tomato planters and weeders, who were paid 50 cents an hour. Truck drivers to haul the goods were paid the best: $1 an hour.

But Western Farm and Produce lost a large portion of the strawberry crop to wet weather conditions, so returns on its first harvest were a considerable disappointment. Soon it was cutting back its operations.

Confusion soon set in, especially as the Japanese leasees began to settle into the camps. In most cases, the farmers had reached agreement with Western Farm to continue paying them through the harvest, so they could in turn make their lease payments to the landowners. A few had been released of their lease obligations altogether, and so the company itself became responsible for paying the rent.

But Western Farm fell down on both counts. First, it began receiving letters of complaint from the landowners who had released the Japanese from their leases, demanding rent for the land the company was working. The company paid up for a few months in some cases—it contested others—and then quit paying altogether after the summer.

Then the Japanese internees, with War Relocation Authority officials backing them, began demanding their unpaid rent. In some cases, the company made partial payments, but even those ended after 1942.

And, with only a handful of workers available for the harvest, it became clear that Van Valkenburgh's grand scheme to become "the successor to the Bellevue Vegetable Growers Association," as Western Farm and Produce Inc.'s letterhead suggested, was a money-losing proposition, and the operation quickly dried up. The crops were abandoned. The company kept hiring tomato planters and weeders through July, but there is no indication that either the tomatoes or the second lettuce crop were ever harvested. Nor is there any indication the company continued to operate in any fashion in Bellevue thereafter.[25]

When the Nisei came back three and four years later, it was obvious that only a fraction of the crops they had planted were harvested. The farms had lain fallow since they had left.

And the Strawberry Festival, that great gathering in tiny Bellevue of thousands of people from all walks of life and from all around Puget Sound, was gone forever.

The internment camps were constructed hurriedly at ten sites in seven western states. The Tule Lake camp was the largest single camp, capable of holding 16,000 internees; however, the Poston, Arizona, camp was divided into three separate sites that totaled a capacity of 20,000. The majority of the camps were designed to hold 10,000 people each: Minidoka in Idaho, Manzanar in California, Topaz in Utah, and Jerome and Rohwer in Arkansas all fit in that category. Gila River in Arizona, comprising two sites, totaled 15,000; Heart Mountain in Wyoming was built to hold 12,000; and the Granada camp in Colorado held 8,000.[26]

Populations constantly were in flux, but at its peak in summer 1943 the Tule Lake camp population totaled 18,800. Most of the Seattle and White River Japanese were located at the Minidoka camp in southern Idaho, which topped out at 9,900, while the Bainbridge Island community was part of the 10,200 peak population at Manzanar.[27]

The War Relocation Authority filled the camps with evacuees from the processing centers as soon as the barracks were built. By November 1, 1942, the evacuation had been completed, and nearly every person of Japanese descent on the Pacific Coast—114,490 in all—had been placed behind barbed wire and under armed guard at remote locations in six western states and Arkansas.

Virtually all the Nisei recall the first sight of camp—seeing the barbed wire and the guard towers, with machine guns pointed inward. "The thing I remember most about the camps was that they told us it was for our own protection," recalled Tosh Ito. "But when we got to the camps we saw the barbed wire, and the guns pointed inward. Why would the guns point inward for our protection?"

Anger, despair, disgust—all floated freely throughout the camp at Tule Lake. The young people were bored and restless and outraged. The elders were heartbroken. Some Nisei called the camps "military prisons"; and what hurt the most, many said, was seeing their parents, who had worked so hard all their lives, "locked up like animals," as Rose Matsushita put it.

The Tule Lake camp, in many ways, effectively marked the end of the Bellevue Nikkei community. The Eastsiders had remained more or less grouped together through the evacuation and assembly centers, but when placed in the relocation center, the community was essentially split in half. About 30 families were placed in blocks 58 and 59, in Ward VI, while the remaining 30 were in blocks 68, 69, and 70 in Ward VII. Mutsuo Hashiguchi, who had taken a leadership role in the JACL back in Bellevue, was named manager of Block 58.

"The Bellevue community—and I believe the Hood River [community] also—they sort of divided it into two groups," recalled Tosh Ito. "I know we lived in the section called the Alaska area [in Block 59], which was on one side of the fire break, and the rest of the camp was on the other, other end.

And then half of the Bellevue people were on the opposite end pretty much. And Hood River was basically divided in the same manner, and I often wonder what reason there was not to keep the one community intact, rather than splitting it more or less in half. Maybe it was to disperse and get them separated for some reason."[28]

Whatever the reasons, the evacuees often operated in a complete vacuum of information, depending on how tight-lipped their camp administrators were. The camps became hotbeds for all kinds of wild rumors. Some of the evacuees worried that massing their numbers together made the Japanese an easy target for elimination. "The rumors were going around that American planes were going to drop a bomb on us and kill us," recalled Akira Aramaki. "I expected that. Because up to now, why should we be going to camp? We looked at everything in the worst way."

Most wondered what would become of them; their future, after all, didn't look particularly promising in the United States. "In there, we kind of enjoyed ourselves, playing baseball games and everything," said Aramaki. "But you start thinking seriously, 'Where am I gonna go after this? We're not gonna be here forever.' Well, I decided I was going to go to South America and start a new life. This country, no more. I was gonna go to Brazil.

"Yeah, there's no place like here. But at that time, I didn't want any part of it. I didn't know what was gonna happen."

The departure of families like the Matsuokas from the camps was very much by design. From the initial stages of the War Relocation Authority's plans, resettling the evacuees in places inland was a stated goal. Even before the evacuation itself, the WRA had attempted a "voluntary relocation" that largely failed but essentially created venues for the Issei and Nisei to move away from the coast. This effort resumed as soon as the relocation centers opened, providing farmers in labor-hungry areas of Idaho, Utah, and Montana with workers to help with their harvests.

However, the WRA hoped to prevail upon the internees to do more than just provide farm labor; it intended to completely resettle the Japanese in cities in the Midwest where they posed no security threat and where they likely would be dispersed, making them more prone to assimilation. The WRA's second director, Dillon Myer, made resettlement one of the agency's top priorities, and signed a full-fledged program into being on September 26, 1942, providing internees with services that would enable them to move out of the relocation centers and on to new lives somewhere out of the exclusion zones.[29]

However, the mere relocation of some of the evacuees with farm operations in the West created a stir. In Montana, the situation was stark: the war effort had drawn 57,000 men—10 percent of its population—out of the state's workforce, creating a manpower shortage that inspired farmers and sugar beet processors to plead for the use of Japanese internees. But local jingoes created a furor; letters to the editor decried any efforts to bring "the enemy" to Montana, where all kinds of mischief they could cause was easily imagined—plunging the West into an inferno by intentionally setting forest fires was a favorite scenario.[30] In the Bitterroot Valley, local efforts by the sugar companies to bring in a contingent of Japanese evacuees caused a stir during a local meeting.

But eventually common sense (or economics) prevailed, if begrudgingly. As the *Phillips County News* editorialized:

> Newspapers of the area have, with one accord, jumped all over the proposal to send these people here. The words have been different, but the music has been the same—WE DON'T WANT 'EM! But why isn't it sensible to ship them to sparsely populated areas where they can be watched closely, where defense industries are few, and where army and navy drafts are making serious inroads in the labor supply? . . . As we see it, it is still possible to hate the innards of every Jap ever born and still make use of them. The United States is widely reputed to be a practical nation and, as we view the matter, this is an excellent time to demonstrate it. Hate the Jap, if you will, but also admit that he is a good worker, a natural farmer, and a human commodity which this region is going to need if it is to continue as a substantial supplier to the war effort.[31]

By mid-summer, the majority of Montanans, including the governor, had reached the same conclusion, and the recruitment effort was under way.

Like his older brother, John Matsuoka—who had shipped out to Pinedale and then Tule Lake with the rest of the Japanese community in the White River Valley—decided the farming route sounded better than staying in camp, so he too joined up with a sugar beet crew and found himself in Townsend, Montana. "My older brother [James] had another crew, and they just about shooed them in the chicken house—'And that's where you're gonna stay'—Ha! And he told 'em, 'The heck we are,' and pulled out of there, and joined us. So we had a big crew.

"We got through topping the beets on our contract, and the neighbors came over, asked us to top his. 'OK.' Same price, you know. So much a ton. So we went over there and knocked off their field. Well, we still had time before the train was going to take us back. And so another guy says he wanted his beets topped, you know. And the guy we worked for, he says, 'Ha! He's the one that didn't want any Japs in Montana!"

"So we told him, 'OK, that's all right.' I said, 'We'll top his beets anyway. Not for him, but for the use of the sugar, for the war effort.'"

Dillon Myer's resettlement program hardly went according to plan. Within the camps, it created a political whirlwind that never really settled for the duration of the camps' existence. No sooner had it been proposed than the charge arose that the government intended to evade responsibility for the thousands of people it had evacuated and simply foist them upon an unreceptive white populace. And outside the camps, political pressure grew in Congress to keep the internees locked up. Groups like the American Legion assailed the plans as "coddling the Japs."[32] At its September 1942 national convention in Kansas City, the legion passed a resolution " . . . that we go on record as being opposed to any special privileges being granted Japanese in these camps and that they be denied the privilege of leaving these camps under any pretext for the duration of the war."[33]

The WRA's program of encouraging the evacuees to develop a community built on democratic principles continued in the relocation camps and became more extensive, and that too wound up causing more difficulties than officials envisioned possible. Both Myer and his predecessor, Milton Eisenhower, had relied heavily on advice from the Nisei leaders of the Japanese American Citizens League, and so it was not surprising that those Nisei involved in the JACL often wound up with powerful managerial positions within the camps, notably in the key roles on the community councils and as block managers.

As the months of internment set in, so did a well-nursed sense of resentment toward the JACL among many of the evacuees. Thanks to the organization's history of voicing support for the evacuation, many of them now viewed the Nisei leaders as lackeys of their tormentors in the federal government. Moreover, the Japanese cultural tradition of deferring leadership roles to the elders was bulldozed by the WRA policy that forbade the Issei—being noncitizens—from holding official positions in the camps, and this created further anger, also directed at the Nisei councilmen.[34]

The volatile situation first bubbled up on November 19, 1942, in the camp at Poston, Arizona, where a community council member was severely beaten and a crowd of evacuees prevented the removal of the two main suspects, shortly thereafter declaring a general strike that eventually dissipated. However, the violence grew serious two weeks later at Manzanar, on December 6. A crowd of angry evacuees, led by pro-Japan Kibei, rioted through the camp, attempting to lynch various JACL leaders, but they were thwarted when the leaders could not be found. Instead, they confronted a group of frightened military policemen who tossed tear gas into the crowd to disperse it. A scene of complete chaos ensued, with rioters fleeing and then returning, and soldiers firing randomly, first into the air and then into the crowd of evacuees. There were ten evacuees hit by bullets, two of them fatally.[35]

Similar tensions were rising in Tule Lake, and they reached a head in the summer of 1943.

By January of that year, the War Department (at least partially because of prodding by WRA officials) had decided to create a segregated unit of Nisei soldiers. In a letter to War Secretary Stimson, Roosevelt proclaimed: "No loyal citizen of the United States should be denied the democratic right to exercise the responsibilities of his ancestry. The principle on which this country was founded and by which it has always been governed is that Americanism is a matter of mind and heart; Americanism is not, and never was, a matter of race or ancestry. . . ."[36]

All this may have come as a surprise to the 70,000 or so Nisei citizens being held at the internment camps. For some of them, at least, it offered a ray of hope that the gates of the camps were cracking open. Meanwhile, for many others, the inherent hypocrisy became a focal point of their anger over the government's treatment of them.

Many of the young Nisei men, like Joe Matsuzawa, had signed up for military service when Japan attacked Pearl Harbor. They were as eager, perhaps more so than others, to prove their willingness to fight for their country. Matsuzawa even recalls being accepted, and holding a going-away party. Then, the word had come down: all men of Japanese descent had been reclassified to IV-C: Enemy Alien. Some who were already in the army at the time were sent home under the reclassification.

To most of those former enlistees, now in the camps, Roosevelt's announcement thus came as welcome news. But for many within the military establishment, questions still lingered about where Nisei loyalties lay. So in the first weeks of February 1943, WRA officials distributed two slightly different pieces of registration: one, titled "War Relocation Authority Application for Leave Clearance," was for female citizens and all Issei; the other, Selective Service Form DSS 304A, was distributed to all male citizens 17 and older. Both forms were 28-item questionnaires, with short blanks to fill in answers. The last two questions were the kicker. In the Selective Service form, they read:

> Question 27: Are you willing to serve in the armed forces of the United States on combat duty, wherever ordered?
>
> Question 28: Will you swear unqualified allegiance to the United States of America and faithfully defend the United States from any or all attack by foreign or domestic forces, and forswear any form of allegiance or obedience to the Japanese emperor, or any other foreign government, power, or organization?

The WRA form for women and Issei asked two slightly different questions:

> Question 27: If the opportunity presents itself and you are found qualified, would you be willing to volunteer for the Army Nurse Corps or the WAAC?
>
> Question 28: Will you swear unqualified allegiance to the United States of America and forswear any form of allegiance or obedience to the Japanese emperor, or any other foreign government, power, or organization?

Not surprisingly, most of the Issei—forbidden from ever obtaining American citizenship—felt compelled to answer the questions "no," since renouncing Japan would render them people without a country. Moreover, a number of

Nisei, and particularly Kibei, were outraged by both these questions. Since they had been forcibly removed from their homes and detained in concentration camps without due process, some of the young men found it gallingly arrogant of the government to expect them to fight in the military, especially as their parents stayed behind barbed wire. Many were deeply embittered at a system that had promised them inalienable rights and had stripped them away, along with everything they had owned, on the basis of their ancestry; they wondered why they should swear loyalty to a nation that had betrayed them.

"If the U.S. Constitution and Bill of Rights didn't apply to me by putting me in camp and classifying me as IV-C, enemy alien, then why should the Selective Service laws apply to me?" wondered Jim Akutsu, a draft resister.[37]

So a number of the internees, both Nisei and Issei, chose to answer the final two questions on their forms with "no." How the questions would be answered, in fact, became the paramount political issue in all the camps. Those who answered "yes" to both were often treated as pariahs, especially by the very vocal traditionalist factions in the camps—namely, the often (though not always) pro-Japan Kibei, and the substantial portion of the Issei who favored Japan in the war.

At Tule Lake, the agitation reached a fever pitch.[38] The JACL activists at the camp organized a quiet meeting of former chapter officers at one of the blocks to discuss the questionnaire. However, the mere fact of the meeting infuriated the traditionalist faction, who viewed the JACL leaders as *inu*, or informers. Seichi Hayashida, who had been active in the JACL in Bellevue, showed up only briefly: "Then I left shortly after that. They didn't have any trouble, but they would have, if they'd have kept it up."[39]

At a camp gathering the traditionalists organized the next day, the air was rife with denunciations of *keto* ("hairy ones," a derogatory reference to whites) and pro-Japanese nationalism. Anyone who dared contravene the prevailing sentiment was threatened: "Let's bag this guy, beat him, and roll him in a ditch!" a Kibei was heard to say in the direction of a would-be moderate. That evening, gangs of pro-Japanese nationalists roamed the camp and assaulted people who were believed to be "sympathizers" of the U.S. government. A Christian Issei minister was severely beaten, as was a Kibei editor of the camp newspaper, the *Tulean Dispatch*. Another Christian staved off an attack by barring his door.[40]

Hayashida feared he might be one of the intended targets that night. "I heard they were out looking for JACL leaders. They heard about the meeting we had. They were gonna beat up on 'em. And these were anti-American, pro-Japanese, non-JACLers. I heard they were from the Sacramento area. . . . [But] they didn't bother me."

They did, however, come looking for his neighbor. "They accidentally knocked on my door, because the doors were just that far apart. My neighbor on my one side of my door, he was an Issei, but he had a son that volunteered for the Army, and that was the reason why. . . . [But] they didn't get in and they didn't get it done. . . . I don't know, someone scared 'em out. But everyone had an idea where they were from."[41]

Similar agitation struck at other camps: Heart Mountain, Granada, Topaz, Jerome, Minidoka, and Poston all became divided by protests and threats. Fearing more outbursts of violence at all the camps, WRA officials decided to act on plans long in the works to "segregate" the camps: all of the "no-no" respondents would be separated out and transferred to a single camp—namely, Tule Lake. Any "yes-yes" respondents at Tule could transfer to another camp if they chose—and most, though not all, did. They did not, after all, wish to be around when Tule Lake became filled with angry political activists itching for a fight with "*inu*" like themselves.[42]

The remnants of the now-divided Bellevue community—a considerable number had followed Tom Matsuoka's path out of the camps through farm work—mostly jumped at the chance to transfer to Minidoka, since most of them had family, friends, and associates in the Seattle and White River communities who had been placed there. The farmers from communities like Bellevue were more conservative anyway, and had studiously avoided involvement in the politics of the camps as well as they could. The Minidoka camp was noted for being peaceable.

In making the jump to Minidoka, the old Bellevue Nikkei community effectively vanished. Most of the Eastsiders who transferred to Minidoka aligned themselves with whoever from the larger Seattle and White River communities they already knew in the camp. And after the camps closed, these alignments largely determined where they wound up resettling, since they constituted the evacuees' few remaining connections to their former lives. In effect, what was left of the Bellevue community was essentially absorbed into the much larger remnants of the Seattle and White River Nikkei.

Not all of the old Bellevue residents transferred to Minidoka. Some, like Enji Tamaye, chose to remain.[43]

"We were given this loyalty oath to either sign or not sign, and my parents decided that they would not sign," remembered Chizuko Norton, Enji Tamaye's daughter. "And their decision was, 'You allow us to become U.S. citizens and then we will.' But as my father said, he refused to become a person without a country, even if that other country did do this horrible war act on the United States."[44]

Likewise, Togoro Suguro signed "no-no," so the family remained at Tule Lake, and his young son Ed found himself a spectator to the unfolding drama at the camp. During the month of October 1943, some 9,000 segregants from other camps arrived at the relocation center. Their arrival "kind of changed the atmosphere of the camp," remembered Ed. "It became a rather charged camp. There was a great deal of agitation and conflict with the administration. They just couldn't go along with the confinement. And there were some pro-Japan groups there."

The majority of the families that had answered "yes-yes" on the questionnaire had requested to transfer to other camps, though a substantial number of those who did answer affirmatively refused to relocate. This created a volatile situation with the arrival of the "no-no boys," as the pro-Japanese faction came to be called. When a truck carrying farmworkers overturned, killing one of the men, his funeral became a political scene, with some 800 men who operated the camp's farm (most of them "no-no" declarants) announcing they were going on strike because they didn't want to be feeding any of the "yes-yes" evacuees: "They wanted . . . Tule Lake labor and produce to be used only for Tuleans who had determined to be Japanese and not for the other evacuees who had determined to be Americans."[45]

Soon the negotiations spilled into more violence. A gang of militants invaded the camp hospital and severely beat a Nisei medical officer who had made a point of disagreeing with their positions. Three nights later another group of young "no-nos," out to stop a rumored shipment of Tule-grown vegetables to other camps, formed a long chanting line that ran along the fire break. Soon they encountered a group of security officers and a fight broke out; reinforcements were called in, and soon a tank with a contingent of soldiers was on the scene. The next day a tank was placed at each corner of the camp and more soldiers arrived. Some 350 of the militants were arrested and placed in stockade.[46]

Though her father, Enji Tamaye, had replied "no-no," Chizuko Norton and her family did their best to stay away from the pro-Japanese faction. She does, however, remember attending Kibei-sponsored classes in Japanese language that she found useful. But the agitation was frightening: "We heard a lot and there was a lot of violence going on," she says. "Not so much in our block or ward it seemed. . . . We did observe a lot of this demonstration as they serpentined down the fire break, yelling and all."[47]

The agitation gradually settled down, though it flared up later in small but unmistakable ways. The manager of the camp store, an "old Tulean" named Takeo Noma, was stabbed to death by several men wielding a short sword in the early summer of 1944, and it was widely believed to be retaliation for his work in countering the pro-Japanese faction; the murder was never solved.[48] The arrests of the chief agitators eventually culminated in their resettlement in Japan, largely at their own requests. After the Justice Department held renunciation hearings in late 1944, some 20,000 people in the camps would come to request they be repatriated—or in the case of many Nisei, expatriated—to Japan. But in the end, only 4,724 of them would actually depart from the camps and try to resume their lives in a war-ravaged country many of them had never seen.[49]

Chizuko Norton was close to one such Kibei family who chose to be sent back. "They had two little boys," she recalled. "So I did go to where they were all congregated, being readied to take them onto the trucks to take them to where they could get a plane or a boat or something to get back to Japan.

"And they, like we, were cautioned that they could only take that which they could carry in their two hands as well as on their body. And they had a little toddler who was not even two and a little babe in arms, and this little toddler had diapers strapped to his back as well as his front. I felt so bad. We cried and cried, but they were determined to go."[50]

Minidoka, it seemed, was a world away from Tule Lake. Most of the Japanese from Bellevue had little compunction about transferring; the Hayashidas, Hashiguchis, Yabukis, and Shiraishis all had leapt at the chance to get out. The Minidoka camp, plunked down in the middle of a vast expanse of sagebrush of south-central Idaho's high desert plateau, was similar in climate to Tule Lake, though the temperatures were a shade lower. The political climate was a great deal cooler; there was little agitation here—and indeed, a somewhat congenial sense of community.

Figure 4.2. A couple of young incarcerees wend their way through the muddy pathways of the Minidoka WRA Relocation Center in the spring of 1943. Courtesy of Wing Luke Asian Museum/Hatato Family Collection.

Southern Idaho was an appropriate setting, as it were, for the limbo-land that was the internment camps. Like most of the camps, it was on a tract of land most remarkable for its sheer unattractiveness.[51] Simultaneously striking and wretched, alternatively harsh and healing, the landscape reflected the emotional life of the camps. In almost all seasons, the wind blows across the desert plateau with only sagebrush for a windbreak, turning any unpleasant weather into a hellish day. In the cold of winter, when the temperature drops to 20 below zero in a typical cold spell, the howling winds turn even a clear day into a drifting blizzard. In the summertime, the wind can provide a kind of relief from the searing heat, but it forces the dust into every nook of your home and every pore in your body. And yet, at its best, the landscape can exhilarate; the desert sunsets are often spectacular, and the cool early mornings feel almost purifying. The open plain where the camp was located was a trackless and endless stretch of sagebrush, and yet the simple quiet of the land had its own virtues for the Japanese. Still, these inevitably were overshadowed by the guns in the guard towers.

"It's harder than we can say, the way we felt," said Mitsi Shiraishi. "We'd look out on a beautiful day, and we'd see that little thing [the guard tower] that soldier is watching us from up there. It's something we can talk about, but we can't tell you exactly how we felt.

"For the younger people, there was anger, there was sadness; for the older people, not knowing what tomorrow would be. We didn't know whether we would come back to the same place or not, so everyone that we went to say goodbye to, we'd have to sit down and cry."

Many evacuees began finding a few routes out of camp. Some were allowed to leave the camp to join labor crews on farms throughout the western states, as the Matsuokas had already done. Others, finally reclassified I-A, signed up for military service or, eventually, were drafted. But the majority remained in the camps. Gradually, they settled into a semblance of normalcy.

Life was maintained in row after row of tarpaper crackerboxes. There were 500 barracks arranged in 44 blocks, and each block would have its own mess hall, laundry, and toilet facilities. The camp itself was on a plot about two and a half miles long and a mile wide.

Families tried to turn their cramped living quarters into something like a home. A number were Buddhist and set up their own worship areas in a corner of the room. Standards of fastidiousness they had observed at their homes were observed in the camps as well; most of the apartments were kept neat as a pin. While the camps were anything but pleasant, and a number of Americans openly advocated making their conditions harsher, the camps under the WRA never came close to the kinds of atrocious conditions that flourished at similar concentration camps in Europe (which became extermination camps) or Japanese prisoner of war camps. Food was comparatively plentiful, and the residents were allowed some freedom of movement, mostly under the auspices of limited one-to-three-day passes that let them travel to the nearest town, Twin Falls.

Still the commercial center for that part of the state, Twin Falls was then only a town of 10,000 whose population was matched by the 10,000 residents of the Minidoka camp. But unlike the camp, there were shops and eateries and freedom in the town. So camp officials issued substantial numbers of the passes that enabled the Nisei in the camp to shop and stroll the streets of Twin Falls.

The remote little farming town, located in the middle of a vast open plain, was understandably a little provincial; the uniformly white population had rarely encountered anyone "Oriental." For the most part, people in Twin Falls were curious and tried to be welcoming, but cultural animosities were alive and well even in remote locations like this. Shopkeepers complained that it was rude for the Japanese youngsters to speak English to them and then use Japanese for conversing with their friends, and the Kiwanis Club took up the cause, making an official protest to the camp director. He in turn enlisted the camp newspaper, *The Minidoka Irrigator*, to explain to the evacuees how to be more sensitive to the sensibilities of their local hosts. A camp-wide campaign involving ministers, block managers, and Buddhist priests then spread the word to the Nisei youth.[52]

The Nisei for the most part complied readily, because a trip into town was their greatest treat. Mitsi Shiraishi worked in the camp mess hall and saved her money for those chances to get out. "I think we got $16 a month for working there," she said. "We would save our $16 checks and then go shopping. With our meager savings, we could still go out there, and it was a big treat for us. You had to have a pass.

"And oh, eating that milk shake at the dime store lunch counter. That was really thrilling. I thought we'd never get to do that again."

Mitsi even was able to eventually get permission for her dog to join her in camp. "They wrote to me from the general's office," she said. "Sure enough, the day came when I could get her. Mrs. Bovee put her on a train.

While she had the dog, she kept a little diary of what she and the dog did today, where they went, who they met, what they did. She sent me the diary to let me know the dog was all right. She was wonderful."

Mitsi's mother, who at first had resisted going to the camps, soon became entrenched and had no intention of leaving. "It was a relief to have somebody bring you your food," Mitsi recalled. The free time allowed elderly Issei to take English classes or learn how to make crafts items—or, for some of the men, to gamble constantly.

The food became better, especially after some of the evacuees joined the mess hall crews. "There were so many good restaurant cooks in there," mostly from the Seattle area, said Shiraishi. "And they would take turns being the chefs in the mess halls. So they more or less competed. The chefs would do the best they could with what they had. So we were very fortunate that they would cook different styles of Japanese and American food. And so many people would take advantage of eating here or there, wherever there was good food."

The system ran fairly smoothly, but on a more elemental level, it actually encouraged the dissolution of the traditionally strong family core in the lives of the Japanese. Younger Nisei, particularly teenagers, spent most of their time eating at various mess halls with their friends instead of with their families. Evenings were no longer spent together. One described the result as "not so much a breakdown, but a loosening of the bonds of the family."[53]

Life settled into its own rhythm in the camp. A number of elderly internees died and were buried there. Some children were born there. And, since it became a place where young people had a chance to meet and court, a number were married there.

Akira Aramaki met his bride, a Sacramento woman, at Pinedale, and married her at Minidoka. Seichi Hayashida likewise met his wife at Pinedale and married her at Tule Lake, in what he says was the first wedding in the camp. Michi Tsushima met a young man from the White River area named Tom Nishimura while at the Pinedale camp, and they continued the courtship at Minidoka. They were married by the Rev. Emery E. Andrews, a Seattle minister noted for defending the Japanese, at a little Baptist church in Twin Falls.

Life went on in the camps, and sometimes it came to an end there.

Cano Numoto and his wife May had been married less than two years when they entered the camps; they took with them a young daughter named

Jenny. They had stuck together through the evacuation process and into the camps. But after reaching Minidoka, Cano decided to try to find work outside on the farms, while his wife and daughter remained in camp.

He worked around at a few farms, including one in the Nampa area east of Boise, where he struck up a friendship with the Caucasian landowner. But while he was out of the camp, May began reporting to the infirmary with a high fever. Camp doctors couldn't find a cause. Cano's friend in Nampa urged him to get May out of the camp and get her checked by a better doctor. When he offered to drive to the camp with his car and get her, Cano took him up on the offer.

Cano went to camp and closed up his residence there, and took his wife back to Nampa. "We loaded up all our personal stuff, and when we got to his place, we stayed there a few days, while their doctor checked her out," Cano recalled. "I think the moment the doctor saw her face, he knew right now what she had."

The doctor told Cano he wanted to run some tests at the hospital and keep May there for observation. "Two days later, when I went up to see her, the nurse in the office said, 'Oh, would you have time to see the doctor? He'll be in at 10 o'clock. He'd like to talk to you.' "I said, sure, fine. That's when he gave us the bad news. She had lupus."

The disease May had contracted, possibly through the frequently unsanitary conditions at the camp, was lupus erythematosis, a slowly progressive autoimmune system disease that begins with skin lesions and eventually progresses to the internal organs, particularly the heart. If diagnosed properly and early enough, its advance could, even then, be halted. But in May's case, the help came too late.

Cano, at the doctor's suggestion, telegrammed the Mayo Clinic to see if she could be admitted there. "I got a telegram right back: 'Stop! Stop! We can't help her.' Oh, boy. That's when my heart really sank. I knew they couldn't do anything. They can't help her. There's no hope, you know. That was the worst news I could get."

A short time later, May died. They buried her in nearby Caldwell. Cano returned to the camp at Minidoka with Jenny in tow and tried to sort out his life.

Cano's case was not uncommon for the camp residents. A number of them say life in the camps was tolerable, unless you had the misfortune to become ill or hurt.

"You really put your life in your hands if you got sick or injured," said Ed Suguro. Suguro, only a boy at the time, was playing on some bars at the camp when he slipped and fell and broke his arm. "They didn't set it right," he says. "I did not have a cast. They just taped it, immobilized it, and that's all." To this day, when he holds out his arm, the forearm looks like a bow that has been bent in the middle.

However, other evacuees praise the work of the medical staff at the camps, short-staffed as they often were. When Chizuko Norton's mother fell ill, the medical workers went the extra mile to help.

"She became ill in 1942 . . . she was aching, her neck and all. . . . I remember her walking and my friends and I walking behind her, and you could tell how she was in pain. And when she was not able to do much it was recommended she have bed rest at home. And a very nice Issei lady, who was a visiting nurse, would come every day to help her. And another Nisei person, who was a nurse's aide, would come, until the point where they decided that she should be hospitalized. And she was hospitalized there during the time that I was working, and I'd go see her. And she was there for six months before she died. . . . They did what they could at the time, and I thought that the doctors there were excellent."

Stuck in Tule Lake, her mother's death forced Chizuko to renew her relationship with her father and sister. "And I think it was OK. It was good that we needed each other during that time, and we became really close. In fact, we used to laugh a great deal that all three of us grew up together."[54]

The routes out of the camps via farmwork were especially popular with the Bellevue Nisei, because it was a familiar life for them, although the style of farming—big tracts with only a few crops and much greater productivity—was something new. Sugar beet and potato farmers throughout southern Idaho, Montana, and Utah were glad for the available labor, and the farmer evacuees were glad for something to do besides sit in the camps and wait for something to happen.

Seichi Hayashida hooked up with his former neighbors, the Hashiguchis, and they formed a crew working on a sugar beet farm near Caldwell. "We went out together to this farm in Caldwell," he said. "But I stayed there for four years and learned how to farm, and did all the tractor work. I didn't do much handwork.

"It was entirely different from the kind of farm I did in the Seattle area. And big—and the crops are different than we raised, we never raised sugar beets. . . . So it was a different kind of farm, different methods, and a lot bigger area, lot bigger acreages. We had a ten-acre farm and that was pretty good—pretty good size, all one family could manage. But out there it was hundreds of acres we were talking about."

Al Yabuki took a similar route: "I was out in Weiser, Idaho, for one harvest season, bucking lettuce, and bucking spuds and onions. That's really hard work. . . . I'm small; these truck beds, you're standing up and the truck bed is up here at chest level. And here I was bucking spuds up from the ground and throwing them up on top.

"Boy, I said, this is too tough for me. Let me get up on the truck and stack the bags on the truck. Well, I thought that would be much easier. Here were three or four guys on each side of the truck feeding the bags, and there were two of us trying to load them, stack them up on the truck. Oh boy, that almost knocked me out."

"That kind of stuff is real tough," said Joe Matsuzawa. "I worked in a sugar factory down there in Utah, doing the same thing. They'd come off the truck, and you'd have to stack them. I think they were 30 stacks around. And they'd go way up high. And they'd keep coming.

"There were four or five of us, and you had to keep the belt running. If one fell on the ground, or fell off there, and no one caught it, then you'd just have to run all the time to get caught up. I kind of blacked out a couple of times, during break time. They only had one break, see, during the night."

As more men found work, and still others joined the military, the camps gradually took on a different character. Women, elderly, and the young became the majority. Older Issei and young Nisei provided the largest numbers of the male population.

Many began to speculate about when the camps would close. They were being told by officials that they would remain interned until the war was over. But there were emerging signs that the closure might come sooner.

Probably the most significant, and the least recognized, of those signs were the gold stars that began appearing in the windows of grieving Issei parents, as word arrived from the war that their sons had been killed fighting overseas. Their numbers mounted dramatically as the war dragged on.

Though hardly anyone recognized it at the time, those signs became the driving force that ultimately closed the gates of the camps of infamy.

Chapter 5

Going for Broke

"If we are to clinch the case for ourselves, and if we are to be embodied in the American grain so conclusively that we can never again be smeared and reviled by the bigots and the home fascists, there is no course but for the eligible among us to try like hell to get into the uniforms of Uncle Sam's fighting forces."

—*Editorial in the* Minidoka Irrigator, *January 1943*

KIM MUROMOTO AND KIYO YABUKI WERE BOTH 19 YEARS OLD AND itching to get out of the camp at Tule Lake, even before the unrest there started. So in January 1943, they found work at a farm in Weiser, Idaho, while their parents stayed behind. They started out in the early planting season.

"He was doing the plowing in the nighttime, and I was doing the plowing in the daytime. All of a sudden, he told me, 'Well, I'm going to leave you.'

"I said, 'Well, where you going?'

"He said, 'Well, I volunteered for the service.' And that was that."

Kiyo Yabuki had answered his loyalty questionnaire "yes" on the crucial last two questions, like the majority of the Nisei. And he had decided the indentured servitude that was farm life for the Japanese camp internees was not for him.

WRA Director Dillon Myer had been pressing Assistant Secretary of War John McCloy since July 1942 to change army policy to allow for a unit of all-Nisei fighting men. In November of that year, a meeting of JACL officials and War Relocation Authority and War Department officials concluded that the Nisei should be allowed to volunteer for the war effort. McCloy took up the cause with Secretary of War Henry Stimson, noting that a Nisei unit from Hawaii—the 100th Battalion—was already in Wisconsin for special training; he recommended drafting men out of the relocation centers to join that force. The plan to form a new Japanese American combat team was given the official blessing of Stimson and President Roosevelt, and General George Marshall announced it on New Year's Day 1943; the 442nd Regimental Combat team was activated on February 1.[1]

It was in hopes of determining whether the Nisei in the camps were willing to join the war effort that the WRA thus devised the ill-fated 28 questions that stirred up so much anger in the camps and drove a wedge through the heart of whatever communities had been built there. Amid that turmoil, some 1,200 Nisei agreed to sign up for armed services if they were called—well short of the WRA's hoped-for goal of 3,600 volunteers, but enough to sustain the program.

Lt. Gen. John L. DeWitt, one of the driving forces behind the camps' existence, opposed the move, particularly since he doubted the efficacy of the loyalty oaths. The camps, after all, were predicated on the notion that it was impossible to ascertain the true loyalties of Japanese Americans. What good would a mere oath be in the face of such duplicity?

"There isn't such a thing as a loyal Japanese, and it's just impossible to determine their loyalty by investigation," DeWitt told Provost Marshal General Allan Gullion. He warned McCloy that loyalty reviews would be "a sign of weakness and an admission of an original mistake. Otherwise—we wouldn't have evacuated these people at all if we could determine their loyalty."[2]

Others who had earlier backed the evacuation began to realize that DeWitt was right—but now his logic was twisting back on him. Col. Karl R. Bendetsen, who had masterminded the logistics of the evacuation, protested the loyalty oaths vigorously. But even he began to voice private doubts about the evacuation. He told an aide to McCloy: "Of course [the problem of determining loyalty] is probably true of white people, isn't it?" To distribute the loyalty oaths, he remarked, would be to "confess to an original mistake of terrifically horrible proportions . . . I would find it hard to justify the expenditure of $80 million to build relocation centers, merely for the purpose of releasing them again."[3]

But by then, it had already become clear how greatly DeWitt's credibility had fallen. After he argued against furloughs and leaves for soldiers in the "exclusion zones"—which included every soldier stationed on the West Coast—and publicly chastised his superiors for the Nisei combat-unit plans while testifying before Congress, he was transferred out of the Western Defense Command and promoted, as it were, to commandant of the Army and Navy Staff College in Washington, D.C.[4]

The ranks of Nisei soldiers began to fill—slowly at first, but steadily. And Bendetsen's fear that the internment would be proven a huge mistake was soon realized.

Kiyo Yabuki and Ryomi Tanino were among the first in line. Yabuki had signed his form "yes-yes," registered to join the 442nd, and then transferred out of Tule Lake to Minidoka: "I signed up in Tule, too late, and then I was called after I moved over to Minidoka, in Idaho. My sister was in Minidoka, and the idea was to get my mother with my sister. When I was there, I worked for a farm just outside of camp, until I got the call-up."

Tanino, the valedictorian of Bellevue High's Class of '41, was eager to join, too. He had been away at Washington State College in Pullman when the war broke out. Since Pullman was outside of DeWitt's exclusion zones, he had been able to remain there while his parents were shipped off, first to Pinedale and then Tule Lake.

Tanino said that for the most part, his fellow students at WSC refrained from treating him differently after Pearl Harbor: "In fact, a lot of them were sympathetic," he said. But fears of military spying even spread to the collegiate level. "I used to be in ROTC," Tanino recalled. "They kicked me out of the ROTC, after the war broke out, because I was Japanese American.

"It made me mad. I went to the administration and bitched about it. I think there was about two, three of us. As I recall, they put us back in. Our fellow students were saying, 'Oh, God, you guys are sure lucky—you don't have to get up at 6:30 in the morning!'

"But the reason they gave for kicking us out was they were getting into an area where they were going to be dealing with new types of weapons. And I found out that the new type of weapon was a bazooka. And a year later I was lugging it up the hills of France."

Tanino signed up to join the U.S. Army in October 1943. "It was sort of strange. When the draft board gave me my notice, you know, they classified me as IV-C, and IV-C was an enemy alien. So I went to the draft board to complain about that. So they told me, if you want, you can volunteer. Because I think by then it had already opened up for us."

Joe Matsuzawa's number came up with the draft early in 1944. Matsuzawa actually had been drafted once before: "My number came up and I was drafted. . . . That was before the war. But between the time that I was to report for duty, the war broke out. Well, that put me in another class again. I was I-A once, and this was IV-something: Enemy Alien." This time around, his status was again I-A. He left his farm job in the Utah sugarbeet fields and joined Uncle Sam.

In the camps, the decision to join—or not—drove a wedge deeper through the respective communities. On the one hand, numerous Nisei who signed up described the persecution they and their families faced for joining the army, since they were viewed as *inu* by the traditionalists who held sway in several of the relocation centers; in a number of cases, they were transported out of camp immediately to avoid conflicts.[5] Equally courageous, though, were the draft resisters who tried to stand on their rights as citizens. Among these was a group of would-be draftees at the Heart Mountain camp; they organized as the Fair Play Committee, demanding that their rights be restored, the camps closed and the exclusion ended, before they would submit themselves to the draft:

> We, the members of the FPC are not afraid to go war—we are not afraid to risk our lives for our country. We would gladly sacrifice our lives to protect and uphold the principles and ideals of our country as set forth in the Constitution and the Bill of Rights, for on its inviolability depends the freedom, liberty, justice, and protection of all people including Japanese-Americans and all other minority groups. But have we been given such freedom, such liberty, such justice, such protection? NO!! Without any hearings, without due process of law as guaranteed by the Constitution and Bill of Rights, without any charges filed against us, without any evidence of wrongdoing on our part, one hundred and ten thousand innocent people were kicked out of

> their homes, literally uprooted from where they have lived for the greater part of their life, and herded like dangerous criminals into concentration camps with barbed wire fences and military police guarding it, and then, without rectification of the injustices committed against us nor without restoration of our rights as guaranteed by the constitution, we are ordered to join the army thru discriminatory procedures into a segregated combat unit! Is that the American way? NO![6]

The government acted swiftly and ruthlessly in suppressing the Heart Mountain resistance. Some 63 members of the Fair Play Committee were shortly arrested for draft evasion, and convicted quickly in a mass trial at a Cheyenne courtroom. Sentenced to three years in prison, the Supreme Court would later refuse to hear their appeal. The FPC's leaders, meanwhile, were charged with conspiracy, though their conviction that summer would be thrown out as unconstitutional in late 1945. Nor were the Heart Mountain resisters alone; nearly 40 men at Minidoka also refused to register for the draft, and there were a handful of others who chose the same route at other camps. Their courage, however, was similarly nullified by railroaded court proceedings that made a mockery of the American system of justice. The Minidoka men's case, for instance, was overseen by a federal judge—Chase A. Clark—who as Idaho's governor only a few years before had been one of the politicians who had forced the Roosevelt administration to detain the evacuees in concentration camps, with several public declarations of his personal hatred for all Japanese, citizen or no. Meanwhile, the entirety of the resisters' legal appeal was based on attacking the constitutionality of the internment itself; yet Clark not only refused to recuse himself, he assigned attorneys to the men's cases by forcing local Boise lawyers to handle them free. Few of these lawyers put up any kind of serious defense, and one even denounced his client in the courtroom.[7]

In such a milieu, it was not surprising that the initial response to the army's recruitment pitch was less than enthusiastic. However, that would change in the coming months. The inclusion of Japanese Americans in the draft in January 1944 intensified the enrollment, but by then the attitudes of many Nisei about the war had settled in favor of the call-up (though obviously this was not the case for others, especially the dissenters). If there was anyone to thank for this, it may well have been the 100th Battalion from Hawaii.

The 100th was made up of Hawaiian volunteers who had signed up for service immediately after Pearl Harbor. Because the army command in Hawaii had resisted any efforts to evacuate Japanese citizens—doing so would have wreaked economic and agricultural disaster on the islands—the Nisei there were still eligible for the military, though they formed a segregated unit.

"They kind of stuck together, because they were kind of discriminated against in Hawaii, too, you know," recalled Joe Matsuzawa. "Their way of doing things was, they would gang up on you; they wouldn't go one-on-one. If one guy got in trouble, they all got in trouble. That's the way it was. Even down in Camp Shelby."

Because the 100th had been in continuous training, it was the first Nisei unit sent to Europe. They arrived in North Africa in August 1943, attached to the 34th Red Bull Division, a unit made up of farm kids from Iowa, Minnesota, Nebraska, and the Dakotas. The Red Bulls shipped out of North Africa, however, before the 100th saw any action, and soon arrived in southern Italy for the campaign there.

They took part in the drive from Salerno to the Volturno River, where they encountered heavy resistance. After punching across the river, the unit proceeded north to Foggia, a campaign that culminated in an all-out assault on the abbey at Monte Cassino, an ancient Benedictine monastery atop a mountain where the targeted German unit had made its last stand. The fighting was so fierce that ultimately the abbey was reduced to rubble by the assault. Despite nearly taking the abbey, the 100th suffered so many casualties that it was forced to withdraw for reorganization. It later took five divisions to finish the job.[8]

These exploits created a wave of headlines back home, covering the Japanese Americans in unexpected glory. A UPI account from Italy glowed with descriptions of soldiers "smiling about the job." A *Life* magazine full-page photo depicted a Nisei soldier wounded at Volturno with bandages covering his eyes. Another account from Washington described the War Department's report: "These soldiers are as far away from the stereotyped picture of the evil-doing sons of Japan as the all-American boy is from the headhunter. They obviously believe in what they are doing, and look calmly secure because of it. They are in the habit of enjoying life like any good American. They like the world they live in.

"They don't ask for anything . . . they're fighting, with the rest of us, taking their regular turn."[9]

The sudden wave of positive public sentiment gave McCloy the green light to deploy the 442nd unit that had been training for months. On October 12, 1943, he wrote to his assistant chief of staff: "I think that the experience of the 100th in Italy should prove that Americans of Japanese descent, properly screened, are no menace to our security, and that our army can function perfectly well with them fighting side by side with us, at least in the theatres where we are not opposing Japanese."[10] By March 1944, the first soldiers recruited from the ranks of the evacuees were shipping out to Europe to complement the ranks of the 100th.

The recruits had been training since the summer of 1943 at Camp Shelby, Mississippi. They went through the typical training every grunt endures on the road to soldierhood. "It's about like Pinedale only it's worse," recalled Joe Matsuzawa, "because all the training we did was in the muggy, humid swamps. And there were chiggers there, and mosquitoes, and copperhead snakes, and we'd have to crawl around in there. But I think physically it was tougher than combat."[11]

The only difference for the first batch of Nisei was that they trained with wooden guns, and were kept under surveillance, because some officers doubted their trustworthiness. Finally, as news of the 100th's successes came in, the day came when the Nisei were allowed to train with real guns, and the soldiers celebrated. They knew then that, finally, they would be allowed to fight.

And fight they did. By the time the war was over, 731 of them were killed or missing in action or died of their wounds; another 3,713 were wounded and received purple hearts, while 597 earned bronze stars and 249 silver stars—though, until recently, only one Congressional Medal of Honor.[12] The 442nd became the most decorated unit of its size in World War II, with 18,000 medals, despite its late entry into the war. Yet the unit never contained more than 4,500 men at any one time.[13]

Ry Tanino and Joe Matsuzawa both were with the 442nd Regimental Combat Team when it arrived in Europe on June 7, 1944—one day after D-Day—at the demolished harbor in Naples, Italy. The next day, it moved on to

Anzio, where it joined up with the smaller 100th Battalion, which had been hit hard by the Cassino campaign. The 100th became officially assigned to the 442nd as its First Battalion.

At boot camp, there had been friction between Hawaiians and stateside Nisei, the latter derisively calling the islanders "buddhaheads," pidgin for "pigheads," while the Hawaiians called the mainland boys "kotonks," a word meant to evoke the sound of empty coconuts hitting the ground. At Camp Shelby, some of the friction had escalated into full-scale brawls. But the realities of war turned the discord into a harmless rivalry. Within a few days after the Hawaiian-dominated 100th Battalion was joined with the mainland-dominated 442nd, they were engaged in combat, and the veterans had to help battle-harden their brethren. There was little time for internal enmity.

They proceeded north and inland from Anzio and through Belvedere uneventfully until June 26. The first squads out that day from Belvedere met with German units, to their considerable surprise. Communications were in disarray, and the soldiers left themselves exposed to tank fire on several key occasions. Moreover, they were encountering enemy troops where they didn't expect to, partly because radio links had broken down.

"They really gave us a beating the first day, you know," remembered Tanino. "I think some signals got mixed up. Our company was supposed to be back in reserve. So we were just kind of walking down the road. Then I recall coming to a bridge.

"We were just starting to cross that bridge when they opened fire on us. If they had waited another 30 seconds, until the whole company got on that bridge, they could have wiped us out. But they started firing just as the first people got on that bridge, and we scattered all over.

"I was just starting onto the bridge, because I remember looking down. I think the one thing that I really remember was that as I got on that bridge there was a dead German soldier, and his face had been blown off. And the funny thing is, I didn't really feel sorry for him. I thought, 'Gee, here's a guy, a young guy, probably has parents—I felt sorry for the parents, and the brothers and sisters, but I never felt sorry for him. Because he was dead. That was the first dead German I saw."

It was also Tanino's first exposure to live fire: "When we all scattered, I was laying in the bushes, and I could see the machine-gun bullets hitting the leaves as they went over."

In most of these encounters, the Germans generally retreated a short distance and then settled in, bending but not breaking. After three days, the fighting at Belvedere finally ended when the Germans pulled out. The 442nd moved north again, this time toward the town of Luciana, with the objective of controlling the seacoast town of Livorno.

In the way was Hill 140, a German stronghold that posed a major problem for an advancing army. The enemy's fortified position atop the hill allowed them to fire at will at the open countryside around them. On July 2, 1944, the 442nd waded in to face the hail of mortar and gunfire.[14]

"Myself, I was on Hill 140, which was one of the hardest-fought battles," recalled Joe Matsuzawa. "I was activated the night of July Fourth, and boy, did we see fireworks!" The casualty count was so high at Hill 140 that it was afterward nicknamed "Little Cassino."

"A lot of people died," Matsuzawa said. "I saw guys . . . dead, exploded. Guys that I knew." He doesn't like to talk about it.

After three days of pitched battle, the Germans finally succumbed when artillery fire from the battalion's Cannon Company arrived, and summarily devastated the enemy positions. The scene of hundreds of German corpses that resulted was described by some veterans there as too horrifying for even the battle-hardened to stomach.

Shortly after Hill 140, Matsuzawa obtained a transfer to a transport unit, which meant that he worked as a mechanic or driver for the rest of the war. He rarely saw action again.

The 442nd kept pushing the Germans back in successive engagements, overtaking Livorno on July 18. The unit spent the next few weeks away from the front as part of a general cleanup force for the campaign northward. Shortly after the Allied forces crossed the Arno River in September, the 442nd was sent to France.

Kiyo Yabuki, part of a replacement unit, caught up with the 442nd as it crossed into the Arno Valley. The campaign completed, the unit shipped north to Marseilles, France, and then traveled by cattle cars to the Vosges Mountains.

The Vosges in mid-October were a radical change in climate for the soldiers from the warm, dry environs of Italy. More like Yabuki's native

Northwest, the range on the French-German border was rainy, forested, and cold, especially as wintertime approached. Blankets and coats suddenly were at a premium.

The 442nd's objective was Charmois-devant-Bruyères, a little village in the Rhone Valley. Allied forces had laid siege to the German fortification at Bruyères, under the control of the much-feared Waffen-SS troops, on September 30, 1944. The 442nd arrived on October 14 and began their assault the next day.

The Germans held Bruyères by virtue of having heavy artillery positioned atop four hills around the town, which had vital transportation links the Germans were seeking to keep out of Allied hands. The first task was to take the hills gradually and the town with them, hitting all of them with steady shelling. As the soldiers advanced through the dense forests to the hilltops, Germans from sniper positions opened machine-gun fire. Minefields were spread through the greenery, as well as booby traps; the most lethal surprise came in the form of "Bouncing Betties," or "nutcrackers," landmines that would explode five feet off the ground in an umbrella of shrapnel that destroyed everything in their path. From above, artillery and rocket launchers rained a variety of shells down on the men: "screaming meemies," which sounded like someone's hysterical shriek; and most feared of all, the "tree bursts" that came when shells exploded in the treetops, showering shrapnel that pierced the head and body with fearsome force.

Ry Tanino had moved up from rifleman and was now toting a bazooka for Company F. "I remember going into Bruyères. I think a German company got in between us and someone else in the night. And I remember—God, it was an awful fight, I tell you. There were dead Germans all over the place.

"As I recall, I woke up that morning, and I was getting out of my foxhole, and I was sort of stretching, you know, and I looked over, and it was maybe, from here to that house there [30 feet], I saw another guy standing up. I looked, and you know, it was a German helmet.

"And the next thing I knew, someone else must have spotted someone else, because rifle fire broke out all over the place. I got back in my foxhole. I could see some people running, and they'd disappear. Just as I'd fire, it'd seem they'd disappear. I found out there was a little gravel pit, and the Germans were running and jumping into the gravel pit. It wound up quite a fight—80 or so dead Germans."

On October 18, the 442nd finally overtook two of the hills. That evening, the first patrols of Nisei soldiers were entering the town, and they had secured it entirely by the end of the next day. The two remaining hills fell in quick succession.

Tanino and his partner were still having a little trouble figuring out the finer points of operating a bazooka. "I remember coming in to Bruyères. They had logs across the road to stop the tanks. We heard this tank coming down the road.

"So I come up, and I see this tank rolling down that road, and I was waiting, oh, a couple of yards, for it to get closer. And I had this assistant to put the shell in. And he was getting ready to put the shell in. And I still remember this—on the bazooka you put two wires across the end. And those two wires were too short to get around; it was a defective shell.

"'Oh, God,' the guy said, 'I can't get the wire around to hook it up.'

"'Well, take it out,' I said. By the time he had taken it out, this tank was rumbling down and was getting closer. About that time I changed the shell. And the tank comes around and starts going away.

"And by the time we had it hooked up the tank was gone. We had a clear shot at a tank and it got away."

Eventually the German fortress was overrun, and the villagers of Bruyères turned out to meet their liberators. They were somewhat astonished to find Japanese men in American uniforms—these "strange American soldiers," as one local called them. But that evening, they celebrated their liberation with a feast of wine and sausages for the Nisei.[15]

The Bruyères villagers made friendships with the soldiers, who gained a reputation for kindness, particularly toward the village children. "They gave candies to my son, cigarettes to my husband and they paid me for the cabbages which they took from my garden—they even asked permission to do that," remembered one resident years later.[16]

Kiyo Yabuki couldn't clearly recall the location of all the places he fought, just that it was "bloody fighting." After Bruyères, it all became a blur.

"I don't know," he said. "When you're in battle, you never know where the battle line is. All we could tell is—we were there."

After Bruyères the villages came fast: La Broquaine, Belmont, Biffontaine. Much of the fighting in the French borderlands took place on wooded hillsides. Again, the treetop shrapnel became the greatest danger. Ry Tanino was taken out of action for awhile when a shard hit his leg.

"The funny thing is, most days, you could dig a foxhole just big enough for your whole body," he recalled. "This particular day, I had one that was really deep and I fit in like that. I still got it.

"This was just outside Bruyères. When the mortar started coming in, I could hear them coming in. It was a two-man foxhole, and we were both in there. And I think it burst up there, and it came right down. I managed to get out of the foxhole and get to a first-aid station. I was out about three months."

"There were times when you contacted the enemy, but a lot of the casualties were caused by artillery," recalled Kiyo Yabuki. "Those things are a distance away.

"I learned, or had been told, that if you can hear it, you don't have to worry about it. It's the ones you don't hear, that's the one that's going to hit you."

Kiyo said he didn't hear the one that hit him: "I just felt it."

They became known as the "Lost Battalion"—275 Texas boys who got caught nine miles behind enemy lines in the Vosges Mountains of the French borderlands and had no way out. "They were pushed so much by the general, who wanted to advance, advance, advance," recalled one veteran of the battle. "Their battalion advanced so far, the men didn't have protection in the rear and they got isolated. The general had to get somebody to do the rescuing."[17] The 442nd, just a few miles west of them, got to be that somebody.

Two other battalions had already been sent in to effect the rescue—which entailed charging into enemy territory with little in the way of backup—and had been beaten back. The Texans were isolated atop a ridge near Biffontaine and St. Die, and the rescue required advancing through enemy lines to the ridge and opening an escape route.

Some soldiers described the push through the enemy lines as "going through a narrow corridor with the enemy on your right and left, laying down a barrage of mortars, small arms fire, artillery, everything."[18] The Germans hid in the dense forest underbrush beneath camouflaged machine-gun nests that allowed victims to walk past before the gunner popped up out the trap door and opened fire. And there was the steady barrage of tree bursts and screaming meemies and mortar fire.

Staying alive inside the battle became a matter of luck. "Actually, in the combat, you die many times . . . every second, every minute you're there, I think you're afraid . . . you're afraid of lots of things that's going to happen because you are always in danger," recalled one veteran. "There's no such thing as safety. When everything happens, the barrage comes, then the enemy starts coming at you, or you start going after the enemy—you know you're going to get it one way or the other. Usually the percentage is against you because the enemy is waiting for you and you're trying to root them out and this is the whole thing. And, as I said, you got to get it sometime.

"But on this, you've really got to be lucky; fate has to be with you. Some of them say the bullet has my name and all that, but I think if you're in the right place at the right time or if you're in the wrong place at the wrong time, you're going to get it."[19]

Kiyo Yabuki's unit, trying to push through the lines, came under a heavy barrage. All the men had hit the ground and were crawling forward. Out of nowhere the shrapnel came whistling in from the treetops and hit him in the legs.

"That's when I really realized how important mothers are," Yabuki said. "Because as soon as I got hit, my immediate thought was crying out to my mother. But I realized that was being too babyish, so I think I changed it to 'Mama Mia!' That's what I cried out. But in my mind, I was thinking of my mother."

Someone, he's not sure who, came to his rescue. "There was a tank, a tank close by, and after the medics came, they took me, and put me underneath the tank, so I would be protected. I stayed conscious, as far as I can remember. It hurt bad, but they gave me morphine to quiet it down. The rest of the squad I was in, they carried me down to the Medic station, and from there, they took me to the field hospital."

Doctors weren't sure if he'd lose at least one leg, but both were severely damaged at the knees. Kiyo Yabuki's war was over.

Indeed, the 442nd incurred extraordinary losses as it worked its way up that hillside through entrenched German positions. At one point, Maj. Gen. John Dahlquist of the 36th Division of the Seventh Army—the man whose strategy had created the need for the rescue—arrived on the scene with his aide and a colonel, just as the men were immobilized by heavy enemy fire. He ordered the soldiers: "Get off your asses and move!" No one obeyed. He moved forward himself—and his aide was killed almost immediately. The general quickly returned and let his soldiers decide on their own when to advance.

At that point, the advance had reached a dead end; artillery support was too far back, and the terrain would not admit tanks. The men attached bayonets to their guns and began a banzai march up the mountainside. At that moment, a soldier named Barney Hajiro—who had just been court-martialed and transferred over a minor offense, and had reached a breaking point of disgust—yelled, "To hell with everything. Just go for broke already!" and charged the Germans, firing away. Electrified, the other men stampeded behind him, yelling and firing, and slowly succeeded in clearing the way to the ridgetop. Hajiro endured only a minor wound.[20]

Soldiers from I Company were the first through to reach the Texans. Finally, on October 30, after four days of fighting, the 211 men of the Lost Battalion greeted their rescuers and were escorted to safety. The Nisei soldiers who had made it possible suffered 2,100 casualties in the process. "Go for broke!" became the 442nd's official slogan.

Just as Kiyo's war was ending, Kim Muromoto's was beginning. Yabuki left the farm in Weiser, Idaho, as a volunteer. Muromoto was drafted awhile later, along with several others from the same farm. He arrived in the Rhineland in November 1944, just as Yabuki was shipping out. Muromoto came as a troop replacement a few days after the final charge through enemy lines had succeeded.

"We were so depleted of men—we did have some replacements, but there weren't enough of us," Muromoto recalled. "There were six or seven in my platoon when I joined them, that were there already. Normally, there were 36."

The 442nd took up positions on the French-German borderlands, in the vicinity of the old Maginot Line fortifications that had been overrun by German tanks in the early days of the war, during which time they saw little action and enjoyed a quiet Christmas. "We were on defensive units then," Muromoto recalled. "Then, in January, another replacement unit came. So we were pretty well up in numbers. But then we lost our 522 Field Artillery. . . . They went up north to help Patton. We went secretly down to Marseilles. Then we went back down to Italy."

The Po Valley campaign, the U.S. Army's final push in northern Italy, was just beginning. It was mostly a diversional assault, intended to spread the Germans thin. Earlier that month, the Allies had broken through the Siegfried Line and were overrunning western Germany. Hitler was in full retreat. Still, the German troops fought as hard as ever. Soldiers on both sides continued to fall.

The 442nd arrived in late March. Ry Tanino, finished with his rehabilitation, was there, too. "In the last campaign, I was really scared, because I knew

Figure 5.1. Soldiers in the 442nd's "I" Company relax in their bunker in the Maritime Alps on Christmas Day 1944. Clockwise from left: Kim Muromoto, George Morihiro, Tad Mayeda, Charles Mori, George Nakamura, and Danny Kiyoshi. Courtesy of Kim Muromoto.

the war was going to be over," he said. "You had to climb those mountains. As I recall, there was a stretch of about a hundred yards on one side of a mountain. The Germans were over there, and we could see the bullets flying. And yet we had to cross [in front of them]. You could see they weren't that accurate.

"And then we got to the other side, and we were still sort of caught in the flat. When you're out in the flat, there's not much you can do. We were crawling to get over the hill, and then when we hit that open area, we were all running across. Towards the end, those were the scariest moments."

Kim Muromoto recalled the strange randomness of death on the battlefield. "We were going up one hill above Carrara. There was an outpost there. The hill took you right straight down into Carrara. Every time you made a movement there was machine-gun fire. So they went up there with 36 men, and came back with 16. Two got killed, and the rest didn't.

"The fella right next to me got killed. He was from Hawaii. He was laying on the trail, and the rounds from the machine gun came and caught him in three different places. I lucked out. I didn't get wounded."

Muromoto figured he was blessed with a charmed life. "We were going up another hill, and the fella right next to me got hit right in the ear. I was right behind him. He says, 'Boy, you don't know how close you came.' You could see the bullets coming right at us."

Much of the Italian campaign took place on steep, arid mountainsides, with troops slowly working their way up rocky, brush-covered slopes while dodging enemy gunfire. Artillery barrages kept coming, too.

"We were on this one hill, late at night, and my partner and I decided we would dig our foxhole into the bank a little bit to protect us," Muromoto recalled. "The lieutenant gave me first watch. I was watching from about midnight till about 1:30. And this one guy from Hawaii said, 'Well, I'll sit up and be watch with you.' I say, 'That's great,' so we sat there and we talked and talked, and finally, my watch was over, so I went back to my foxhole.

"About 2 o'clock that morning, we got a couple of replacements, and one young fella, he got into the foxhole of the fella that I was talking to, and ours was dug into the wall. And we caught a terrific barrage that night. And they both died. I didn't even know this one fella. He'd only been with us about an hour. Tree-burst came in and came right straight down.

"I don't remember much of the bombardment that we took. My partner, he thought I was dead. Because there was a bunch of rocks and dirt and everything that came down from the concussion. He put his ear to my nose and said, 'Ah, he's still breathing, so I guess he's all right. He must have had a rough night, so he's still sleeping.'

"I don't remember a thing. I don't know if I slept through it or if I got knocked out from rocks or something."

Masami Inatsu had been a popular guy back in Bellevue. Handsome and devil-may-care, he'd been a star player for Tom Matsuoka's baseball teams, and enjoyed a reputation as something of a ladies' man.

His father, Yoshio, had arrived in Bellevue in 1914 and had cleared five acres in the Wilburton area that the family farmed until he died in 1920. His mother remarried, and the family moved to the Newport area a little farther south. Mas, as he was called, married early, and became one of the first Nisei in Bellevue to hold legal title to land.

"If Mas couldn't make a guy laugh, nobody could," recalled Alan Yabuki, Kiyo's brother. "He was a joker, very jolly. He was well-liked, the life of the party. He'd even get some of those State Patrol guys smiling."

Forced into the camps, Mas Inatsu had joined the 442nd a month or so behind Joe Matsuzawa. He caught up with the battalion in France, then promptly shipped out to Italy.

"I heard that the outfit was up in one area in Italy," recalled Joe Matsuzawa. "I went to visit them . . . they were bivouacked there, see. And I was driving a truck going to Northern Italy and I stopped in. I tried to get back in, see. Get back in with the outfit.

"Old Mas, they had just gotten back from France. They were gonna make this push up to northern Italy, and that's what he was saying; he says, 'We're gonna go up to northern Italy.' He gave me a bunch of stuff, you know, bracelets and cameos, things he'd picked up, cheap stuff. He wanted me to give them to his wife.

"I sent it to her. I got a letter back thanking me for sending it, and at the same time she told me he got killed. I was over there and didn't know he got killed."

Kim Muromoto had seen Inatsu only the day before he had died. "I remember seeing him on a truck coming in to where we were bivouacked. I waved at him, and said, 'Hi, Mas!'

"I could see where they were camped. It was a really bad place. I remember telling someone, I wouldn't want to be camped there, because it was up on this hill that was right in line for fire from the Germans. And sure enough, that night they shelled that hill. And that's when Mas was killed."

Mas Inatsu was the only Nisei from Bellevue killed in action with the 442nd. But even that distinction failed to preserve the honor of his memory.

Michi Nishimura, who returned to Kirkland after the war, recalled a white schoolmate named Jack Shoemaker. Some years after the war, Nishimura hired Shoemaker for some cabinet work in her home.

"When he was working here, we were talking about the internment, and he said, 'Well, you know, there were people in Bellevue who were spies, who were working for the Japanese.'

"And I said, 'Oh no, there wasn't, Jack. The Army has investigated and they had never found any Japanese who were spying and sabotaging.'

"And he said, 'Mas Inatsu, he was one of the spies.' And I said, 'Oh, no, Jack, that's a mistake.' I just couldn't change his mind."

The war for Ry Tanino and Kim Muromoto ended in the Po Valley. The German forces in Italy surrendered on April 25. The Allies were moving into Berlin. Hitler committed suicide on April 30, 1945, and on May 7, Germany officially surrendered.

"Oh, I was relieved," recalled Muromoto. "It was almost hard to believe."

The war's end in Europe left the men of the 442nd more numb than joyous. When they heard the news, there was little celebration. Instead, the soldiers simply stopped in their tracks, sorting out the relief from the sudden wave of grief for lost friends that washed over them, mingled with a particular bitterness. Many of them still deeply resented the circumstances of their service, particularly the fact that many of their parents remained behind barbed wire at concentration camps while their sons were dying and being wounded for the sake of a government that imprisoned them. The resentment was intensified by the widespread perception that their battle unit had primarily been used for spearheading attacks, a distinction reserved for "expendable" troops whose numbers the generals didn't mind depleting.[21] The reward for their patriotism in the face of persecution had been to be sent out to face near-certain death in almost every campaign.

The soldiers remained in Europe for a few weeks as they mopped up and enjoyed a little R&R. They found that fighting and dying on the same battlefields had made the Caucasian soldiers color-blind. Muromoto remembers an officer with the 36th Division who had befriended some Nisei with the 100th while the units were attached at Anzio.

"They got to be real good friends there," Muromoto said. "So after the war, we were stationed in Florence for awhile, and this great big captain would come to our outfit. And he'd take off his bars so he could go into the bars with our guys. That's the way it was."

Ry Tanino had survived the entire campaign with the 442nd, but death still managed to touch him. He was stationed with a mop-up unit in the town of Lecco, on Lake Como, when he got the bad news from his brothers who were still in the camp at Tule Lake: "I was in Italy when my mother died. She died of cancer in the camp. I think she knew she had cancer when she went in the camp. Dad never wrote. My brothers wrote. The war was over by this time. I found out within a few days. I got the message through the Red Cross. I knew she was sick, but at that time, I was so young, you don't really think about people getting sick and dying. It hit me pretty hard. And I wanted to go home and they wouldn't let me."

Eventually, the soldiers returned home to a hero's welcome. Gen. Mark Clark lauded the 442nd in the press as "the best soldiers I've ever had." Gen. Joseph Stillwell—who'd had a front-row view as DeWitt's hysteria sparked the evacuation—declared: "They bought an awful hunk of America with their blood. You're damn right those Nisei boys have a place in the American heart, now and forever."[22]

On their return to the United States, President Harry Truman hosted the ceremony as the proud soldiers marched down Constitution Avenue to the Ellipse. Truman—who himself had been a skeptic of the evacuation—awarded the 442nd the Distinguished Unit Citation, telling the men: "You fought for the free nations of the world with the rest of us. I congratulate you on that, and I can't tell you how very much the United States of America thinks of what you have done. You are now on your way home. You fought not only the enemy but you fought prejudice and you have won."[23]

The tales of the 442nd's valor became one of the most prominent news stories of the winter of 1944–1945, and as Page Smith observes, "its effect on public opinion is hard to overestimate."[24] Magazines and newspapers were rich with articles detailing their heroism and bravery. The blood toll had been paid, and with it came a gradual acceptance that the Nisei were finally, unquestionably, American. As the War Relocation Authority's report put it: "Their performance had the effect, not instantaneously but gradually, of quieting the voices of all but the most rabid of the American racebaiters, and of enlarging materially the ranks of forces of good will that were determined to see that the families of Nisei fighters were accepted as full Americans."[25]

Perhaps more important, the Nisei soldiers returned to find the internment camps mostly emptied. That was another battle they had won.

From the start, the opening of the armed services to Nisei volunteers and draftees was closely linked to efforts to close the camps. WRA Director Dillon Myer, who harbored grave reservations about the wisdom of the evacuation, had initiated the camps' resettlement program with a view to eventually reopening the West Coast to Japanese, and indeed believed the program's success depended on ending the exclusionary ban. When he was unable to persuade officials in Washington to take this route, Myer turned to the task of encouraging army registration as another way out of the camps.

The agitation at Tule Lake and elsewhere had inspired another round of Japanese-bashing in the halls of Congress, where the lecterns were pounded serially by senators and congressmen demanding to know why the relocation centers weren't being run with a tighter fist. In early 1943, Washington's Democratic senator, Mon Wallgren, sponsored a bill to wrest the War Relocation Authority from the hands of the Interior Department and place it back in the lap of the War Department, where it had originated. Myer appeared at the hearings for the bill and announced not only his opposition to the power play, but that he also favored ending the exclusion on the Pacific Coast, saying the evacuees could never be persuaded to leave the camps until the ban was lifted. A brief uproar ensued. President Roosevelt himself came to Myer's defense, and the bill was shot down, but so was Myer's proposal to end the exclusion—for the time being.[26]

The performance of the 442nd fighting unit, however, proved beyond question to everyone—both the public at large and officials in Washington—that Nisei citizens were fully as loyal as other Americans. The high casualty rates they suffered and the reports of their impressive bravery in battle had begun to change sentiments back home. The evidence continued to mount that there was no reason to continue the ban.

In late 1943 Myer raised the matter with Stimson again, but this time, he had support in the person of Attorney General Francis Biddle, an opponent of the internment from the start. Biddle began arguing to President Roosevelt that the camps should be closed. "The present practice of keeping loyal American citizens in concentration camps for longer than is necessary is dangerous and repugnant to the principles of our government," he wrote. "It is necessary to act now so that the agitation against these citizens does not continue after the war."[27]

Nonetheless, Roosevelt waffled, if only because it was now 1944 and there was an election. Returning the Japanese to their homes was still highly unpopular on the West Coast, particularly in areas where former Japanese farmlands had since been taken over by white farmers or developers looking to convert their farmlands into suburbs. This was the case both in the Seattle area and in California, where Roosevelt felt he needed the votes. Congressmen Henry Jackson and Warren Magnuson both made public their opposition to returning the Japanese to the West Coast, especially since the war continued in the Pacific.[28] But the president's fears proved groundless, since he won reelection handily. And shortly afterward, the Supreme Court gave the administration real impetus to close the camps for good.

Several Nisei had already challenged the constitutionality of the military restrictions placed on them and the evacuation itself, but until 1944 had enjoyed no success. Minoru Yasui—the son of the Hood River businessman interrogated so harshly at Fort Missoula—had intentionally challenged the curfews in Portland in 1942 and had been arrested, and had managed to forward his case to the Supreme Court. Likewise, a University of Washington senior named Gordon Hirabayashi both violated the curfew and refused to report for evacuation, but had successfully challenged his conviction to the highest level. And a welder in San Leandro, California, named Fred Korematsu was caught trying to evade evacuation by hiding his identity (even going so far as to have plastic surgery) and living with a non-Japanese girlfriend, but was only sentenced to probation, which raised questions about whether it could be appealed. The Supreme Court ruled on the first two cases in 1943, and on Korematsu's in 1944; and in all three it turned thumbs down on the Nisei protestors. If nothing else, the rulings were consistent, justifying the three men's convictions on familiar grounds—namely, that wartime conditions justified the evacuation.[29]

The ruling that finally cracked the shell, though, was handed down the same day as Korematsu's. It came about as the result of a Caucasian lawyer's visit to an assembly center. The Sacramento chapter of the JACL had persuaded a local attorney to handle the case of Mitsuye Endo, one of a number of clerical workers—she worked in the Department of Motor Vehicles—who lost their jobs in 1942 when the California State Personnel Board fired all persons of Japanese ancestry. When he went to visit her at the assembly center at Tanforan, he was so shaken by what he saw—the conditions were too similar to a prison, he felt—that he decided that his client should provide a test case to fight the internment on constitutional grounds. In July 1942 Endo's lawyers filed a writ of habeas corpus challenging the government's right to exclude her from her home in California, but the case languished in district court for nearly a year. When the district court judge did rule on it, he summarily dismissed it, citing the Supreme Court's earlier rulings.[30]

However, ACLU lawyers took up the case and successfully wrung an appeal from the Supreme Court. And on December 18, 1944, the ruling—titled *Ex Parte Mitsuye Endo*—came down: Endo could no longer be detained by the WRA, and she was free to return to her Sacramento home; the WRA had "no authority to detain loyal citizens." A scathing concurrence from one justice found "that detention in Relocation Centers of persons of Japanese ancestry regardless of loyalty is not only unauthorized by Congress or the Executive but is another example of the unconstitutional resort to racism inherent in the entire evacuation program. . . . Racial discrimination of this nature bears no reasonable relation to military necessity and is utterly foreign to the ideals and traditions of the American people."[31]

That ruling proved to be the clincher for the camps. Secretary of War Stimson had already recommended, in March 1944, that the camps be closed; and Interior Secretary Harold Ickes, to whose purview the War Relocation Authority had been shifted early that year, wrote to President Roosevelt (with whom he played cards regularly) a report that was caustic in its assessment of the camps, concluding: "I do say that the continued retention of these innocent people in the relocation centers would be a blot upon the history of this country." But Roosevelt decided to wait until after the election. So on December 17, 1944, an army press release anticipating the Supreme Court ruling leaked the government's announcement that it had lifted the exclusionary ban against Japanese on the Pacific Coast, two and a half years after the last Japanese had been evacuated.[32]

⟡

The news of the closures—scheduled to occur within six months of the announcement—caused yet another round of chaos and protest within the camps. Many of the elderly Issei were understandably frightened about the prospects of returning to communities where they had once lived but now had nothing to return to. Many of them had sons serving—or lost—in the 442nd and had themselves grown beyond the age when they could care for themselves. Nearly all of the evacuees remaining in the camps were faced with the prospect of starting completely from scratch, and most were understandably frightened.

Camp officials began encouraging younger evacuees from urban areas to return first and scout out their old communities, with an eye to reconstructing some of the old infrastructure. Local churches picked up the effort and began serving as liaisons for the early returnees. When they came back to camp, it was often with encouraging words about the prospects for starting over.

Most returned to their hometowns, though many had no homes there to return to. Others, like the Matsuokas, chose to remain in the Rocky Mountain states like Montana, Idaho, Wyoming, and the eastern portions of Oregon and Washington, where farming was more promising and the neighbors more accommodating.

Many had already found other routes back out of camp. "I knew that Idaho farm life was not for me," said Al Yabuki. "So after the season, I said, No more of this, so I moved up to Spokane. I said, my direction is back to the West Coast. So I can get a little closer to home."

Spokane had always been outside the exclusion zone (though early in the relocation process, when "voluntary evacuation" was being sought, anti-Japanese agitation had reared its ugly head there, as it had in many inland rural counties of the Pacific Coast) and some Japanese Americans had managed to make their way there already, often with an eye to returning home to the Seattle area. "So I went to Spokane, and I was there for a little over a year, working in a greenhouse, which was a little more to my liking," Yabuki said. "I wrote to my brother-in-law, 'Come on up to Spokane to see if you can't find a job or like it up here.' He stuck around up there for a little while, and he got a job in a laundry.

"He says, 'OK, let's call the rest of the family up.' So we called the rest of them up to Spokane." A year later, they were able to return to their home at Hunts Point.

Though some congressmen wanted the camps shut down by June 1945, the WRA took a more tempered approach because of the fears of so many internees, and gradually moved them out so that all of the camps were closed by January 1946, except for Tule Lake, which remained open until March to deal with lingering repatriation questions.[33] When it came time to close the gates, a number of reluctant evacuees refused to leave. Water was cut off, and internees shown the gate. In one case at Minidoka, an elderly Issei man was taken to Shoshone, the nearest town, and given money for a train to Seattle. He instead simply threw the money on the ground and walked back to the camp. He was put on another train at Shoshone. Another Minidoka family, the Takagis, had to be forced aboard the last evacuee train with their suitcases, shopping bags, and carton boxes packed with their belongings.[34]

But for the returning soldiers of the 442nd, the camps' closure was nothing but good news. By the time they reached stateside, most of their parents had either returned home or had gone to stay with relatives, or had found their way to temporary housing provided by a few compassionate churches. The demise of the camps, perhaps even more than victory against the Axis, was chief among the Nisei men's hopes when they enlisted. Years later, that is what most of them remember, and is their enduring source of pride. In describing the 442nd's military exploits, Kim Muromoto echoed Harry Truman: "We fought two wars—the war against Germany and Japan, and the war against prejudice."

The 442nd won both wars—though in 1945, the losers of the war at home were not quite aware of it yet.

Kiyo Yabuki spent the better part of a year recovering from his wounds. After some initial worries, both legs healed—well enough, in fact, that Kiyo eventually became a postal carrier. He delivered to Bellevue addresses until his retirement in 1989.

He was hospitalized at a military installation in Vancouver, Washington, for most of the year he spent in rehabilitation.

"One time, when I was in the hospital in Vancouver, there was a couple from Portland that used to come visit the patients at the hospital," he recalled. "I guess I made a remark about the rain coming from Portland, and it really ticked this lady off. I was just joking. Knowing that I was of Japanese ancestry, she made a remark about Japs, that, 'You're just fortunate that you're alive. A lot of our boys were killed.' I couldn't argue with her on that one. I was just too slow with any kind of comeback. Maybe it was a good thing I didn't.

"Then again, being sensitive to discrimination, it really made me kind of shrink back. Even with the uniform on, you had the feeling you were in the wrong."

Bedridden for much of his time in Vancouver, Kiyo was glad to return home when he finally was released. His older brother, Alan, was trying energetically to resurrect their home and greenhouse at Hunts Point, since both had been ruined during their stay away.

Kiyo decided one day that his army uniform needed dry-cleaning, so he took it down to a Bellevue cleaning service to get it done.

They refused to serve him—because he was Japanese.

Chapter 6

The Long Road Home

"DO YOU WANT JAPS FOR YOUR NEIGHBORS AGAIN?" the flier shouted.

"Free MASS MEETING—Monday, April 2, 8 P.M., Bellevue."

The sheets appeared the spring of 1945 on street-corner lampposts, telephone poles, on bulletin boards, and in barber shops around town. Some people handed them out at their gas stations. The March 29 edition of the *Bellevue American* trumpeted the event. The large headline in the lead position on the front page read: "To Hold Mass Meeting Monday—Protest Return of Japanese."

The meeting was to be held in the auditorium at Overlake Elementary School. "It is expected," the news story read, "that representatives from communities throughout the Eastside will be present." George H. Crandell, an attorney who lived on Hunts Point, was to be the featured speaker.

Only a few years before, in 1942, Crandell had been on the other side of the fence, gaining some notoriety by defending two Seattle Japanese businessmen who had been prosecuted by federal authorities for allegedly making false statements while filing for an export license. Crandell argued persuasively in court that the men were victims of anti-Japanese hysteria in the wake of Pearl Harbor. The case ended in a mistrial.

Now, it seemed, Crandell—who crossed the new floating bridge daily to his practice in Seattle—was eager to fan the same old flames he once decried. He alleged that a "Jap spy ring was operating on the West Coast" and that the return of the Japanese from the internment camps would pose a military threat until the war with Japan was over.

"Dozens of local organizations are springing up along the Coast in the so-called Japanese 'hot beds' where they were thickly colonized before the war," Crandell told the *American*. "Each organization is trying to keep the Japs from trying to come back into that particular area. . . . Unless we do something about it, the Japs are going to move in with us. And surely none of us want that."

Crandell, like others in the Puget Sound area, had even grander motives. "We've got to do more than keep the Japs out of our own back yard. That won't solve anything. We've got to get them off the entire Pacific Coast, and we've got to do it legally and peaceably. But we've got to do it permanently, and it can be done if we're all willing to put a shoulder to the wheel."

The *American* also obliquely hinted at economic interests behind the gathering: the meeting, its story said, was sponsored by "a large committee of Eastside business men and women who oppose resettlement of the Japs in this area."

The agitation in 1945 wasn't the first time Bellevue's white citizenry had been stirred up about the impending return of their former neighbors from the internment camps and battlefields where they had spent the duration of the war. Two years before, in June 1943, Bellevue had been electrified by rumors that the Japanese were "sneaking" back to their farms.

The scare, such as it was, may have been started by Joe Matsuzawa, who recalled that he was in Bellevue around that time visiting friends while on furlough from the army. The Saturday visit to the Eastside—mostly looking up old friends and visiting a few old haunts—took only a couple of hours. But later accounts indicated that his presence had raised some local eyebrows.

The next day, a Chinese farmer named Woo Boo, who owned a small family farm on Vashon Island, showed up in downtown Bellevue with his teenage son. He had earlier contracted with a landowner to operate a truck farm that had been evacuated by a Japanese family, and his visit to Bellevue that Sunday was occasioned by his preparations for spring planting. But their truck broke down on Main Street, and the farmer and his son spent much of the afternoon trying to get it running. Charles Bovee, working that Sunday in his real estate office, came out to help them. But he mistook Woo Boo for a Japanese man, and told others that he had seen Japanese farmers apparently coming back to Bellevue. The next day, the rumor was all over town.

Farmer Howard Johnstone came into Bellevue that day and visited a tavern "to use the telephone. I was setting up a fellow to see about buying a hog. So Earl Decker comes up to me and he says, 'How do you like that!' I said, 'How do I like what?' And he says, 'The Japs are coming back to town to take over their farms.' I thought he was kidding. But they said they wasn't kidding. O. D. Russell, he used to be the marshal, he said, 'I seen them myself.' And Bill Crooker, he said he certainly seen one too."

Johnstone set about feverishly working to keep catastrophe at bay. He called the sheriff's office and the FBI, who told him they knew nothing of any Japanese returning to Bellevue. So he approached Charles Bovee about drawing up a petition, and Bovee readily agreed. In a flurry of excitement, the petitions—protesting the return of any Japanese to Bellevue—were circulated through town, and 500 signatures collected in only a few hours.

However, A. J. Whitney, publisher of the *Bellevue American*, decided to investigate the rumors, and discovered the sources of the rumors were harmless Chinese and the hysteria, once again, quite groundless. As the Seattle *Post-Intelligencer* report a few days later put it, "The movement died aborning because of the unfortunate lack of Japanese."[1]

The absence of the Japanese from their longtime communities during the war had not necessarily made hearts grow fonder for them. Indeed, though the frequency of the hysteria was certainly lessened by the fact the Japanese were no longer present and visible, the war-born hatred of all things "Jap" had transformed them into demon-things in the popular mind, and the dearth of daily, real-life examples to the contrary only made things worse.

Headlines reporting on the war front regularly referred to the enemy "Japs"—as did headlines reporting on events in the WRA's relocation centers. Consistent with popular sentiments prior to the war and during the evacuation debate, letters to the editor as well as political pronouncements made no differentiation between the citizens who once had been their neighbors and the foreign enemies their sons were fighting.

Washington's congressional delegation had a particular propensity in this regard. In addition to the damage already wrought by Democratic Senator Mon Wallgren, who had chaired one of the early congressional committees recommending evacuation in 1942, Congressman Henry Jackson, a respected

Everett Democrat, took up the anti-Japanese cause with particular relish for the war's duration. Not only was he an enthusiast of the evacuation, he was a stern advocate of the campaign to keep the Japanese from returning to the Pacific Coast—both during and after the war. He was often seconded in this regard by his Seattle colleague, Democratic Congressman Warren Magnuson, who had a habit of raising groundless alarms about an imminent invasion of the Pacific Coast by the Japanese.[2]

But it was otherwise anonymous men like Joe Matsuzawa who spurred Jackson to headline-grabbing action. In May 1943, Jackson began protesting in Congress against the army's policy of allowing Japanese American soldiers to visit the Pacific Coast on furlough; apparently, wearing an American uniform wasn't assurance enough of Nisei loyalty. Jackson sponsored a resolution calling for a complete investigation of "the Japanese situation," and his congressional colleagues were critical of the use of any Japanese Americans in combat. Rep. John Costello of California sounded the familiar refrain that "you can't tell a good Jap from a bad Jap."[3]

Jackson penned a speech that he never delivered on the subject, but it was clear he was opposed to Japanese Americans ever returning to his home district:

> What is to be the eventual disposition of the Japanese alien and native . . . is the second aspect of this problem of the Pacific. Are we to return them to their former homes and businesses on the Pacific Coast to face the active antagonism of their neighbors? Shall they again, as happened in World War I, compete economically for jobs and businesses with returning war veterans?[4]

The House Committee On Un-American Activities chaired by Texas Democrat Martin Dies (known as the Dies Committee) also joined in on the action, partly at the urging of Jackson and others. A New Jersey Republican named J. Parnell Thomas flew out to Los Angeles and, without visiting a camp, declared that the WRA was pampering the internees. Thomas also demanded the agency halt its policy of "releasing disloyal Japs"—that is, end its policy of relocating evacuees in jobs outside the camps.[5]

The Dies committee hearings provided a steady stream of scandalous headlines for a few months, bolstered by the reports of the unrest at Manzanar and Tule Lake. The most sensational of these reports involved a former motor-pool driver named Harold H. Townsend—described in press reports as "a former official of the Poston, Ariz., relocation center"—who told the credulous congressmen that Japanese subversives were secretly conducting army training drills inside the relocation centers so that evacuees could spring to the aid of an invading Japanese army when it attacked the coast.[6] What the reports also neglected to mention—besides the lack of a shred of evidence for Townsend's claims—was that not only had Townsend been present at the violence in Poston, but he had been fired for panicking and fleeing the scene.[7]

Dies himself held press conferences demanding that the WRA bring back all the Japanese it had relocated out of the camps and keep them interned for the duration of the war, claiming he had evidence that race riots in Detroit the week before had been the secret handiwork of an officer in the Japanese Army.[8] Subsequent headlines detailed more wild allegations, including tales of elderly Issei secretly plotting a kamikaze attack on local forests, setting the West ablaze[9]; caches of food being buried in the desert in a plot to aid the invading Japanese[10]; and claims that the Japanese internees were being fed better in the camps than were American G.I.s (which may have been true, since much of the evacuees' food source was the camp farms they operated).[11] Dies wrapped up his exploration of the "Japanese question" later that summer by reiterating demands that the WRA alter its policies—but besides making headlines in the press, these pronouncements had little apparent effect on the changes that were already in motion at the WRA. And the Dies Committee would soon be more stridently focused on the looming "Red Menace."[12]

The interest groups chimed in as well. The American Legion joined in on the rising anti-Japanese sentiments with its denunciation of the WRA's policy of "coddling the Japs,"[13] and longtime anti-Asian groups like the Native Sons of the Golden West (whose demeanor historically suggested vigilantism) became active in agitating alongside newer groups like the Pearl Harbor League. Some of these groups distributed signs proclaiming: "We don't want any Japs back here—EVER!" These signs gained prominence in places like Kent, in the heart of what had been a thriving Japanese community in the White River Valley; the town's mayor, a barber, displayed the warning prominently in his shop, and earned a *Time* magazine appearance for it, pointing at the sign.[14]

⁂

In Bellevue, the group that George Crandell formed to organize the April 1945 meeting called itself the Japanese Exclusion League. It sported rhetoric nearly identical to the kind once heard from Miller Freeman's old organization, the Anti-Japanese League, though updated to reflect the war-flavored sentiment of the times. Freeman himself was involved with this latest incarnation as well.

It is impossible to tell whether Miller Freeman intended for the two abiding focuses of his life—combating the Japanese, and building an Eastside metropolis—to coalesce at this point, or whether it was pure serendipity, but it is clear that they did. It had become obvious, with the completion of the new Lake Washington Floating Bridge, that cleared land in the Bellevue area would soon be held at a premium as the town's imminent transformation into a Seattle suburb took hold. The main occupants of that land at the time were farmers—and their numbers were dominated by the 60 or so Japanese farmers. It was equally clear that this population would have to be displaced before development could occur. As historian Lucile McDonald put it, in describing the demise of the Bellevue Strawberry Festival: "The festival continued to be staged annually until the Second World War sent the Japanese farmers away . . . and the opening of the first Lake Washington bridge made land too valuable for growing berries."[15]

There is no indication that, when Freeman testified before the Tolan Committee in 1942 as a fierce advocate of evacuation and internment, he did so with an eye toward postwar economic development on the Eastside, though Freeman had been acquiring property steadily since his move to Medina in 1928. Considering the tenor of the times and of his remarks, it seems more likely that he favored the internment out of the same motivations that had spurred his long battle with the "Yellow Peril."

But Freeman remained unusually active on the "Japanese question" even after the evacuation was accomplished. He wrote often to local Justice Department and FBI officials to report what he deemed to be inappropriate activity by the evacuees. More significantly, he began building a bulwark against the possibility the Japanese might return. And there was clearly an economic component to this line of argument.

In 1943, he wrote to Rep. Warren Magnuson—though Freeman was a Republican National Committeeman, he and the Seattle Democrat apparently had a long and friendly acquaintance, as well as shared views on the Japanese—decrying Dillon Myers' attempts to undo the exclusion zones, and urging Magnuson to take steps to prevent the return of the Japanese to the Pacific Coast. Magnuson replied on June 14 with a chatty letter about their families that concluded:

I hope you noticed my recent statement on the Japanese. It was occasioned by the calling to my attention of a certain group who were trying to oust General DeWitt because of his Japanese views. I know DeWitt, and I disagree with him on many things, but I wanted to take that opportunity to add my bit to the fact that the Japanese issue goes beyond DeWitt and even though we might scare up a "fiddler's dozen" of loyal Japanese, I could see no sense in any coddling of their problem, in particular after we have gone to the enormous expense of removal from the Coastal areas.

You and I know that as the Japanese get desperate, wilder things are apt to happen, with plenty of opportunity for sabotage in our area, and by far the most important thing, on which I entirely agree with you, if we start to coddle them now during the war period, they become reintrenched in our post-war problem in the North Pacific area. I don't want them involved in that development.

The leadership of the House the other day came to me for consultation on Congressman Jackson's resolution to make a thorough investigation of the Japanese problem. They were inclined to pigeon-hole the matter on the grounds that the FBI could take care of all such problems relating to the Japanese. I pointed out that the real purpose of the resolution was not to the direct war question of sabotage and espionage, but rather one of dealing with the whole question as it involves our post-war world and their position in it in our area. I expressed the opinion to them that in view of this problem, I hoped action would be taken to set up this Select Committee. I can inform you, off the record, that Congressman Jackson thinks the same as we do on this question.[16]

Freeman continued to hammer any attempts to reopen the exclusion zones to Japanese, and was utterly dismayed when the end of the ban was announced in December 1944, well before the war in the Pacific was over. He again sprang into action and began a letter-writing campaign to try to stave off the return of Japanese to the Seattle area. One correspondent, like Freeman, questioned the rationale for the change in policy:

As a proof that the Japanese were loyal to us along the Coast, they point out that one Battalion (last November) had fought admirably, which is true. But as a matter of fact the French Foreign Legion and any number of Americans as well, including Mr. Lindeman and myself to a minor degree, were with the French in the last war. Yet none of them, I believe, felt deep love and zealous interest in supporting the authority and interest of France. We were

> mercenaries, so to speak. We did not feel that deep love, which is called patriotism, for France. The fact that these Japanese Americans who are very brave men and who fought well, is no proof that their relatives, uncles and cousins and fathers, most of them were born in Japan and worship the Japanese emperor, loved our country and were zealous in supporting its interests and its authority. On the contrary, they tolerated subversive propaganda and shut their eyes to the fact that the Japanese government had spies operating under our noses. I know something about those spies and I know who some of them were.[17]

The new Japanese Exclusion League was organized that spring with help from Miller Freeman and others. The core ideology seems to have been built off the bones of Freeman's old Anti-Japanese League, which had gradually ceased activity after the passage of the Asian Exclusion Act in 1924. Freeman was a financial supporter of the new entity, but most of its leadership represented fresh blood in the anti-Asian movement, men named Dale Bergh, C. G. Schneider, Ralph Hannan, and Arthur J. Ritchie. And their June 1945 newsletter, dubbed the *Japanese Exclusion League Journal*, made their agenda quite explicit, describing the JEL as "an organization dedicated to legally, peaceably and permanently ridding this Coast and, ultimately, this country of the Japs."

The newsletter was chock-full of various attacks on the Japanese. A Bainbridge Island resident named Lambert Schuyler attacked Japanese strawberry farmers:

> "The beating that the Japs gave Bainbridge acres amounts to assault and battery," Schuyler told the *Journal*. "The fact is that the Japs made their fortunes here by mining the soil—leased soil. Take a good look at our so-called berry fields today. Most of them will not even grow good weeds. At best they will produce very inferior berries. And it will cost plenty to restore them to any kind of farming. The reason: chemical fertilizers and no crop rotation. . . .
>
> "Don't believe it, either, when someone tells you that the Jap has brought wealth to our community. Actually, they mined this region. They made money, but they lived in filth and poverty. They did their spending in Jap stores, put their savings into Jap hotels and grocery stores in Seattle,

sent the balance to Japan to help build battleships. They didn't build us up. They tore us down. We want no more of them. . . .

"We can raise better strawberries ourselves than the Japs can. With the help of machinery and crop rotation we can produce them just as cheaply, too. Here is opportunity for some of our farm boys, returned from the wars. In strawberries we have natural advantages of soil, climate and market.

"Keep the Japs away and the white farmers will make money in berries just as they did before the Japs came in and drove them out of business."[18]

A *Journal* editorial titled "A Program That All Can Back!" outlined the League's political agenda:

Almost daily letters come into the headquarters of the Japanese Exclusion League from persons who are anti-Jap but who confess their inability to go along with the League's program because "it sets a precedent that will undermine the fundamentals of the Constitution and imperil other minority programs."

Let's re-inspect the program and see:

Item 1. Induce the government to keep all Japs out of the Western Defense Command until the war is over. That's just good sense, with a war on. If only one among them was a saboteur, the exclusion of all, to prevent his dirty work, would be justified. And we heard a man, close to the military intelligence service, say in a public speech that six known Japanese spies were now operating in Seattle alone.

Item 2. Deport all alien Japs and all disloyal Japs. Who will argue that this is either un-American or unnecessary?

Item 3. Stimulate interest in a national post-war election (so the soldiers can participate) to amend the Federal Constitution and provide that, after a certain date, NO MORE descendants of persons not eligible for citizenship may automatically become citizens merely because their alien mothers were here when they were born.

Japanese now constitute only one-tenth of 1 per cent of our population. No great danger there. The peril lies in permitting fast-breeding races that are not assimilable to go unchecked, and to make American citizens of them as fast as they are spawned. Give them a few years and they will make good of their boast of dominating America. And they'll do it without firing a shot. They will VOTE OUR COUNTRY AWAY FROM US.

If that kind of law is un-American, we set a bad precedent many years ago. We had such a law once. And we kicked it out the window.[19]

This position was explored in greater depth in a pamphlet that Lambert Schuyler published independently: *The Japs Must Not Come Back!* Schuyler's core arguments were not very distinguishable from those offered twenty years before by the exclusionists:

> As a nation we stand prejudiced against orientals. This is something which our bleeding-heart idealists have overlooked. They claim our basic laws, the principles upon which America rests, are unanimously in *favor* of regarding all men as equals. The fact remains, however, that according to our statute books all men are created equal *except those with yellow skins.* Any race, color or creed, say our laws, may become naturalized citizens of our country except the Japanese, Chinese and Hindu. These are judged unfit for assimilation in our society.
>
> Mind you, we on the Pacific Coast are glad of it. What irks us is the loop-hole in our Constitution through which orientals may purchase the farm next door to us and defy us to kick them out. The loop-hole is this—all *babies* are created equal providing they are born in the United States. The Japs, Chinese and Hindus are no exception to this rule. Oriental babies born here are automatically American citizens. . . . Obviously this is a contradiction of principle which cannot be justified within the bounds of either religious or political idealism.[20]

For Schuyler, in keeping with the anti-Japanese tradition, the tenets of white supremacism and pseudoscientific racial eugenics were paramount:

> The dividing lines between the races are necessary to prevent mixed breeding. The white race *does* want to survive!
>
> There is no dodging it. This is a white man's country. The white man runs it. And he is not going to let his own rules of behavior drive him from his own soil. So, as long as we remain a people of spirit we will refuse to sanction the mixing of colored blood with ours. Japanese in America will never be the social equals of the whites for the simple reason that they are not assimilable. Germans? Italians? Jews? Yes. We can assimilate any of the whites. But the colored races are different. We reserve the right to reject from our midst those who are not patently assimilable.[21]

His final solution: designate a passel of Pacific islands permanent territories of the United States, and then remove all persons of Japanese descent to this new permanent homeland. Of course, no one of Japanese blood would be permitted to become a permanent resident of the mainland afterward.[22]

As is often the case with well-laid plans, the Bellevue "mass meeting" of Monday, April 2 didn't quite run according to script. Much to the dismay of the Japanese Exclusion League, some people actually showed up to voice their opposition.

As expected, the Overlake Elementary community hall was filled to overflowing with about 500 people. The parade of speakers began with assurances—soon shattered—that the organizers supported the principles of free speech. Crandell launched into his expected diatribe against the evacuees, concluding that "the one and only way to solve the Japanese question is to exclude them forever from all American territory!"

League executive A. E. McCroskey of Seattle added that the entire nation "is fully aware of the danger of giving American citizenship to those who have proved unworthy of it time and again."[23] He then went on to make a pitch for league memberships, asking for a show of hands from all "who favor exclusion of all American-born Japanese from this country," and about 400 hands went up. Ritchie, who had previously tried to make a quick buck by selling busts of FDR by a "famous Northwest sculptor," held up for the audience door prizes he promised to give away: busts, created by the same artist, of "America's No. 1 Jap hater"—and as he peeled away the tissue, the image of Gen. Douglas MacArthur was revealed.

However, there also were about 100 people in the crowd who apparently weren't ready to sign up at all. Some of them began questioning the league's positions, and two women began heckling the speakers. In response, McCroskey decided free speech wasn't such a good thing after all and threatened to oust their antagonists, telling them to "hire your own hall to heckle in . . . and if there are any more outbreaks you will be ejected."

The outburst apparently put a damper on the evening, because at the end of the night, only 200 or so of those who had raised their hands stayed to put up their $10 for a Japanese Exclusion League membership.[24]

A similar fate befell the would-be organizer of an anti-Japanese effort in Seattle announced the same day as the Bellevue gathering. Lloyd Young, who ran a glass shop in South Seattle, announced he was going to cobble together a local chapter of the Remember Pearl Harbor League, though his dues would only cost $5. But that mattered little to the 150 or so University of Washington students who showed up at his meeting that Thursday to distribute pamphlets and ask questions making clear their opposition to his plans. The opposition far outnumbered the would-be league members. The students refrained from heckling the speakers, but spontaneous laughter erupted at times—as when a speaker declared that white pioneers had "taken this country away from the Indians and now the Japs are trying to take it away from us." The would-be organizers were taken aback by the opposition and said little afterward. No record exists of any further activity by the league in Seattle.[25]

The interest appears to have waned almost as quickly in Bellevue, despite the reported sponsorship of the first meeting by "business men and women." In the edition of the *Bellevue American* following the meeting, no account of the gathering itself appears, except for a discussion of it in a front-page editorial by editor A. J. Whitney.

Whitney backed away from his earlier pro-exclusion tone, though his inclinations against the Japanese were still evident—reflective, perhaps, of his long association with Miller Freeman, who actually purchased a minority interest in the paper a few years later. He bemoaned, for instance, the fact that there was little anyone could do to stop Japanese citizens from returning to their own land. "We were unable to discover anything that could be done about relocation—except protest," his editorial in the April 5 edition observed. "But, even a protest is effective, and we believe that it is honest and fair to notify in advance those Japanese who are planning to relocate here that many people here do not want them to return now."

Whitney was also aggravated by the fact that the internment camps had been closed before the end of the war in the Pacific, and seemed inclined to the Japanese Exclusion League's suggestion of a national plebiscite: "We are of the opinion that the War Relocation Authority . . . made a terrible mistake in trying to force the relocation of the Japanese on the Pacific Coast during the war. Instead, we believe the Japanese should have been encouraged to stay where they were until peace is established, and the nation can attack this grave problem in a rational manner."

He did, however, suggest that a proposal to pass a constitutional amendment to exclude all Japanese from the country "presents many difficulties." And he noted that he "holds no brief for the Japanese Exclusion League," adding: "We do not guarantee the men who are organizing the league. We cannot tell you how the money [collected for memberships] will be spent."[26]

Within a week, a counter-meeting had been organized. Whitney was in full retreat. A headline in the lead positions of the April 12 *American* announced yet another "Town Meeting," this one to be held in the Bellevue School Auditorium on April 19. The meeting, the story declared, "indicates that East Siders believe in fair play and want to know all the facts on the problem of American citizens of Japanese descent."

The story listed organizers from each Eastside community. All were important civic, business, and church leaders, and all wanted the other side of the debate heard. The Bellevue contingent included Charles Bovee, whose wife had been the kind overseer of Mitsi Shiraishi's dog (and who also had sparked the Japanese "panic" two years before).

Again, several hundred attended. Support for their Japanese neighbors' rights was voiced. "I'm not for or against any group," said speaker John Fournier, publisher of the weekly newspaper in Kent. "But as a newspaper publisher and King County businessman, I am deeply concerned to see that the Constitution is upheld and the rights of citizens respected." Other speakers questioned the motives of the exclusionists. Some observed that many of the anti-Japanese backers were businessmen who stood to gain by having the Japanese lands remain vacant.[27]

The tide changed quickly in Bellevue as the town's deeper nature manifested itself. Among longtime Bellevue residents, Miller Freeman was—discreetly—viewed as an overbearing self-promoter and a rich man with little in common with the average rural Bellevue resident. Moreover, many of the former neighbors of the Japanese, who had lived among them and attended school with them, were repulsed by the jingoism they were witnessing. They knew better.

"There were people around here that were madder than all get-out about the Japanese," recalled Robert Hennig. "I didn't particularly feel that way. I was mad at what happened at Pearl Harbor, but as far as the Japanese that lived here, it wasn't their fault.

"I know one guy, lived over here on 24th, and he says, 'Well, if a Jap ever came to my house, I'd shoot him right off the bat.'

"And I said, 'What the hell for? . . . You ever realize that there's a bunch of them over there in Europe, 442nd, the most highly decorated bunch in the Army? . . . They're fighting for us.'

"Well, he—he was a knothead anyway."

Of course, Hennig had a cautious perspective on the entire internment episode, considering his own German ancestry: "I always had to laugh about it, because—I said, they shipped all the Japanese out of here, Japanese descendants—they'd never been near the country of Japan—and here I am a hundred percent German descent and they didn't even look at us."

Bellevue at the time was largely populated with working-class people like Hennig, and his attitude about their Japanese neighbors was relatively common, though often unspoken. As the weeks went by, that view prevailed. The Japanese Exclusion League dropped entirely out of sight; there was no evidence that it organized any further meetings or published any more newsletters. And the *American*, as expected, never was able to report how the membership money had been spent.

Despite its apparent failure, the Japanese Exclusion League at least might have been able to claim that it had its intended effect: of the 60 or so Japanese families who had been evacuated from the Eastside, only 11 came back. Nearly all of those who did were landowners; the bulk of the remainder had leased their farmlands.

The league itself, however, had very little in fact to do with the displacement of the Eastside Japanese, except insofar as it was an extension of the larger forces at work. For the vast majority of Nisei farmers and their families, there was simply nothing worth returning for. Rather, economic forces—many of them put in motion by the same factions that seem to have used the jingoism for their own ends—achieved what the Japanese Exclusion League intended.

When the Lake Washington Floating Bridge was finished in 1941, it opened up the area's development potential, which was considerable, since the land-clearing work provided by the Japanese farmers made for relatively simple conversion to commercial and residential use. Most of the Eastside lay untouched during the war, but land tracts were acquired and plans were laid for a modern Bellevue complete with large shopping centers.

Kemper Freeman, the second son of Miller Freeman and, by 1945, chair of the Overlake School District board, spearheaded those plans. He had begun buying property along Main Street in the 1940s, but what he had in mind was a major development. He traveled to other cities in the West and

Midwest, looking over the new brand of large shopping centers that were springing up in suburbs elsewhere.

He obtained the key property for his idea through his father, Miller Freeman. James Ditty, the city father who had first envisioned Bellevue as a city, offered in writing to sell Miller Freeman a tract of land on the southwest corner of 104th Avenue and Northeast 8th Street for $40,000, but Freeman thought the price was too high and turned him down. Before the 30-day limit on the offer expired, though, Kemper persuaded his father to proceed with the deal, figuring that the price would only go up in negotiations.[28]

Ditty apparently realized his mistake and tried to back out of the offer, but was bound by the letter. Kemper Freeman took over the property, and by mid-June 1945, excavation began on his envisioned shopping center. He obtained expedited approval for the center, despite a shortage of wartime building materials, because federal officials thought the center plans, which included a movie theater, would provide entertainment for soldiers and workers at the nearby shipyard in Kirkland.[29]

The key step for Kemper Freeman came, however, when he landed a Frederick & Nelson store for the center. The prestigious Seattle department store announced its plans to locate at Freeman's development in September. Work began immediately on the store. Freeman rapidly lined up a succession of other businesses to move into the shopping center, including a grocery store, a restaurant, even a barber shop. The movie house, called the Bel-Vue Theatre, opened March 10, 1946; its first feature was *Doll Face*, starring Vivian Blaine and Perry Como.[30]

Originally Freeman called his development the Bellevue Shopping Center, but by 1946, its name had been transformed to Bellevue Square. It became the most visible, and most significant, symbol of the transformation of Bellevue from a sleepy farming town to a modern suburb.

The Japanese farmers who had cleared the land actually owned very little of what they farmed, since laws and economics prohibited them from doing so. Of the 60 or so families in Bellevue at the time of the evacuation, only 13 were landowners.[31] As they trickled back to the Puget Sound area, beginning in early 1945 and through mid-1946, only those lucky enough to have bought property before the war found the door still open in Bellevue.

Many of the white landowners who had leased to Japanese farmers before the war decided, after watching the land sit fallow for four years, not to put the lands back to use as farms. They had other plans.

"If we didn't own the land, then we couldn't come back," said Alan Yabuki, whose family owned a greenhouse in the Yarrow Point area. "They had designs on the property; they probably knew it was going to be developed. There was no sense in trying to come back."

Clyde Hill, which had been largely leased property that produced much of the famed Bellevue strawberry crop, was being developed with homes for upper-income residents. Farming areas in Eastgate and Lake Hills became tract housing developments. And the leased farmlands north of old Bellevue had become the city's new downtown.

This effect was felt all along the Pacific Coast in rural areas that had been occupied by Japanese before the war. When the evacuees returned from the internment camps to the coast in 1945, there was a marked shift away from those kinds of communities as families tried to put their lives together again. Doing so was a much simpler proposition for families who were able to work from the relative shelter provided by the core Japanese communities in urban areas. The opportunities to reoccupy their old farmlands were rare, so many former farmers wound up taking urban occupations. Those who remained in farming often did so in places like Idaho, Montana, and Wyoming, where the initial quiet suspiciousness gradually gave way to open respect.

The numbers bear this shift out: Washington State's Japanese population dropped from 13,889 before the war to 9,694 in 1950, a decline of 4,235; but Seattle's Nikkei population, in the same period, had only lost 1,197. In the meantime, the Japanese population's rural–urban distribution shifted dramatically, from 60 percent urban in 1940 to 80 percent in 1950.[32] This trend was generally consistent throughout the coastal states: In Oregon, only 40 percent of the Hood River Nikkei community returned to the valley, while many relocated instead to Portland; the Russellville community, which declined in the 1930s, appears to have been extinguished altogether.[33] In California, one study found that only one-quarter of the former Japanese American farmers had returned to their former occupations by 1947.[34] Nonetheless, the former strawberry farming communities of Gardena, Agnew, and Watsonville managed to revive themselves to some extent during the 1950s, thus avoiding the fate of the Northwest Nikkei truck farmers, at least for awhile. However, nearly all the old farms have been consumed by the demand for suburban neighborhood tracts in the ensuing years, just as in Bellevue.

For most families returning from the camps, an urban life was nearly the only choice they had. For one thing, their old leased farms were now largely out of reach.

For Enji Tamaye's family, now reduced to the father and two daughters, returning to Seattle was the only real option available. They had remained at Tule Lake until it was clear the war in the Pacific was about to end, leaving finally in August 1945: "When the war came to an end we could hardly wait to leave," recalled Chizuko Norton. "There were a few Japanese businesses open on Jackson Street [in Seattle]. And I remember very vividly the three of us sitting on the train, carrying my mother's ashes.

"And what we discussed, that's all I could remember, not where we would live and what we would do, but what we were gonna eat. And we were hoping that it would be breakfast so we could have waffles and ham and eggs and that kind of thing. So we went to a Japanese café on Jackson Street called Jackson Café and had our first meal as free people. And it was exciting."[35]

For the Nisei who still owned land on the Eastside, returning wasn't easy. First they were confronted with groups like the Japanese Exclusion League—people Akira Aramaki recalls as "a bunch of flag-waving kind of guys."

"We caught wind of that," recalled Ed Suguro. "None of us ever talked to anyone about it. We never asked around or inquired about that to anyone. After the war, we wanted to be very low-key. We didn't want to be very obtrusive. We didn't want to stir up any trouble. And we didn't want to make it any worse."

"When we came back to Bellevue, 'No Japs Wanted'—those signs were all over," said Aramaki. "I went to see my good friend Fred Vinje. I used to help him during the nighttime at Lakeside Supermarket (the Eastside's first large grocery store). I went to see him, and by God, he hid and went in the back room, because he didn't want to be seen with a Japanese in front of his customers. Afterwards, he tried to make amends. He admitted he felt sorry and he felt real ashamed. I shook hands with him."

Kiyo Yabuki (who had already been refused laundering service for his uniform) recalled being intimidated by the anti-Japanese signs. "The thing that really scared me when I came back," he said, "was when I went to this restaurant to eat. I never thought about anything. I went in and sat myself down at the counter. And I looked up, and it says, 'No Japs HERE!' I thought, 'Uh-oh, boy, I wonder if they're going to put poison in the food or something.' I was too scared to go out. So I just stayed there. But they did feed me, though. I was really wondering there for awhile if they were gonna feed poison to me."

Those few Nisei who did return to Bellevue went quietly about rebuilding their lives. Most had to start virtually from scratch. Many found their homes had been burned.

"We didn't go back to where we lived," said Mitsi Shiraishi. "That burned down, so what furniture we didn't take that was left in there, that all burned. We never knew how it burned down. I think it was set. To get rid of the 'Japs,' I think it went with the flames."

The Shiraishis weren't alone. The Hirotakas, the Matsuokas, and several other families returned to find their homes burned down. There were no explanations, only suspicions.

The Matsuokas first got word about their home while working on the farm in Montana. They had asked a friend, a Filipino named Johnny de Los Angeles, to keep an eye on the place.

"They were on the way to my house," Tom Matsuoka recalled. "Johnny said he went to get his wife in Redmond, and they were coming back, and saw smoke. Gee, it looks like our place, you know. And he really hurried. He came up there, and where it was burning in the kitchen; that's where it started. Somebody must have helped Johnny. They dragged out the piano. That's when they got the old chair. And some pictures. I asked Johnny how it started. He didn't know."

Losing the house made it nearly impossible for Tom Matsuoka to return to Bellevue. He stayed with his brother-in-law, Tok Hirotaka, in the summer of 1946 while he checked out the remnants of the place, and looked into the possibility of rebuilding. "They told me, 'You're gonna have a hard time with this house,'" he recalled. "Because the deal with it was, everything was rationed. So you had to put the application in. And maybe if you come back and put the application in, maybe in a year's time, it will come. Oh, it makes one mad!

"So I went back to Montana, and I talked to the wife and kids, and I said, well, they can stay here. . . . And the family, they don't mind to stay."

The Matsuokas remained in Chinook, Montana. With the money from the sale of their Bellevue place, they bought the Lundeen place in 1946 and farmed it for the next 33 years. The children grew up attending school in Chinook and college in Bozeman.

It wasn't easy, because Chinook was not a welcoming community at first. Teachers at the school, they say, were cold, though their fellow students sometime went out of their way to say hello. And, recalled Rae, "the town was even worse, I must say. I never—well, the word 'Jap' was very derogatory and we didn't hear that much in Bellevue, but in—now, Chinook, I mean, this is a sort of, not a Wild West town, but of course, it's different. And there were signs and of course, we would have to walk through the town. I know I did because I would have to wait for my brothers. This was probably later on and you would walk down the main street and a lot of the—not a lot, but several establishments [had signs]: 'No Japs Allowed." And that was . . . I don't know. They must pick it up from each other. They feed on each other, and that lasted all through the war years."[36]

School wasn't a lot better. "That's what I can't forget," said Tom. "They had a really hard time. Like Rae, she had the highest grades ever Chinook High School had before, but they don't give her her valedictorian. And . . . I heard some of the teachers [were] against that, and some teacher said [to disqualify her] just because she is a 'Jap.'"[37]

Rae remembered it well, too: "Well, it was before graduation, and I guess they always pick the valedictorian, salutatorian. And the superintendent, he called me in, and he told me that, 'You should be the valedictorian, but you're not going to be.' Because they decided, they—and I think this is the school board now . . . and I think they decided that I could not be valedictorian because I had not been there the full four years. And that was it."[38]

Despite rough spots like this, they settled into the community and found that life under the Big Sky suited them well. "I stayed 48 years, you know, in Montana," said Tom Matsuoka. "Oh, but that was not so bad a place for to live. You know, Montana, people is a nice. Naturally, the weather is bad, but the people is really nice.

"I had company from back East, one of the boys' relations came and they stayed one time. And she, Mrs. Hanawasake, wanted to walk in the morning. And she [went] out to walk in the road. And she said, 'I don't know how many people stop and want to take me to where I am going. I have to tell them I am walking.' Oh, so I said, 'Montana people can't understand walking.'"

Kazue tried to bring a touch of the lush gardens of her childhood to the dry plains. "She had a beautiful garden," recalls Rae. "She grew flowers. I don't know where she found the time, but she always managed to do that. She transformed that farm place where we lived in Montana. She did all of that, the planting of the flowers. It was always really spectacular.

"And people in that area really didn't garden like that. And they noticed, you know, how they would raise flowers and put in all these big beds of flowers. It was really quite spectacular. . . . And people would come by and take a look at their garden. She was very proud of that on top of everything else."

The Matsuoka family became not just members of the community but beloved fixtures in the town of Chinook. Tom was named Montana Farmer of the Year in 1966. And their long-ago life in Bellevue became a dusty memory draped in sorrow.

The vandalization of homes on the Eastside may not have been reserved solely for the Japanese. Clark Jenkins, a neighbor and friend of the Hirotakas and Matsuokas, stored most of the families' valuables in his attic while they were interned at the camps. And the Jenkins' home, too, burned down under suspicious circumstances, though there was never any evidence that their sympathies for their neighbors were the cause.

Nonetheless, whites who stuck up for the Japanese, said Joe Matsuzawa, "took a lot of abuse. They would be called 'Jap lovers' and unpatriotic."

Yet there were enough of them to provide a bulwark against the tide of racial hatred the returning Japanese Americans encountered. Eastside Nisei all can recount at least one Caucasian friend who stood up for them and assisted them, both before and after the war. Their names—Clayton Shinstrom, Sam Boddy, Clancy Lewis, Charles Bovee—often were associated with the founding of Bellevue as a modern city.

"You found out who your friends were," Rose Matsushita said. "In Bellevue, during the internment, very few spoke up for us during that time."

Japanese homes that remained standing often were vandalized, and everything of value taken. Mitsuko Hashiguchi was in for a nasty shock when she and Mutsuo came back in the summer of 1945 to scout out their old farm, hoping they could resume their old lives: "Well, we came home all right," she said. "But then it was a nightmare. And we couldn't see how in the world we could ever do that. It wasn't burned down or anything. It looked like the cows and pigs and everybody had walked in and out—filthy, and the main part is, we didn't have any water, because the well was all filled with all kinds of junk. Everything you could think of was in that."

Vandalization wasn't the only loss. "Everything was stolen. We had storage room where we had all our things. In the back of our building there was another building, and we put everything in there and just locked it all up and nailed it down and everything so it would be there when we got back. So a lot of my wedding things like silver and everything—we included all of that because there was no place else to keep it, you know—and put it all in there with all our things.

"American friends told me the day we moved out, they came in truckloads and just cleaned out all the Japanese homes, anything they could get into. And they just took it, is what they told me."

Still, the Hashiguchis determined to make a go of it. The Whaleys, who owned the auto garage at Midlakes—"They were real good to us"—let the family use as much water from their source as they needed. "So I think for a couple of months we stayed at my father-in-law's—they came home first to Seattle. They were in Minidoka so they came straight home over here. So we stayed at their place, and then from there we worked out of, to see if we could get our place cleaned up so we could at least live in the house."

As bad as the house was, though, it was a minor task compared to their fields. "Oh, yeah, grass was just all over every inch of the fields. You couldn't even get in there or do anything with it. But you know, to rebuild our soil so we could be farmers again was the biggest job that you could ever do. And there wasn't any money to do it. But we had faith and whatever we made over there on the farm, on the farm over there in Idaho. So we all put our outfits together—my brother and my dad and mom. But to restore that field was something. It took us about five years and tons and tons of cow manure. And we had it hauled to the railroad track—we ordered it and bought it that way. But it was tough."

And even with all that work, the Hashiguchis never could make their farm the success it was before: "It never came back to normal, no way. That's why we farmers all gave up in 1953. 'Forget it!'" The few who came back to the Midlakes row of farms sold out to Great Northern Railroad that year and took up nonfarming jobs in Bellevue.

Their next-door neighbor, Seichi Hayashida, came out from Caldwell in 1945 to collect his things, since he had determined to stay in Idaho and farm there. But he too had a rude welcome: "When I came back, it was all gone—it wasn't gone, but there was a man in there that leased the farm, which was all right in my case," he said. "But I said, 'I came for the stuff I left behind.' And a lot of it I had under lock and key—tools.

"He said, 'You can't take that.' He says, 'It's mine. I bought it from the government.'

"I said, 'Who'd you buy it from?'

"'From the government.'

"I said, 'The government didn't own it, it's mine.'

"So he goes back into the house and he comes back out with a long list of stuff that he bought, and it's a government bill of sale on there, marked 'paid in full.' So he said, 'You can't touch it.'

"I never got paid for it. I probably could have sued the government, but I wouldn't have gotten any more out of it. It probably would have cost more than it was worth."[39]

Alan Yabuki came back to what he called "a few surprises." His family's Hunts Point greenhouse was in shambles, largely, he believes, the byproduct of a couple of tough winters. But the home was ransacked, equipment stolen. There was virtually nothing left.

Akira Aramaki recalled the reaction of the acquaintance to whom he rented his family's farm during the internment. "He said, 'The Japs aren't coming back, this land is never gonna be back—we're gonna have this land.' Boy, that made me mad. No matter what happened, I was gonna get that land back. And I did. I didn't have to fight him for it.

"But they took all my tractors, all my irrigation pipe, and took it to their farm. They just ransacked the house. Because we had it all locked up in the rooms. And I didn't think they'd take it. But they took it."

Doors were closed that, before the war, had been open. Nisei farmers quickly found that no one would buy their produce.

"When I got back, I started growing things on the farm again," recalled Aramaki. "And when I took my things to Everett, I couldn't get anyone to buy. Some of them may have wanted to buy, but they couldn't, you see. They said, forget about coming to Everett. It was tough, I tell you."

Jobs were not easy to come by either. Rose Matsushita, salutatorian of the 1939 Kirkland High School graduating class, enrolled in a business course in Spokane after the evacuation ended and graduated in May of 1945. "Boy, were we naïve," she said. "Nothing, no jobs anywhere. In January, we decided it was hopeless, and we came back to Seattle.

"We did housework when we got back here. No one would hire me for office work. You got suspicious after awhile. You'd go in and apply, and they'd say, 'Sorry, the job is already filled.' Then, two weeks later, the ad for the job was still in the paper."

But though hardly anyone had noticed, the war itself had caused a sea change. The old slander—promoted through decades of "Yellow Peril" theorizing and scapegoating—that held all Japanese in America guilty of treason had been shattered, permanently, by the haunting images of blood sacrifice by the Nisei soldiers of the 442nd.

There was, for instance, the widely seen newsreel featuring Gen. Joseph Stillwell, hero of the China-Burma front, presenting a posthumous medal to a woman named Mary Masuda on December 5, 1945. When she had returned from the internment camps to her old home near Santa Ana, California, Masuda had been greeted by a deputation of locals who informed her she was unwelcome back in town. What they did not know was that her brother, recently killed in action with the 442nd in Italy, had been awarded the Distinguished Service Cross—and it was this medal that Stillwell pointedly traveled crosscountry to Santa Ana to present to Masuda before a national audience.[40]

With images like these fresh in the public's mind, the Japanese American Citizens League rebounded from its pariahhood in the camps to become the foremost advocate for Japanese in America. Reversing its course for most of the war—when it had actively worked against legal challenges to the evacuation and internment[41]—the JACL began working to provide legal counsel to people seeking reparations for their losses in the internment, as well as to lobby for overturning the laws that forbade Japanese immigrants from becoming citizens. At the same time, it began a persuasive public relations effort to gain broader acceptance for the Nisei and Sansei, emphasizing their Americanness and their desire to assimilate. These efforts were bolstered once again by the veterans of the 442nd—the thousands of soldiers returning from the war, with GI Bills fresh in hand, were often able to escape their parents' poverty and settle into middle-class lives. Job opportunities, particularly in professional and white-collar fields, that had been closed to Nisei before 1942 gradually became available.[42]

The JACL's lobbying efforts culminated with the passage of the Immigration and Nationality Act of 1952 (also known as the McCarran-Walter Act), which overturned the language of both the 1870 Immigration Act and the 1924 Asiatic Exclusion Act by eliminating race as a consideration in both immigration and naturalization.[43] During the war, Chinese and Filipinos—who had been America's allies in the war—had already seen the gates of naturalization open, thanks to legislation passed in 1943 and 1946 that overturned the laws that had previously excluded them. But the new legislation recognized all Asians as being worthy of immigrating to the United States—and more important, of becoming its citizens.

In the end, what is perhaps most striking about the anti-Japanese campaign that was mounted at the end of the war was its sheer ineffectiveness. Just as in Bellevue, the efforts to deprive citizens of their rightful places was remarkably short-lived up and down the coast, in striking contrast to the long life this racial agitation had enjoyed in previous decades. Besides the dramatic image and economic changes for Japanese Americans wrought by the sacrifices of the 442nd, several other significant factors were at work: the hard work of the evacuees and their desire to assimilate; the rapidly shifting racial demographics of the postwar coastal population, which saw dramatic increases in a wide variety of racial minorities, thereby masking the relatively small numbers of Japanese returning; the effective campaigning of the JACL; and finally, the quiet efforts of thousands of whites who worked to achieve what they perceived as justice for the Japanese in America, particularly church groups and liberal organizations that worked in local communities to buffer the returnees from violence and face down the hatemongers. The response to George Crandell's big Bellevue meeting of 1945—when the many friends the Japanese had made over the years finally stood up for them and vocally opposed the would-be exclusion—was repeated up and down the coast.[44]

Bellevue officially became a city in 1953, after a long and relatively spirited debate about the pros and cons of cityhood. Many of the 6,000 or so residents weren't keen on giving up their mostly rural status, but the advantages of cityhood won out; on March 24, some 885 voters easily outpolled 461 opponents of the plan. Charles W. Bovee, who had a reputation for defending

Figure 6.1. Honoring his role in getting the Mercer Island Floating Bridge built, Miller Freeman pays the final toll on the bridge in a broadcast public ceremony in 1947. Courtesy of Seattle Post-Intelligencer Collection, Museum of History and Industry.

the Japanese but who also had played a key role in the "scare" of 1943, became the town's first mayor.[45]

The city had grown in leaps and bounds, nearly tripling in size over the previous decade. At the center of the growth was Bellevue Square, which served as an important business magnet, shifting the downtown district northward from the old Main Street alignment. Businesses spread out into the Midlakes area.

In adjacent areas like Clyde Hill and points north and south of Bellevue's core, housing developments sprung up. They mostly offered clean new homes in neatly groomed neighborhoods to Seattle residents searching for a more rural environment. The rapidly growing business core flourished as it provided the new residents with a growing array of services.

Indeed, developers advertised the advantages of a suburban home in one of the new tract developments just across the lake: "Imagine yourself in a country setting, just 15 minutes from work!" read one newspaper real estate ad. Some of the Eastside developments, particularly in Robinswood and Somerset, were built specifically because of their proximity to the four-lane highway. The developments were relatively easy to construct, in large part because the tracts had been cleared and farmed by Japanese immigrants.

The floating bridge had transformed the areas along the Sunset Highway into virtual neighbors to downtown Seattle, and access was even more attractive and simple after the toll expired in 1947; the event was marked with an elaborate ceremony, and Miller Freeman was given the honor of paying the last quarter, in recognition of his role in getting the bridge built. Freeman died in 1955 at the age of 80, his dream of a suburban Bellevue well on its way to reality.

Bellevue enjoyed steady growth over the next 30 years as Boeing employees and much of Seattle's white-collar workforce emigrated out of the urban setting and moved to the Eastside. Demand on the Mercer Island bridge grew to the point that the state built another floating span, farther north, from the Montlake district across to Evergreen Point in Medina. Bellevue's neighbors, Kirkland and Redmond, likewise became home to sprawling residential developments.

Gradually the entire Eastside became the primary suburb of Seattle. Businesses moved there, particularly white-collar clerical operations. The nationwide chain of Safeway grocery stores set up its regional distribution center in the Midlakes area, precisely where rows of Japanese families had once farmed.

With Frederick & Nelson at its core, and the Bon Marché supplementing its business, Bellevue Square became more than a mere shopping center. Kemper Freeman chose to push a more upscale image by being selective about the types of businesses that could place there. Shops at the square eventually grew a reputation tony enough to rival any downtown Seattle store's. It became a covered mall in the 1970s, and it remains the steadiest symbol of downtown Bellevue's wealth. Even the financial collapse of Frederick & Nelson in 1991 hardly caused a blink on the part of its owners; Kemper Freeman, Jr., the square's current proprietor, simply went out and recruited Saks Fifth Avenue to take its place.

It was in the 1980s that Bellevue truly came into its own as a suburban city. Tall steel-and-glass office structures formed a distinctly modern skyline along the eastern shores of the lake. Redmond's Microsoft Corporation became the world's premier software manufacturer and soon was pouring dollars into the local economy on a scale that rivaled Boeing's. With a home-grown economic engine, and services to equal anything offered by its urban neighbors in Seattle and Tacoma, the Eastside became an entity almost unto itself, though its cultural offerings still lag far behind those of grungy old Seattle. Land and home prices on the Eastside now outpace comparable markets in Seattle residential areas; the once-worthless stumplands are now some of the richest real estate in the Puget Sound region.

Reminders of the Japanese farmers are few and far between, though city fathers still sponsor an annual Strawberry Festival that resumed in the 1970s; it is, by all accounts, a pale imitation of the original gathering, and few if any of the strawberries eaten at it are grown in Bellevue. Virtually every physical remnant of the original festival has been wiped out. Only John Matsuoka's farm was still operating until recently—though at age 85 he decided to put away the plow at last. He announced in the fall of 2000 that that year's harvest was his last.

You can still find the tree the young Nisei boys say they climbed at the old Japanese school, in what is now the Vue Crest neighborhood almost adjacent to the Bellevue Square area. If the boys' initials were once carved into its bark, as they claim, those marks have since grown over.

One structure remains: the old produce warehouse next to the railroad tracks. Recently refurbished, it houses a real estate firm, a window shop, and a cleaner's shop.

The site of the Japanese clubhouse, which symbolized the community more than any structure, now has an arterial street providing access to Bellevue

Square running through it. The remainder of the clubhouse property is a parking lot for a travel agency.

The tracts of land where Tom and Kazue Matsuoka farmed, as well as those farmed by the Aramaki, Suguro, and Ito families and most of the other Midlakes farmers, are now occupied by the sprawling Safeway distribution center.

Interstate 405, the north-south freeway route for Eastsiders, cuts through the Hirotakas' family farm. The remnant of their property is now a Ford dealership and the site of a hotel, a restaurant, and some offices.

The Peterson Hill tract, which had been home to a large number of Japanese farmers, was never reoccupied after the war. In the mid-1950s, it was purchased by the Glendale Country Club, a private Seattle organization, and converted into a posh golf course. Unlike many other courses in that climate, it became almost immediately successful, in no small part because the clearing and tilling work of the Japanese farms made it easy to convert the land to grass fairways.

Joe Matsuzawa's old family farm is now the site of the expansive Bellevue Cottontree Inn, the city's main site for conventions prior to completion in 1993 of the Meydenbauer Convention Center.

The land that Ryutan Kurita was prosecuted for farming under the Alien Land Law in 1923 is now the site of the downtown Bellevue Post Office.

Mitsi Shiraishi's former homesite on Newport Way is now occupied by a business complex. One of the businesses offers Shiatsu therapy.

The Itos' family farm is similarly occupied by businesses, mostly real estate and accounting firms, that are tenants of an office and residential complex.

But most of the remaining sites where Japanese farmed—the first and second Japanese schoolhouses, the Yabuki, Numoto, and Tsushima greenhouses, the Muromoto and Mizokawa and Tanino family farms—have now become upper-middle-class residences, mostly new homes with carefully manicured lawns and sprinkler systems. Their former occupants would probably hardly recognize them, and their current tenants might be shocked to discover that their backyard had once flourished with strawberries, peas and corn grown by Japanese farmers.

Their community wiped out, the few Nisei who did return to Bellevue persevered. They took up their parents' mantle and rebuilt the Japanese community. Their parents, the Issei immigrants who had cleared the land and worked the soil that became Bellevue, had become mere shadows of their former selves.

"I think it kind of broke his spirit after he was arrested and taken away," said Michi Nishimura of her father, Asaichi Tsushima. "Because he never was the same after he came back. He went to Japan one year, to visit. He went back because he was the oldest son of his family. I guess they have some kind of tradition that the oldest son inherits the land, in Japan, and they're responsible for the land. Anyway, he went back, and he stayed—he didn't stay too long. He came back.

"Then, about three years later, he just decided, well, he was going to go back there to die. I don't know—I really think he lost his spirit during the war. He never was bitter. I just had that feeling . . . I guess a lot of people were disillusioned." Asaichi Tsushima returned to his birthplace, Okayama, and died there at the age of 91 in 1969.

Michi and her husband, Tom, were like the other Nisei who returned: They worked hard, kept a low profile, made friends, made good neighbors, and as the years passed, found that they had become accepted as regular members of the community.

In that way, the Nisei dream—to be accepted as full Americans—eventually came to pass.

Akira Aramaki built up a successful real estate business. Kim Muromoto and his partner, Hiroshi Mizokawa, started the Bellevue Nursery and operated it for 30 years. Mitsuko Hashiguchi—who was widowed in 1963 when Mutsuo died of cancer—went to work for the Bellevue School District and eventually became head of its food services department. Cano Numoto went to work for the Boeing Co. and eventually retired to his small home in Bellevue, where he maintains a thriving garden. Rose Matsushita also went to work for the Bellevue School District.

Tok Hirotaka worked his farm and the land he bought from Tom Matsuoka for a few years, then worked a number of odd jobs as a landscaper and nursery specialist. He died at the age of 89 in 1999.

Joe Matsuzawa, who came back to Bellevue for a year or so after the war, wound up re-enlisting by signing up for the Air Force when it was established in 1947. Assigned for many years to radar bases in Japan and the Pacific, he retired in 1965 to the Lynnwood area north of Seattle. Matsuzawa died peacefully at his home May 6, 2001.

Mitsi Shiraishi found work sewing garments in Seattle, while she remained on the family farm and took care of her parents. After they died, she was finally free to marry, and did so in 1970. She passed away at the age of 85 in 1997.

Most of the rest of them are long retired now. They say the shadow of the old racism still lingers, in subtle shapes. And the old fears still surface sometimes.

Rose Matsushita said the observation of the fiftieth anniversary of Pearl Harbor in 1991 touched old nerves. "It brought it all back again," she said. "I used to be afraid to go shop for fear of abuse. Just a couple of months ago, when Pearl Harbor was celebrated, it happened again. I was surprised that I would feel that way after all these years. It's scary."

And they still look back on the war years with pain.

"Where was everyone when we needed them?" wondered Matsushita. "They were afraid of their neighbors. . . . Most of us take the easy way out. It's human nature. And I think most of us have allowed for that. But the pain, the hurt of the internment was more than we should have had to take. Especially for my parents, who sacrificed so hard for so long—and to lose everything they had. . . . It still upsets me."

But when they remember those years, often reluctantly, virtually all of the Nisei preach a kind of forgiveness: "I'm not one to dwell on the past," said Michi Nishimura. "I think this is something that happened, and you may as well forget, because you can't do anything about it now. Except try to make sure it doesn't happen again."

The old feelings of dread resurfaced in 1988 when Congress voted to pay the internment camp survivors $20,000 each as a redress for the evacuation and internment. With the debate prior to the vote on the redress, the old arguments that they had heard during the war resurfaced. Some congressmen again suggested that Pearl Harbor had justified the internment, failing again to distinguish between citizens and a foreign military.

Sen. Jesse Helms, a North Carolina Republican, proposed an amendment to "provide that no funds shall be appropriated under this title until the government of Japan has fairly compensated the families of men and women who were killed as a result of the . . . bombing of Pearl Harbor." Another Republican senator, Alan Simpson of Wyoming, remarked: "An apology is way overdue, but coupling it with money takes away some of the sincerity." Despite their objections, the bill passed.

But even that failed to rebuff some of the internment's defenders. When the Washington State House of Representatives prepared to pass a resolution noting the fiftieth anniversary of the internment in the spring of 1992, the same arguments were heard again.

"Oh, it's real good to sit back here and fifth-quarter quarterback," said Rep. Darwin Nealy, a LaCrosse Republican and a World War II veteran. "Sure it was tough on the Japanese, but we had fear, and I can understand what happened with our leaders at that time. They (Japan) had just devastated Pearl Harbor.

"There was a tremendous amount of inequities, and I'm sorry for it, and most all of us are sorry for it. But you have to put yourself in that position. Our leaders were taking precautions and I guess they probably took more than they needed."

Nealy's remarks sparked an emotional rebuke from Rep. Gary Locke, a Seattle Democrat who later was elected Washington's governor—the first Asian American (he is of Chinese descent) ever to win a governorship. "Yes, we were in a time of fear," Locke said. "Yes, we were in a time of war. Yes, Americans lost their lives in the Pacific Theater. But we cannot blame American citizens simply because they are the same race as the enemy."

But along with the bad old feelings that resurfaced, it was with the redress that the victims of the internment found themselves able to begin talking about their experiences. For years, they had buried their memories of the camps with the shame and pain it had come to mean for them.

"My neighbor lady, after the redress, she wanted to ask some questions," said Mitsi Shiraishi. "And I say, 'Madge, do you realize that I never talk about the camp days or anything? We just want it to be a thing of the past, you know.' I only hope it will never happen again to anybody."

Tom Matsuoka retired from farming in 1968. He turned 65 on August 1, 1968, and walked in to their home from the day's work and announced his retirement that day to Kaz. They moved into town, and Tom got a part-time job with the county road crew for awhile. "You had to do hard work sometimes, but it was pretty easy and good pay for the most part," Tom said.

They settled into the life of affectionate retirees, people with so much passed between them that words weren't needed to communicate. His daughter, Rae Takekawa, said they never were a demonstrably affectionate couple: "They didn't show it—none of us do. We're quite reserved. Let's say we're not demonstrative.

"I think they were both strong personalities. Every once in a while they would have their arguments—they both had their opinions, and they both believed that they were always right, you know. And sometimes that didn't go over so well. But they were always together, always the united front. A team."

Kazue discovered an untapped artistic streak late in life, said Rae: "She was very good at art. She didn't pick this up until I think they retired, until they went into town in Montana. She started taking lessons, you know, classes, and she was very good. . . . But she was very quick. My dad said that she would get started and she would just keep going. She was just so quick at doing the work of the painting."

He tended a one-acre "garden" that helped fill the tables of many of their neighbors come harvest time. Kaz liked to play bridge with the neighbor ladies, but Tom didn't join her as a partner very often. She liked to second-guess the way he bid, he said. They lived that way for the next 18 years.

"Mom was one of those people who wouldn't go to a doctor," said Rae Takekawa. "She got really sick after eating out one night, and we took her to see the doctor. It turned out she had a badly infected gall bladder. She died about a month later. It was May 12, 1986; the day before had been Mother's Day, and we had all called her and talked to her that day. It was cardiac arrest."

Kazue was 80 years old, and had led a remarkably full life. But it was difficult for Tom to let her go. He recalled that night vividly.

"Around midnight, she woke me up, and said she needed to go to the bathroom. So I get up, and I help her go to the bathroom, you know. And that was it.

"I got up about six, made her some coffee, and my younger daughter was staying with us, she got up and we got breakfast ready. Should we eat, I said, and she said, 'I don't know, is mother ever going to come down?' I went up and looked, and it just looked like she was sleeping.

"So I came down, and we ate, and after awhile, we thought, this isn't right. So my daughter, she went up and checked, and she was cold, you know. She came down and said something's wrong. I called the ambulance, they came and got her. When they get to the hospital, they say she is dead. They say she had died about an hour before."

They buried Kazue in the town cemetery in Chinook. Tom remained there a few more years, but realized that his advancing years left him vulnerable, especially with no family members around. His children had scattered to towns around the West and Midwest, and he feared that any medical episode would wind up being a burden on his neighbors. And he wasn't ready for a nursing home.

"In a rest home, they're lots younger than me," he said. "I used to go visit friends in rest homes. They weren't the same. Sometimes, you can't even recognize them. I sure give thanks I don't have to go there yet."

Instead, Tom moved to Ridgefield, Washington, because it's a short 20-minute drive away for Rae, who had lived in nearby Vancouver for nearly 30 years. He could still lead an independent life. Ridgefield is a quiet, bucolic town, not altogether unlike the Bellevue of his youth. He still grew a fruitful garden, but it was smaller than his acre plot in Chinook, and he had to contend with slugs again. His growing aches and pains forced him to scale back the size of the garden, too.

His granddaughter in Seattle brought him a dog, a little gray schnauzer that had belonged to a widow she worked with in Bellevue who was unable to keep caring for it. "She tells my granddaughter, 'If you know of anyone who can take my dog, let me know,'" he said. "So she says, 'Oh, my grandpa will take it!' So she brings it to me."

The dog became his companion throughout the day. "Just about every day, I walk the dog down to the post office," he says. "Some days, oh, it's a long way."

Much of his good health seemed to spring from his personality. A lifetime of hardships has not managed to change his essentially optimistic outlook on life. Where many men would have been poisoned by the hatefulness and the ordeals Tom Matsuoka has endured, they were merely obstacles in the distant past for him. Hatred did not seem to exist in his world, and when he was confronted with it, he refused to let it enter.

"He wasn't going to have his life consumed by that," said Rae Takekawa. "People could say things, but I don't think we ever thought any less of ourselves."

Blind fear and peer pressure, Tom believed, were at the root of the injustice he saw in his lifetime: "There was a man who had a team of two horses, and he used to go around with his team, you know, and plow the fields for all the Japanese farmers in the area. And when the war came, he was one of the worst people for going around and saying to lock us up.

"I think a lot of people acted that way because of what the neighbors would think. They didn't want people to think they liked the Japanese. I remember, in Chinook, there was one barber who wouldn't cut Japanese hair. But later I heard it was just because he was afraid of losing customers.

"You know, I never met these men who say bad things about the Japanese. Not that I knew. Maybe I met them and didn't know it. But if I met them, I'd maybe just say, 'Hello.'"

Tom Matsuoka died March 9, 2001. In February he suffered a stroke, and Rae placed him in a convalescent home; but she said he never recovered from the blow, and he eventually succumbed to its complications. Rae herself followed him a few years later; she died of cancer at her Vancouver home on October 8, 2004.

I had interviewed Tom, with Rae's help, for the last time in August 2000, and had dropped off a copy of the first draft of this book to him in December. He looked weaker and moved slowly; the little dog had passed away a year or so before, so he was alone then. But the genial spirit, of course, never flagged.

He asked me in for tea, and we sipped it while he leafed through the pages. (Rae told me later he read it in short order, and of course, offered a few minor corrections.) He smiled and we chatted a little, mostly about the football game on the TV. But I was late, so I shook his hand and left. As we pulled away, he stood in the doorway and waved, as he had every other time I visited him.

Epilogue

The Internment: Race, Memory, and Meaning

WHEN UNITED AIRLINES FLIGHT 175, THE SECOND OF FOUR jetliners hijacked the morning of September 11, 2001, slammed into the World Trade Center, Tosh Ito was watching it on television, like many Americans. But what he thought about in those moments was very different than most—except perhaps for his fellow Nisei. The images on the television made him think of internment camps.

"It didn't take very long," Ito said, for the memories of the evacuation to come flooding back. "It was almost instantaneous, I'd say. By the time the second plane hit, why, I was thinking about what happened."

Ito recognized the immediate similarities between September 11 and Pearl Harbor, raising the specter of a similar reaction against the domestic "enemy," a recognition he shared with most of his fellow evacuees: "It was kind of a surprise attack, and totally unexpected," he said. "I think for most of the Nisei that are still around, it didn't take us very long for it to bring back bad memories."

Rose Matsushita, watching on television at her home in Bellevue, had the same thoughts. "9/11, yeah, I thought: Uh-oh. We're at war," she recalled. "Some of them are here. And they were probably going to go through the same thing we did."

They were hardly alone in thinking this way. John Tateishi can tell you, for instance, about his dream callers.

The calls began a few days after the September 11 attacks. "I got a call one day—this was probably about four days after September 11—from a

Nisei who just started talking, and basically just rambled and rambled," recalled Tateishi, the national director of the Japanese American Citizens League, at his Bay Area office. "And, you know, Japanese Americans, we're raised to be very respectful of our elders. So this man just kept going on and on, and I just sat there and listened to him, waiting to find out, you know, what he was calling about. And then he just said, 'Well, OK, I'll see you.' And he hung up.

"I didn't know this person. And I thought, 'Well, that's a strange a call.' I mean, it was about two hours of phone call."

"And then a day or so later I got another call, and the same thing happened. And it was, I think, on the fourth call I got, when this gentleman was talking to me, and he says, 'You know, I can't sleep again. I'm having bad dreams.'

"I thought what he was referring to was the image of the World Trade Center being hit and collapsing. And as he kept talking I realized what he was talking about were dreams about camp. Of the experience going back sixty years.

"And then after that call, it kept happening, and every time I got a call, I would ask, 'Are you having problems sleeping?' And invariably, the answer was, 'I'm having nightmares again.' I would ask very specifically whether it was about the World Trade Center or about camp, and they would say, 'Oh no no no, the nightmares are about camp, that I had after we left.'"

The Nisei elders' nightmares—replete with barbed wire and machine guns and guard towers—are not mere ephemera. They are, after all, the only American citizens ever to have been herded *en masse* into concentration camps by their own government, not for having done anything, but because of *who they were*. For many of them, the scars of that experience were revived by the trauma following the terrorist attacks on New York and Washington: "This is something that has provoked a very deep psychological response among Nisei," said Tateishi.

Some of this probably was due to the similarities between Pearl Harbor and September 11, at least as traumas to the national psyche. Having lived through the aftermath of the former, when they were publicly attacked, by government officials and politicians as well as by the press, as potential "fifth column" traitors, it probably was only natural that the latter produced concerns that history might repeat itself. Yet the fears touched on something deeper as well.

"I didn't have any bad dreams, but it surely brought up bad memories," said Tosh Ito. The specific memories it engendered, he said, were not so much of the camps but of the outpouring of naked racial hatred that followed Pearl Harbor.

"There was a lot of mass hysteria, a lot of discrimination, and it was not subtle at all. It was right out there," Ito said. "Now, in later years, as things got better for minorities, there was still a lot of discrimination, but it was quite subtle. I think some of us thought maybe it was pretty much gone. But 9/11 brought all of it out again."

It became clear, however, over the ensuing months that the historic circumstances which led to the Nikkei incarceration were not duplicated, neither by the Bush administration nor the public at large. The wave of hysteria that struck shortly after Pearl Harbor, as well as the evacuation itself, both occurred within six months of that attack. In contrast, the government in the post-September 11 environment has been adamant about discouraging racial, ethnic and religious scapegoating, and the public generally has followed that lead, with some notable exceptions. Nonetheless, the concern among Japanese Americans since September 11 has in some regards intensified, because they perceive a gradual drift in a direction that may eventually produce the same result.

They point to increasing agitation among both the press and officialdom blaming Muslims broadly for the terrorism, combined with official actions by the Bush administration that many Nisei internees believe echo the same kinds of gradual steps that led to their own imprisonment. More recently, they can point to attempts by right-wing ideologues to rationalize and defend the internment as somehow justifiable in its time—and by extension, in ours as well.

It matters little to the Nisei that Muslims, not Japanese, are the target this time around. The shadow of the internment camps lingers for nearly all of the former evacuees. Most came out of the concentration-camp ordeal swearing to prevent such a fate ever befalling Americans again, and they now feel duty-bound to speak up.

"I firmly do believe that the Nisei that were in the camps never will forget," Ito said. "It will always be in the back of their minds what can happen to minorities."

"There are things [occurring] that are really disturbing today that in some ways echo what had happened to us," Tateishi said. "I felt that it was our responsibility to speak out and take a very strong position."

What especially concerns the Nisei has been the increasing tide of rationalization of the internment by movement conservatives, mostly in an attempt to justify a fresh round of ethnic profiling measures ostensibly directed at

Arabs and Muslims. The first round of revisionism came shortly after the September 11 attacks, in February 2002, when a powerful congressman suggested that the internment of Japanese Americans had been for their own good.

"We were at war," Rep. Howard Coble, a North Carolina Republican, told an interviewer in February. "They (Japanese Americans) were an endangered species. For many of these Japanese Americans, it wasn't safe for them to be on the street."[1] Coble is not just any congressman, either; he is chairman of a key House subcommittee on national security, one of the people charged with oversight of the new Department of Homeland Security.

Tateishi has heard this talk before. Most disturbing to him, and other Japanese Americans, is the underlying attitudes it represents.

"When Coble made that statement, what I recognized is that kind of age-old attitude about Japanese Americans as perhaps exotic, certainly foreign, can't be understood and they certainly are not one of us. And so because we don't know them, this was a necessary act," Tateishi said.

"And for him to have said that it was for our own protection was really insulting. I don't think he understands how insulted and offended Japanese Americans are by that comment. You just think about the logic of it—you know, if we were being threatened as victims, the solution was to put us into prisons?"

Despite protests from the JACL and other civil rights organizations, including the National Association for the Advancement of Colored People, Coble refused to back down, demanding proof that he was wrong: "I certainly intended no harm or ill will toward anybody. I still stand by what I said . . . that, in no small part, it (internment) was done to protect the Japanese Americans themselves." He said that if anyone could prove to him that such "protective custody" wasn't one of FDR's motivations, then he would apologize for that remark.[2]

A number of historians—notably University of North Carolina law professor Eric Muller, who tracked the case at his popular Weblog, *Is That Legal?*—offered Coble a broad range of concrete proofs that he was wrong.[3] The supporting evidence isn't hard to find; it's addressed directly in the 1983 report of the Congress' Commission on Wartime Relocation and Internment of Civilians, *Personal Justice Denied:*

> This explanation sounds lame indeed today. It was not publicly advanced at the time to justify the exclusion and, had protection been on official minds, a much different post-evacuation program would have been required. [Assis-

tant War Secretary John] McCloy himself supplied the most telling rebuttal of the contention in a 1943 letter to DeWitt:

> That there is serious animosity on the West Coast against all evacuated Japanese I do not doubt, but that does not necessarily mean that we should trim our sails accordingly. . . . The Army, as I see it, is not responsible for the general public peace of the Western Defense Command. That responsibility still rests with the civil authorities. There may, as you suggest, be incidents, but these can be effectively discouraged by prompt action by law enforcement agencies, with the cooperation of the military if they even assume really threatening proportions.

That is the simple, straightforward answer to the argument of protection against vigilantes—keeping the peace is a civil matter that would involve the military only in extreme situations. Even then, public officials would be duty-bound to protect the innocent, not to order them from their homes for months or years under the rubric of a military measure designed to maintain public peace.[4]

The report further demolishes this argument in detail. Indeed, over the years the record regarding the internment has been voluminously examined and detailed, and the verdict has always been clear and overwhelming that protecting the Japanese population from vigilantism was, if considered at all, at best a negligible factor in the decision to intern them.

Nonetheless, Coble refused to either correct himself or apologize (though he did admit: "We all know now that this was in fact the wrong decision and an action that should never be repeated"[5]), and ignored demands he step down from his committee chairmanship. Likewise, neither the Bush administration nor the Republican leadership generally even acknowledged the concerns that were raised. This muted response helped feed the perception among Japanese Americans that government officials are treading down the same path that led to their own internment—more gradually, even imperceptibly, but just as certainly.

"If you're talking about people who should know better, these are usually people in leadership or responsible positions," said Tateishi. "And what they're edging towards is a policy that will echo much of what we experienced in 1942. And we've already taken steps in that direction, with things like the Patriot Act, the kind of racial profiling that's going on, the arrest of

2,000 men right after the terrorist attacks—they are all echoes of things that happened to us back in 1942."

Coble's was only the first in a rising chorus of conservative voices either defending the notion of internment or against Arabs and Muslims generically in a way that echoed the pre-internment hysteria of 1942, suggesting they may represent a "fifth column" in our midst. These voices ranged from nearly all bands on the right-wing spectrum, from columnist Peggy Noonan to religious leader Jerry Falwell to radio talk-show host Michael Savage. Some of these were subtle; others were not.

In July 2002, an already-controversial Bush appointee to the U.S. Commission on Civil Rights named Peter Kirsanow suggested at a public hearing that the public probably would support the detention of Arab Americans in internment camps if another al-Qaeda terrorist attack were to occur on American soil. Were that to happen, "and they come from the same ethnic group that attacked the World Trade Center, you can forget about civil rights," Kirsanow said: "The public would be less concerned about any perceived erosion of civil liberties than they are about protecting their own lives."[6]

The combination of revisionism and agitation for racial profiling reached its fever pitch in the summer of 2004 with the publication of Michelle Malkin's *In Defense of Internment: The Case for Racial Profiling in World War II and the War on Terror*. Malkin, a conservative Filipino American and a regular commentator on Fox News talk shows, made numerous appearances on cable television networks and radio talk shows (almost always without benefit of an opposing historian) to promote her book, which subsequently appeared on the *New York Times* bestseller list.

The thrust of Malkin's argument was that the secret "MAGIC" intercepts of Japanese diplomatic cables (discussed in chapter 3) "proved" that the stateside Nikkei community was riddled with spies and saboteurs, which in turn provided a genuine national-security rationale for rounding them up and evacuating them *en masse* from the Pacific Coast (even though any serious survey of the cables reveals that there was no real evidence of this charge, and moreover there was no substantive evidence that they played a significant role in the decisions made in 1942). Thus, charges that racism and hysteria were responsible for the internment were false, Malkin charged, and the resulting false image of the causes of the internment moreover glossed over the historic need—then and now—for taking appropriate measures to ensure national security. Peculiarly, Malkin's book dismisses racism as a proximate cause without spending even a sentence addressing it; there is no mention of the Alien Land Laws, the Asian Exclusion Act, or the "Yellow Peril" anywhere in her text, nor even a brief passage alluding to the mountain of evidence regarding the role of racism in the internment.[7]

That sort of omission amounts to a grotesque distortion. As this book has detailed, at every step of the long unfolding drama that led to the internment, racism played a significant if not decisive role. These steps included:

- The intense anti-Japanese agitation and resulting disenfranchisement of Japanese immigrants in the 1912–24 period (which included their being denied the right to citizenship), steeped in overt racial hatred and a belief that "oil and water will never mix."
- The passage in 1924 of the Asian Exclusion Act, an explicitly racist law which so angered the Japanese nation that it instilled an implacable anti-Americanism and empowered the military authoritarians who eventually took the nation to war 17 years later. This may not have been, as Pearl Buck later argued, the fatal step leading inevitably to war (there is, after all, no evidence that the nascent campaign to establish democracy in Japan, snuffed out by the act, would have succeeded in any event, as Buck supposed). But there is little doubt it played a fateful role.
- The decision to intern the Japanese, predicated in large part on the predispositions of the key players in the policy, from Franklin Delano Roosevelt to Lt. Gen. John DeWitt to Col. Karl Bendetsen, to believe prewar "Yellow Peril" stereotypes regarding the loyalty of Japanese Americans, and the unmistakable influence those biases played in their policymaking.
- The public agitation for evacuation and incarceration of Japanese Americans, featuring an explicit racial animus, much of which was clearly predicated on prewar anti-Japanese agitation, as well as explicit white-supremacist ideology. (This public racism was most concretely manifested in the refusal by Western governors to admit Japanese evacuees within their borders unless they were placed under armed guard in concentration camps, a demand that brought a screeching halt to the plans for a "voluntary evacuation," and forced the decision to incarcerate the evacuees.)
- The anti-Japanese agitation that greeted the returning Japanese at the war's end, much of it explicitly commingling racial bigotry with economic interests. This agitation played a major role in the permanent

> decline of the Japanese in Pacific Coast agriculture, since most Nikkei farmers gave up any hope of returning to their former lands, as was the case in Bellevue.

A thorough accounting of the entire historical record surrounding the internment clearly reveals that racism played a significant role at every key juncture. This is not to say, by any means, that racism or its associated hysteria constituted the sole cause of the internment. There were many factors that contributed to the decisions, and the resulting policy was in many ways the outcome of a tangled bureaucratic nightmare. Tetsuden Kashima, in his landmark 2004 study *Judgment Without Trial: Japanese American Imprisonment during World War II*, surveyed the broad range of intelligence gathering (not merely the MAGIC encrypts) as well as policymaking in the years prior to the war and found that the internment was the product not so much of hysteria as of the inexorable inertia wrought by policies that had been set in motion well before Pearl Harbor. However, even Kashima makes clear that racist attitudes toward Japanese Americans had a significant role in forming these policies, just as it likely colored the policymakers' interpretations of prewar intelligence about the Nikkei; certainly, the blurring of the distinction between American citizens and Japanese nationals—a blurring based clearly on popular prejudices—was prevalent during the entire course of these decisions.[8]

That same blurring, it must be observed, occurs throughout Malkin's text. In dozens of instances, she refers to "ethnic Japanese" to describe her subjects, a phrase so broad it allows Malkin to lump American-born citizens in with Japanese-born spies. After repeatedly referring to the citizen Nisei as "ethnic Japanese," she uses the same phrase to describe Japanese-born operatives engaging in espionage from inside consulates. The unrelenting appearance of the phrase transforms Malkin's thesis into a twenty-first-century version of the hoary "Yellow Peril" truism reiterated by General DeWitt: "A Jap is a Jap."

Neither, for that matter, is it so easy to parse the effects of wartime hysteria from the outcome of events. The outpouring of racial animus directed at Japanese Americans in the months following Pearl Harbor clearly played a significant, if symbiotic, role in inducing both the president and leading public officials to demand the evacuation of the Pacific Coast, even as much of it, in fact, was inflamed by some of these same officials. The sources of this animus in the three decades of relentless anti-Japanese propaganda are similarly unmistakable, especially considering the leading role of figures like Miller

Freeman in fomenting the hysteria. Most significantly, the hysteria induced the public not only to accept but to embrace enthusiastically a major power grab by the government in wartime—namely, the power of the military to evacuate and incarcerate an entire population of citizens. This is not a power the public might have approved so willingly were it directed at white populations such as the German or Italian American communities, who were not targeted for mass incarceration.

This is the lasting legacy of President Roosevelt's decision to sign Executive Order 9066, which set the machinery of internment into motion. As historian Roger Daniels has observed, it "was a sweeping, and unprecedented, delegation of presidential power to an appointed subordinate. Although, as it turned out, its authority was used only against Japanese Americans, it was an instrument that could have affected any other American. . . . The jurisdiction of the War Department was made to supersede the authority of the Justice Department in such areas, and all executive departments of the government were directed to assist the military in carrying out any subsequent evacuation. With the signing of this order, the War Department had the power arbitrarily to evacuate and incarcerate any American."

The damage was compounded by the Supreme Court when the time came to rule on the constitutionality of the government's actions. The three major wartime challenges to the internment filed by Minoru Yasui, Gordon Hirabayashi, and Fred Korematsu all resulted in high court rulings that firmly established a precedent granting the executive branch unprecedented wartime powers and conferring a constitutional blessing on an act of racial discrimination.

Justice Harlan Stone, writing for the majority in Hirabayashi's case, contended that "the danger of espionage and sabotage to our military resources was imminent, and that the curfew order was an appropriate measure to meet it." (The court did not rule on the legality of the evacuation in Hirabayashi's case, even though that was one of the main referrals to it from the appeals court.) Fred Korematsu's conviction, after wending its way down to the appeals court and back up to the Supreme Court, was likewise upheld the following year by the Supreme Court, on December 18, 1944. Once again, the court declined to rule on the constitutionality of the evacuation, but limited itself to his violation of the evacuation order. And it specifically deferred to the wisdom of DeWitt's findings of "military necessity," ruling that Korematsu "was excluded because we are at war with the Japanese Empire, because the properly constituted military authorities feared an invasion of our West Coast and felt constrained to take proper security measures, because they decided that the military urgency of the situation demanded that all citizens of Japanese ancestry be segregated from the West Coast temporarily. . . ."

The Korematsu ruling concluded by repeating legends that had already been established as false by Justice Department attorneys, though this fact was suppressed at the time: "There was evidence of disloyalty on the part of some, the military authorities considered that the need for action was great, and time was short. We cannot—by availing ourselves of the calm perspective of hindsight—now say that at that time these actions were unjustified."

Justice Robert Jackson's dissent, however, would focus specifically on the complete deference to military authority by the courts, and the problems it posed: "[If] we cannot confine military expedients by the Constitution, neither would I distort the Constitution to approve all that the military may deem expedient. That is what the Court appears to be doing, whether consciously or not."

Some 40 years later, all three men—Korematsu, Hirabayashi, and Yasui—filed *coram nobis* ("error before us") petitions in their respective district courts in an effort to get their names cleared. Korematsu's petition appealing his curfew conviction was granted in late 1983, but the judge in Yasui's case threw out his petition in early 1984. Yasui died that spring, before his appeal could get a hearing, and his case was buried with him.

Hirabayashi, however, won a major victory when Judge Donald Voorhees ruled that the behavior of War Department bureaucrats in covering up the malfeasance of Gen. DeWitt's official rationalizations of "military necessity" constituted "an error of the most fundamental character" and ordered that his evacuation conviction be vacated. When the two cases reached the appeals court, the verdict was even more ringing: Hirabayashi's curfew conviction was vacated as well.

Despite the apparent vindications, however, the legal precedents created by the trio of internment-era rulings have never been overturned. As Frank Chuman, in his *Bamboo People: The Law and Japanese-Americans*, put it:

> In 1943 the justices of the Supreme Court had already concurred in converting a wartime folly into a principle of law: the supremacy of the military judgment over civil judgment and authority in time of war, even though a war might be being fought thousands of miles away from the United States and might already be half won. After 1943 the national policy of the United

States government would be grounded on the legal precedent that whether military intentions be good, wicked, or merely capricious, the actions of the military, if based on "findings" of "military necessity," would be upheld by the United States Supreme Court.

This lingering shadow on American law was forecast in Justice Jackson's *Korematsu v. United States* dissent, in passages that would have an especially prescient ring after September 11, 2001:

> Much is said of the danger to liberty from the Army program for deporting and detaining these citizens of Japanese extraction. But a judicial construction of the due process clause that will sustain this order is a far more subtle blow to liberty than the promulgation of the order itself. A military order, however unconstitutional, is not apt to last longer than the military emergency. Even during that period a succeeding commander may revoke it all. But once a judicial opinion rationalizes such an order to show that it conforms to the Constitution, or rather rationalizes the Constitution to show that the Constitution sanctions such an order, the Court for all time has validated the principle of racial discrimination in criminal procedure and of transplanting American citizens. The principle then lies about like a loaded weapon ready for the hand of any authority that can bring forward a plausible claim of an urgent need.

The Japanese American internment also revealed, as Jackson suggested, a hole in the traditional checks and balances of constitutional powers by granting extraordinary arrest powers over civilians to the military. In wartime, the total deference to the executive branch would lend it nearly comprehensive powers. The post-September 11 response of the Bush administration—declaring the power of military commissions to arrest "enemy combatants," and passing the Patriot Act, which grants immense investigatory powers to the Justice Department—opened another dimension to this: If wartime, as in the "War on Terror," becomes itself a never-ending enterprise, then the executive branch's power becomes potentially illimitable.

The administration already has come under fire from numerous quarters over its assertion of these powers. Besides the JACL and various Muslim American groups, some of the most vigorous dissent has come from the American Bar Association, which has pointedly questioned how citizens can be held without the right to an attorney, or for that matter without any kind of judicial review. Legal scholars have also weighed in with their concerns;

Anita Ramasastry explored the dangers posed by the Bush policies in a 2002 commentary that pointed out that while the White House so far has relied on another Supreme Court precedent, *Ex parte Quirin*—which dealt with Germans caught spying on American soil—to justify its actions, these also closely resemble the *Korematsu* matter: "[In] both cases, the government arrogated itself the right to detain—and detain indefinitely—without court review of its decisions as to who should be detained."[9]

At the same time, some of the administration's critics have raised the specter of the Japanese American internment in ways that are neither fair nor accurate. This was particularly the case in the immediate wake of the September 11 attacks, when law enforcement officials rounded up thousands of Muslim and Arab aliens and detained them indefinitely; these actions were immediately compared by a number of critics to the events of early 1942.[10] But the government's ability to round up and detain a reasonable number of aliens, particularly on behalf of national security, has never been in question. What made the Japanese American internment an atrocity was that it swept up citizens alongside those aliens.

So far, the Bush administration has wisely refrained from even suggesting that an internment of Muslim American citizens is a conceivable course (though former Attorney General John Ashcroft did call for smallish internment camps for "enemy combatants"). Historians of the Nikkei internment, including Roger Daniels, have pointed out that this administration (unlike FDR's) has for the most part distinguished between citizens and aliens in deciding who comes under the military's purview. Most famously, the case of John Walker Lindh—the "American Taliban" captured in Afghanistan—was handled through the criminal courts, not the military.

However, there have been significant incursions by the Bush administration down the same path followed by President Roosevelt, including the arrests of at least two American citizens, Yaser Hamdi and Jose Padilla, as "enemy combatants." These cases point to the larger issue behind the administration's actions, because it has, like FDR, placed in the hands of the military the legal and bureaucratic wherewithal to intern indefinite numbers of civilians, perhaps even entire ethnic or religious populations—depending, as it happens, on the whim of the president.

Malkin and her cohorts couch their defense of the decisions made in 1942 at least partially as a response to the critics of the Bush administration who have raised the specter of the Japanese American internment. To her own critics who charged that in doing so, she was opening the doors for post-September 11 internment camps, Malkin would refer to a key line in her text: "Make no mistake: I am not advocating rounding up all Arabs or Muslims and tossing them into camps, but when we are under attack, 'racial profiling'—or more precisely, threat profiling—is justified."

This is, however, more than a little disingenuous, since Malkin's text is not merely a rationalization for racial profiling but indeed one for mass internment based on ethnicity as well. Beyond the immediate question—Why use a massive violation of civil rights to justify relatively limited measures such as those proposed?—there is the effect this logic has on the discourse: Justifying an action may not be semantically the same as advocating it, but it can have the same effect. And indeed, within a few weeks, the discussion had shifted to the possibility of interning Arabs or Muslims. *U.S. News and World Report* columnist John Leo, while praising Malkin's book lavishly, concluded thus: "It's also reasonable and important to open an honest discussion of internment, past and present."[11] Similarly, Daniel Pipes—a Bush administration appointee to the U.S. Institute of Peace—penned an op-ed piece likewise praising Malkin's text as reopening the way for an honest discussion of potential wartime measures against domestic enemies.[12]

Even if we grant Malkin and her defenders this less-than-persuasive caveat, it remains inescapable that the model of mass internment that emerges from the historical record of World War II does not, as we have seen, offer the slightest shred of evidence that racial profiling is either effective or wise, especially not when it comes to protecting national security and serving the public interest. The overwhelming weight of the postwar evidence is that the internment prevented very little, if any, sabotage or espionage. Moreover, even beyond its transparent unjustness, the damage to the integrity of the Constitution, and the dangerous precedents it set, the internment of the Japanese Americans was an unfathomable waste. It demonstrably undermined the war effort, and proved not to be worth a penny of the billions of taxpayer dollars it wasted.

In addition to the hundreds of millions of dollars the actual enterprise itself cost—rounding up 120,000 people by rail car and shipping them first to "assembly centers"; building ten "relocation centers" in remote locales, and then shipping the evacuees into them; maintaining and administering the centers for another three years, which included overseeing programs to help internees find work outside the camps; feeding, clothing, and educating the entire population of internees during this time; and then helping them to relocate near their former homes once the camps closed—there were $37 million more in initial reparations costs in 1948, and then $1.2 billion more in the later reparations approved by Congress in 1988.

At the same time, the Japanese on the Pacific Coast, who occupied some 7,000 farms in the "Military Exclusion Zone," actually were responsible for the production of nearly half of all the fresh produce that was grown for consumption on the Coast (the Japanese also shipped out a great deal of produce to the Midwest and East). Indeed, Nikkei farms held virtual monopolies in a number of crops, including peppers, snap beans, celery and strawberries, and a large portion of the lettuce market.

As we saw in the case of the Bellevue farms, a handful of enterprising whites throughout the coastal communities decided to try running the Japanese farms with the hope of making a killing from the crops. But labor was so short that not one of these enterprises lasted beyond about five weeks, and none of them had a successful harvest. Nearly all of these farms lay fallow for the next four years. This major loss of production of fresh vegetables clearly harmed the war effort on the home front, and played a significant role in triggering the rationing that came during the war years.

What the Japanese American internment made clear was that there are no guarantees of success with such vast social enterprises as incarcerating entire racial or religious populations, and their costs are extraordinarily high. There is a high likelihood that a Muslim American internment would be every bit as wasteful, and probably as fruitless, as its 1942–45 counterpart.

These are, however, largely pragmatic considerations. There are also civic, ethical, moral, and in the end spiritual dimensions to any such project. Perhaps most remarkable is the fact that what the government, at the behest of a majority of its citizens, inflicted upon Japanese Americans in World War II was also a grievous blow to the integrity of the Constitution. It undermined constitutional guarantees of equal protection under the law, due process, and the presumption of innocence, as well as the constitutional balance of powers. The internment opened up a hole in the Constitution—one that has, in fact, never been fully closed, and so remains relevant to this day.

In the end, moreover, it was an immense and grotesquely ineffective overreaction that deprived nearly 70,000 American citizens of their property and livelihoods on the basis of a threat for which the evidence was scant at best. As law professor Eric Muller explored in a paper for the *Ohio State Jour-*

nal of Criminal Law, "the fundamental error of the internment was not the inference of suspicion that the government drew from the fact of Japanese ancestry, but the enormity of the deprivations that the government imposed on the basis of that inference." This enormity, Muller further argues, can only be explained "by reference to racism." He also concludes that the socio-legal landscape has not changed enough in the ensuing years to ensure that a similar leap from minor to massive intrusions would not occur in the post–September 11 environment: "On the one hand," he writes, "national origin is not an utterly arbitrary factor in all cases. But on the other hand, the government has never done well at confining itself to using that factor in a restrained and narrow way."[13]

Responding to arguments that comparisons between Roosevelt's actions and Bush's were inappropriate, Roger Daniels argued in the *Chronicle of Higher Education:*

> That is an evasion: the kind of evasion that has allowed us to offer apologies for the actions we have taken against those whom we perceive to be outsiders, and then do the same thing to a different group. Time and again, scholars (if not the government) have eventually acknowledged that we, as a nation, have violated the spirit of our Constitution. Time and again, we have gone on to violate it again.
>
> . . . Optimists assure us that a mass incarceration of American citizens in concentration camps will not recur. But reflection on our past suggests we ought not to be so sanguine. To be sure, it was not just the disaster at Pearl Harbor, but the subsequent sequence of Japanese triumphs that triggered Executive Order 9066. But shouldn't we then ask, If successful terrorist attacks hadn't abated after September 11, would the current government reaction have been so moderate?[14]

This is what feeds the nightmares of the Nisei internees: the possibility that history may yet repeat itself in their lifetimes. These fears are further stoked by the rising chorus of voices, from Howard Coble to Peter Kirsanow to Michelle Malkin, revising history and denying the truth of their memories, either suggesting or saying outright that the internment of Japanese Americans was the right thing to do after all. The fact that they defend supposedly "limited" measures like racial profiling by rationalizing the incarceration of 120,000 people only underscores, as Muller suggests, how easily seemingly minor steps can make the leap to atrocity.

Perhaps the most eloquent expression of these concerns came from 95-year-old Fred Korematsu, the Bay Area man whose case before the Supreme Court in 1944 produced the definitive ruling on the internment, a ruling that most legal scholars admit has been "overturned by the court of history." Korematsu, in a September 2004 op-ed for the *San Francisco Chronicle*, wrote:

> It is painful to see reopened for serious debate the question of whether the government was justified in imprisoning Japanese Americans during World War II. It was my hope that my case and the cases of other Japanese American internees would be remembered for the dangers of racial and ethnic scapegoating.
>
> Fears and prejudices directed against minority communities are too easy to evoke and exaggerate, often to serve the political agendas of those who promote those fears. I know what it is like to be at the other end of such scapegoating and how difficult it is to clear one's name after unjustified suspicions are endorsed as fact by the government. If someone is a spy or terrorist they should be prosecuted for their actions. But no one should ever be locked away simply because they share the same race, ethnicity, or religion as a spy or terrorist. If that principle was not learned from the internment of Japanese Americans, then these are very dangerous times for our democracy.[15]

The forced incarceration of an entire minority population of American citizens based on a mass presumption of guilt is only possible when we let our fears make us forget what it means to be American. The meaning of the internment, as told by those who lived it, is this: It will always be the wrong thing to do, whether in 1942 or today.

A Note on Sources

This book began as an in-depth reporting project for the Bellevue *Journal American* (now the *King County Journal*), where I was news editor in 1991–1994. It was published as a series titled *Camps of Infamy* in May 1992, the fiftieth anniversary of the evacuation and internment. Most of the interviews that form the basis of this text were conducted that spring in preparation for the series.

In chronological order, these interviews were with:

CANO NUMOTO: Tuesday, March 3, 1992, at the Numoto home in Bellevue. Cano still has a thriving garden which he tends assiduously. He was particularly helpful in organizing the project, since he directed me to many of the other Nisei and provided me with a copy of Asaichi Tsushima's book. He also was one of the few Nisei to still have prewar photos intact (most lost theirs to vandalism or fires during the war).

TOM TAKEO MATSUOKA, March 11, 1992, at Matsuoka's home in Ridgefield, Washington. This first interview was arranged through Matsuoka's granddaughter, Beth Takekawa. (I interviewed Matsuoka again on August 22, 1994, and on August 31, 2000.) All of these interviews took place in the presence of Tom's daughter, RAE TAKEKAWA, who helped me understand Tom's sometimes heavily accented responses and at times helped him understand my questions as well. I also took the time to interview Rae separately during these interviews, and her insights of course were invaluable. Needless to say, these interviews were very rewarding, both in terms of Tom's wealth of information and his great personal warmth.

TOSH ITO: March 13, 1992, at the Ito home in Bellevue. Ito lives in a rather new home in a relatively new development in northern Bellevue, though it's also less than a mile from the onetime strip of Japanese farms at Midlakes. Tosh is a very genial man and easy to interview—direct and descriptive. Ito also helped me to locate several other interviewees. His daughter, Alice Ito, was instrumental in providing much of the supplemental information for this book in her role as an official of the Densho Project (for whom she conducted a number of the interviews cited in this text).

ED SUGURO: March 13, 1992, Seattle. I was put in touch with Ed through Ron Chew, director of the Wing Luke Asian Museum in Seattle, and we conducted the interview at the museum. Again, Ed directed me to other Nisei who would participate, and we have remained in touch over the intervening years as this project proceeded, with Ed continuing to provide fresh information and contacts.

TOKIO HIROTAKA, HIDEO "AL" YABUKI, JOE MATSUZAWA, AKIRA "MAC" ARAMAKI, CANO NUMOTO: March 14, 1992, Hirotaka residence, Bellevue. This originally was going to be just an interview with Tok Hirotaka, but when I and a photographer arrived, we found a large group of other Nisei assembled instead. Mr. Hirotaka participated, but not as avidly as Matsuzawa or Aramaki, who contributed very dynamically to the interview. (When I tried to re-interview Mr. Hirotaka in 1994, he did the same thing; that interview also included Al Yabuki and two other Nisei.) Though this initial interview was in many respects watered down, it provided me with many key subsequent contacts, two of whom I re-interviewed in 1994: Joe Matsuzawa and Al Yabuki. I spoke with Al on several occasions, and he was kind enough to spend a couple of afternoons driving around through Bellevue and looking up the locations where Japanese farms and schoolhouses once stood, so that I could record what they had become in the present day. Mr. Hirotaka died March 3, 2000, and Mr. Matsuzawa on May 6, 2001.

KIYO YABUKI: March 17, 1992, at Yabuki residence near Fall City, Washington. Kiyo's place is tucked away in a rural setting, and he seems to like the solace. He is very quiet-spoken, and was not eager to talk about what he saw in the war, but willing. His responses were unusually thoughtful but restrained.

KIM MUROMOTO: March 19, 1992, Clyde Hill, Washington. Muromoto lives in a house just a block and a half away from his family's former farm acreage. He wears a large silver belt buckle with the 442nd's logo and slogan ("Go for Broke!") inscribed on it. Kim is obviously proud of his service, and is active in the 442nd's alumni organization. He has plenty of little mementos, some excellent photos, and even some videos. He is, like all of the interviewees, extremely polite and bright-natured.

MICHI [TSUSHIMA] NISHIMURA: March 20, 1992, Kirkland. Michi and her husband Tom Nishimura obviously have lived at their tucked-away place in Kirkland for awhile. The yard—almost an acreage, really—is immaculately landscaped like an unostentatious Japanese garden. Tom is wiry and fit, and Michi seems to be a content person. She was very reluctant to participate, and was the only participant who wouldn't let me take photographs. But once we sat down to talk, she gave an unusually warm and frank interview.

ROSE [YABUKI] MATSUSHITA: March 25, 1992, at Matsushita's residence in Bellevue. Mrs. Matsushita was reluctant to talk because of her feeling that the media often were slanted in an anti-Japanese fashion or too often were factually incorrect. It required some persuasion to get her to participate. She provided one of my more heartfelt and emotional interviews; she was at once cynical and sentimental about what had happened. She sometimes had to stop because the reminiscences made her cry; she particularly felt that her parents had been wronged.

MITSI SHIRAISHI KAWAGUCHI: March 26, 1992, Seattle, Washington. Mitsi was perhaps the most genial of all the Nisei I interviewed, and I noted as well the warmth with which other Nisei spoke of her. She lived with her husband, Kenji, on Beacon Hill, and kept some of her mementos from the internment camps, including an old family chest with the family number on it. She was unflaggingly upbeat, and liked to spend her days tending her immaculate yard, which included a miniature model of Mount Fujiyama and a Buddhist shrine out back. Mitsi died in 1998.

After the series was published in the *Journal American* I decided the material begged to be put together as a book. So in 1994 I set out to fill in the many holes that were present in the newspaper series. I re-interviewed (often briefly, reflected in my sketchy notes) several of the original participants, including Tom Matsuoka, Joe Matsuzawa, Al Yabuki, Cano Numoto, and Rae Takekawa. I also conducted an interview with Ryomi Tanino on August 24, 1994, at the Tanino residence in Seattle.

The project was sidetracked from 1996 to 1999, however, while I went to work on what would be my first book, *In God's Country*, which dealt with then-current events. After it was completed, I returned to this project, conducting more archival research and re-interviewing Tom Matsuoka one last time in August 2000.

I also interviewed John Matsuoka at this time, at his home in Bellevue on August 19, 2000, and Tyrus Matsuoka on August 23, 2000, at his home in Bellevue. Mitsuko Hashiguchi graciously agreed to an interview on August 29, 2000, at her home in Bellevue.

With the help of the Bellevue Historical Society, I also interviewed a series of non-Japanese Bellevue residents who were present during many of the events described here. They include Patricia Sandbo, on August 29, 2000, at the Bellevue Historical Society Winter House; Beatrice Mathewson, at her family home in Renton, Washington, on September 7, 2000; and Robert Hennig, on September 12, 2000, at the Hennig home in Medina, not far from where his family once grew grapes.

Finally, in the aftermath of September 11, I interviewed Japanese American Citizens League national director John Tateishi in his office on Nov. 28, 2002, and reinterviewed Tosh Ito and Rose Matsushita at their homes on Jan. 6, 2005.

All quotations in the text from these persons are from these interviews, unless otherwise noted.

One lingering problem associated with my interviews is the fact that I am a Caucasian of a younger generation and from another state, yet many of the important questions that needed to be asked are of a culturally sensitive nature; and a proper interview might be better conducted by someone with the appropriate background and knowledge. Deadly pauses in the conversations were not uncommon when I was conducting interviews; but in the end, I was grateful at the extent to which most of the interviewees were willing to open up and be frank. That said, there was no getting around the fact that in many cases (as I would realize later) the question I should have asked would probably have been posed by someone who knew enough about events and cultural backgrounds in the first place.

My ultimate savior in this regard was the Densho Project, a Japanese American oral history digital archive directed by Tom Ikeda and operated in conjunction with the Wing Luke Asian Museum. Beginning in 1996, Densho interviewers—most of them Japanese American—began compiling an impressive archive of oral histories, video-recorded for posterity and available in computerized form. (Densho also has a Web site at http://www.densho.org.) Among the many interviews were a number of Bellevue Nisei, including Tom Matsuoka, Rae Takekawa, Mitsuko Hashiguchi, Joe Matsuzawa, and Tok Hirotaka. Also included were interviews with some Eastsiders I had not met—especially Chizuko Norton and Seichi Hayashida. Naturally, these interviews provided an important complement to my own, and the added perspective, I hope, has helped inform the text of the book. The direct use of Densho interviews is cited in the endnotes.

Notes

Prologue: Good Earth

1. See Joel Garreau, *Edge City: Life on the New Frontier* (New York: Doubleday and Co., 1992), pp. 6–9, p. 436. Garreau lists Bellevue as one of his 125 identified "Edge Cities."
2. U.S. Census Bureau, 2000 Census (table: Race, Hispanic or Latino, and Age) and 1990 Census (table: General Population and Housing Characteristics) figures for Bellevue, Washington.

Chapter 1: The Clearing of Bellevue

1. See Lucile McDonald, *Bellevue: Its First 100 Years* (Bellevue: Bellevue Historical Society, 2000), pp. 90–91. McDonald's discussion of the Japanese comprises roughly three paragraphs of the book, and some of her information is inaccurate (e.g., she writes that "the adults built a clubhouse in 1930 and organized a Japanese language night school"; in fact, the Japanese language school was either on Saturdays only or was an after-school course, while night classes attended by Japanese adults taught English primarily and only offered a few courses in Japanese).
2. See Asaichi Tsushima, *Pre-WWII History of Japanese Pioneers in the Clearing and Development of Land in Bellevue* (Bellevue: Private printing, 1991), p. 45. Census figures do not exist for Bellevue in that time period—the Census Bureau did not begin collecting tract data in rural King County until 1950—but Tsushima's figures are borne out by the recollections of Bellevue residents. It is also reflected in a 1924 study published by the Department of Commerce and the Census Bureau titled *Farm Population of Selected Counties: Composition, Characteristics and Occupations in Detail for Eight Counties, Comprising Tsego County, N.Y., Dane County, Wis., New Madrid and Scott Counties, Mo., Cass County, N. Dak., Wake County, N.C., Ellis County, Tex., and King County, Wash.*, by C. J. Galpin and Veda B. Larson. Compiled from data obtained in the 1920 census, it shows that of a countywide farm population of 20,630, some 2,192 were Japanese. The largest age segment was under 15 years (885), and a total of 552 of them owned homes. However, this data would have included the large Japanese American community in southern King County around Auburn and a few other Japanese-owned farms sprinkled randomly around the county, so numbers specifically for the Eastside population could not be extrapolated.
3. See Henry Kittredge Norton, *The Story of California From the Earliest Days to the Present* (Chicago: A.C. McClurg & Co., 1924), pp. 283–96.
4. Ibid., pp.283–96.
5. See Elmer C. Sandmeyer, *The Anti-Chinese Movement in California* (Urbana, Ill.: University of Illinois Press, 1973), pp. 44–46. Also, see Roger Daniels, *The Politics of Prejudice: The Anti-Japanese Movement in California and the Struggle for Japanese Exclusion*, pp. 16–19.
6. From a Knights of Labor pamphlet, "China's Menace to the World," by Thomas Magee, distributed in San Francisco in 1878, p. 1. According to the City Museum of

San Francisco—which includes a copy of the pamphlet at its Web site (http://www.sfmuseum.org/hist/kofl.html)—Magee was "founder and publisher of the 'San Francisco Real Estate Circular,' which had a strong anti-Chinese editorial position as far back as the 1870s. He was still active in San Francisco politics as late as 1906 when he served on the committee to stabilize the real estate market following the Earthquake and Fire. Magee was involved in the attempt to move Chinatown to Hunters Point following the disaster."

7. See James Chan, "'Rough on Rats'—Racism and Advertising in the Latter Half of the Nineteenth Century," Chinese Historical Society of America, 1997, p. 4, available online at http://www.chsa.org/research/ching_conference_excerpt.php. Chan notes: "One recurring theme frequently found in trade cards is 'pigtail pulling.' The Chinese men wore queues that were often pulled or cut for white amusement. This mean-spiritedness shows up in a number of trade cards and hints at the violent tendencies many white people harbored toward Chinese immigrants. Violence was not just targeted against Chinese adults, but against Chinese children as well. Several trade cards in the Ching Collection show Chinese boys with their pigtails being pulled by white boys. A French trade card shows a Chinese boy's queue being pulled so hard that he is decapitated over a sharp rail."
8. Daniels, *The Politics of Prejudice*, p. 17.
9. See Charles Pierce LeWarne, *Utopias on Puget Sound 1885–1915* (Seattle: University of Washington Press, 1995), pp. 15–16.
10. See Art Chin, *Golden Tassels: A History of the Chinese in Washington, 1857–1977* (Seattle: n.p., 1977), pp. 2–4.
11. See Stefan Akio Tanaka, *The Nikkei on Bainbridge Island, 1883–1942: A Study of Migration and Community Development* (Master's thesis, University of Washington, 1977), pp. 24–26, 38–39.
12. United States Census Bureau. Also see Daniels, *The Politics of Prejudice*, p. 1.
13. See Daniels, *The Politics of Prejudice*, pp. 7–9.
14. See Tanaka, *The Nikkei on Bainbridge Island*, pp. 58–72. See also Stan Flewelling, *Shirakawa: Stories from a Pacific Northwest Japanese American Community* (Auburn: White River Valley Museum, 2002), pp. 22–25. See also Lane Hirabayashi and George Tanaka, "The Issei Community and the Gardena Valley, 1900–1920," Historical Society of Southern California, pp. 127–58.
15. See Tanaka, *The Nikkei on Bainbridge Island*, pp. 72–78.
16. *Morning Call*, May 29, 1892. See also Daniels, *The Politics of Prejudice*, p. 20.
17. See Flewelling, *Shirakawa*, pp. 24–25.
18. *Post-Intelligencer*, April 16–20, 1900.
19. *White River Journal*, April 21, 1900.
20. Dr. James Watanabe, *The History of the Tacoma Japanese translated from Tacoma Nihonjin Hattenshi* (Tacoma: Pierce County Historical Society), p. 5.
21. See Ronald Magden, *Furusato: Tacoma-Pierce County Japanese 1888–1977* (Tacoma: Tacoma Japanese Community Service, 1988), p. 21.
22. See Frank Chuman, *The Bamboo People: The Law and Japanese-Americans* (Del Mar, Calif.: Publisher's Inc., 1976), pp. 23–25. See also Daniels, *The Politics of Prejudice*, p. 21.
23. *San Francisco Chronicle*, May 8, 1900.
24. These headlines appeared in the *San Francisco Chronicle* between Feb. 23 and March 13, 1905. This is a mere sampling of the Chronicle's "Yellow Peril" headlines. For a larger sample, see Daniels, *The Politics of Prejudice*, p. 25.
25. "Asiatic Coolie Invasion," The Asiatic Exclusion League, *Proceedings* (San Francisco, May 1905). Available online at the Virtual Museum of the City of San Francisco Web site, http://www.sfmuseum.net/1906.2/invasion.html.
26. See Asiatic Exclusion League, *Proceedings* (San Francisco, 1907–1912), May 1910, pp. 13–14. See also Daniels, *The Politics of Prejudice*, p. 28.
27. See *San Francisco Chronicle*, April 27, 1906, "Chinese Colony at Foot of Van Ness; The Plan to Remove Celestials to San Mateo County is Opposed."

28. There have been numerous accounts of how Roosevelt negotiated the "Gentlemen's Agreement," but Daniels' in *The Politics of Prejudice*, pp. 31–46, is succinct. See also Page Smith, *Democracy on Trial: The Japanese American Evacuation and Relocation in World War II* (New York: Simon and Schuster, 1995), pp. 48–49.
29. See Miller Freeman, *The Memoirs of Miller Freeman* (Bellevue: Private printing, 1956), pp. 1–38.
30. Ibid., p. 50.
31. Letter from Miller Freeman to Dr. Eliot Grinnel Mears of Stanford University, April 1927. Cited in Freeman, *The Memoirs of Miller Freeman*, p. 116.
32. Letter from Miller Freeman to Lt. Commdr. H. H. Hoefs, Sc USN, San Francisco, Oct. 5, 1949. Miller Freeman archives, University of Washington.
33. See particularly Daniels' detailed description of the factors at work in Roosevelt's actions regarding the "Gentlemen's Agreement" in *The Politics of Prejudice*, pp. 31–45.
34. The main progenitor of this theory was the Hearst-owned San Francisco Examiner, which began its "Yellow Peril" campaign in 1906. It was supported by a military hero named Richard Pearson Hobson, who toured the coast in 1907 promoting the theory. Lea's book detailed an invasion of the Philippines—actually long foreseen by nearly every U.S. military expert—very similar to that which actually occurred in December 1941. Lea's book was republished in 1942 as "prophetic" and is still currently available (Safety Harbor, Florida: Simon Publications, 2001). See esp. pp. 149–55, 176–84, and pp. 240–71. See also Daniels, *The Politics of Prejudice*, pp. 70–78.
35. See Congressional Record, Sept. 10, 1942, speech of Sen. Homer Bone of Washington. Bone's speech cites a 1908 editorial by Freeman.
36. See "The Price of Peace," by Major R.C. Croxton, 9th U.S. Infantry, *Harpers Weekly*, Jan. 8, 1910, vol. LIV, no. 2768, pp. 31–32.
37. See Freeman, *The Memoirs of Miller Freeman*, p. 67.
38. *Seattle Daily Times*, "Miller Freeman Sees 'Yellow Peril' Ahead," Aug. 4, 1910.
39. Miller Freeman, "The Japanese Question," *Pacific Fisherman*, Jan. 25, 1909.
40. Tom Matsuoka, Densho Project Visual History Interview, May 7, 1998, segment 5.
41. See David Takami, *Divided Destiny: A History of Japanese Americans in Seattle* (Seattle: University of Washington Press, 1998), p. 17.
42. Ibid., pp. 18–20. See also Tanaka, *The Nikkei on Bainbridge Island*, pp. 81–95.
43. See Flewelling, *Shirakawa.*, pp. 30–35.
44. See Tanaka, *The Nikkei on Bainbridge Island*, pp. 39, 50–51.
45. See McDonald, *Bellevue*, p. 2, and Charles LeWarne's foreword to the 2000 edition of her text, p. 6.
46. Ibid., pp. 2–18.
47. Author's interview with Beatrice Mathewson. The story is also told in McDonald, *Bellevue*, pp. 16–17.
48. McDonald, *Bellevue*, pp. 18–19.
49. See *A Hidden Past: An Exploration of Eastside History* (Seattle: *Seattle Times* Publishing, 2000), pp. 24–25, 30–32, 33–35.
50. See Tsushima, *Pre-WWII History of Japanese Pioneers*, pp. 10–11, 66, 70.
51. McDonald, *Bellevue*, p. 99.
52. Ibid., p. 10.
53. See Tsushima, *Pre-WWII History of Japanese Pioneers*, esp. p. XIII, 1–4, and 12–13.
54. See McDonald, *Bellevue*, p. 113.
55. Editorial, "Their Land and Your Living," *Seattle Star*, July 31, 1919, p. 8.
56. Densho Project Visual History Interview: Tokio Hirotaka, Toshio Ito, and Joe Matsuzawa, May 21, 1998; segment 1.
57. Densho Project Visual History Interview: Chizuko Norton, April 27, 1998, segments 1, 2, and 4.
58. See Robert A. Wilson and Bill Hosokawa, *East to America: A History of the Japanese in the United States* (New York: William and Morrow Co., 1980), pp. 58–71, and particularly p.

69 for a description of the land ownership trends in Washington state. See also Leonard Broom and Ruth Riemer, *Removal and Return: The Socio-Economic Effects of the War on Japanese Americans* (Berkeley: University of California Press, 1949), pp. 69–71. See also Linda Tamura, *The Hood River Issei: An Oral History of Japanese Settlers in Oregon's Hood River Valley* (Urbana: University of Illinois Press, 1993), pp. 70–71, p. 82.

59. Densho Project Visual History Interview: Tom Matsuoka, May 7, 1998, segment 6.

Chapter 2: Strawberries

1. See Masakazu Iwata, *Planted in Good Soil: A History of the Issei in the United States Agriculture* (2 vols.; New York: P. Lang, 1990), pp. 221–50, 539–78. See also Brian Niiya, ed., *The Encyclopedia of Japanese-American History* (Los Angeles: The Japanese-American National Museum, 2001), pp. 392–93, 135, 365. See also John Modell, *The Economics and Politics of Racial Accommodation: The Japanese of Los Angeles, 1900–1942* (Urbana/Chicago: University of Illinois Press, 1963), pp. 95–99, 104–10.
2. See Stefan Akio Tanaka, *The Nikkei on Bainbridge Island, 1883–1942: A Study of Migration and Community Development* (Master's thesis, University of Washington, 1977), pp. 107–09, and Modell, *The Economics and Politics of Racial Accommodation*, p. 112.
3. See George M. Darrow, *The Strawberry: History, Breeding and Physiology* (1965: U.S. Department of Agriculture), pp. 35–89.
4. See Lane Ryo Hirabayshi and George Tanaka, "The Issei Community in Moneta and the Gardena Valley, 1900–1920," Southern California Quarterly, March 1988, pp. 127–58.
5. See John Isao Nishinoiri, "Japanese Farms in Washington" (Master's thesis, University of Washington, 1926), p. 20.
6. See Tanaka, *The Nikkei on Bainbridge Island*, p. 104.
7. See Nishinoiri, "Japanese Farms in Washington," pp. 24–26.
8. See Stan Flewelling, *Shirakawa: Stories from a Pacific Northwest Japanese American Community* (Auburn: White River Valley Museum, 2002), pp. 26–30, 57–64. See also Nishinoiri, "Japanese Farms in Washington," p. 31.
9. See Linda Tamura, *The Hood River Issei: An Oral History of Japanese Settlers in Oregon's Hood River Valley* (Urbana/Chicago: University of Illinois Press, 1993), pp. 82–87.
10. See Hirabayashi and Tanaka, "The Issei Community in Moneta and the Gardena Valley, 1900–1920," pp. 151–53.
11. For a general discussion of the Washington communities, see Nishinoiri, "Japanese Farms in Washington," pp. 12–33, and Iwata, *Planted in Good Soil*, pp. 531–78; for more on Bainbridge, see Tanaka, *The Nikkei on Bainbridge Island*, pp. 103–12; for Vashon, see Iwata, *Planted in Good Soil*, pp. 541–42, 561; and Pamela J. Woodroffe, *Vashon Island's Agricultural Roots* (iUniverse, 2002), pp. 43–44, 72–73; and see further discussion of the Bellevue community below. The strawberry farming phase of the Hood River community is described in Tamura, *The Hood River Issei*, pp. 82–87, as well as Iwata, *Planted in Good Soil*, pp. 514–16. Iwata also discusses the Russellville community on pp. 520–21. For more on the Gardena and southern California communities, see Iwata, *Planted in Good Soil*, pp. 397–407, and Hirabayashi and Tanaka, "The Issei Community in Moneta and the Gardena Valley, 1900–1920," especially pp. 151–53, which also discusses the Russellville strawberry farmers. The Watsonville community is vividly described in a pamphlet by Kathy McKenzie Nichols and Jane W. Borg, "Nihon Bunka/Japanese Culture: One Hundred Years in the Pajaro Valley" (Pajaro Valley Arts Council, 1992), which is available online at the Santa Cruz Public Libraries website, http://www.santacruzpl.org/history/culdiv/nihon1.shtml; Iwata, *Planted in Good Soil*, also describes the Watsonville community. For more on the Fraser Valley Nikkei community, see *A Dream of Riches: The Japanese Canadians, 1877–1977* (Toronto: Japanese Canadian Centennial Project, 1978), pp. 136–37, as well as the Japanese-Canadian Research Collection, Special Collections Division, University of British Columbia Library, available online at http://www.library.ubc.ca/asian/jcrc.html.

12. See "Deport Japanese: Demanded by Secretary of Veterans' Commission," *Seattle Star*, July 26, 1919, p. A1.
13. Ibid.
14. Ibid.
15. United States Census Bureau. See also John Adrian Rademaker, "The Ecological Position of the Japanese Farmers in the State of Washington," Ph.D. dissertation, University of Washington, 1939, pp. 21–22.
16. See Roger Daniels, *The Politics of Prejudice: The Anti-Japanese Movement in California and the Struggle for Japanese Exclusion* (Berkeley: University of California Press, 1962), pp. 46–64.
17. See Ronald E. Magden, *Furusato: Tacoma-Pierce County Japanese 1888–1977* (Tacoma: Tacoma Japanese Community Service, 1998), p. 57.
18. This and similar figures were bandied about frequently during the debate over the Alien Land Act, both in Washington and California. They are simply false; for instance, an official report issued by California's State Board of Control tried to show a birth rate three times that of whites. But as Daniels amply illustrates in *The Politics of Prejudice* (pp. 88–89), this figure was sheer manipulation. In fact, "the long-range Issei birth rate was somewhat below that for contemporary immigrant groups from Europe, and only slightly above the rather low native-white birth rate in the twenties and thirties."
19. See "Scores Effort to Bar Out Japanese," *Seattle Star*, July 25, 1919, p. 1.
20. Madison Grant, *The Passing of the Great Race, or The Racial Basis of European History* (New York: Charles Scribner's Sons, 1922), chapter 14.
21. Lothrop Stoddard, *The Rising Tide of Color Against White World Supremacy* (New York: Charles Scribner's Sons, 1922), chapter 12.
22. There have been numerous studies of the eugenics movement in America. Among the best are Steven Selden and Ashley Montagu, *Inheriting Shame: The Story of Eugenics and Racism in America* (New York: Teachers College Press, Advances in Contemporary Educational Thought Series, vol. 23, 1999) and Elof Axel Carlson, *The Unfit: A History of a Bad Idea* (Cold Springs Harbor Laboratory Press, 2001). See also Prescott F. Hall, "Immigration Restriction and World Eugenics," *Journal of Heredity*, March, 1919: "Just as we isolate bacterial invasions, and starve out the bacteria by limiting the area and amount of their food-supply, so we can compel an inferior race to remain in its native habitat, where its own multiplication in a limited area will, as with all organisms, eventually limit its numbers and therefore its influence. On the other hand, the superior races, more self-limiting than the others, with the benefits of more space and nourishment will tend to still higher levels."
23. Quoted in "The Fight is On!," *Seattle Star*, Aug. 14, 1919, p. 1.
24. See "Seek Body of White Wife of Japanese," *Seattle Star*, June 21, 1919, p. 20.
25. These lead headlines from page A1 of the *Seattle Star* appeared, respectively, on July 29, 1919; July 30, 1919; July 31, 1919; and Aug. 5, 1919.
26. See "Is This To Remain White Man's Land?," *Seattle Star*, July 29, 1919. p. A1.
27. "Civic Mass Meeting Protests Jap Menace," *Seattle Star*, Aug. 12, 1919, p. 1.
28. Daniels, *The Politics of Prejudice*, pp. 94–95.
29. See Magden, *Furusato*, p. 59.
30. See Rademaker, "The Ecological Position of the Japanese Farmers in the State of Washington," pp. 323–24.
31. See Grant, *The Passing of the Great Race*, ch. 11, p. 1.
32. See Stoddard, *The Rising Tide of Color Against White World Supremacy*, in ch. 11, p. 8: "The colored peril of arms may thus be summarized: The brown and yellow races possess great military potentialities. These (barring the action of certain ill-understood emotional stimuli) are unlikely to flame out in spontaneous fanaticism; but, on the other hand, they are very likely to be mobilized for political reasons like revolt against white dominion or for social reasons like over-population. The black race offers no real danger except as the tool of Pan-Islamism. As for the red men of the Americas, they are of

merely local significance." Stoddard goes on to detail the extraordinary misery to which Asians ostensibly allowed themselves to be subjected as laborers. See also H. M. Hyndman, *The Awakening of Asia* (New York, 1919), p. 180: "The white workers cannot hold their own permanently against Chinese competition in the labor market. The lower standard of life, the greater persistence, the superior education of the Chinese will beat them, and will continue to beat them."

33. Rademaker, "The Ecological Position of the Japanese Farmers in the State of Washington," pp. 325–26.
34. Ibid., p. 324.
35. Magden, *Furusato*, p. 61.
36. Ibid., pp. 61–62.
37. Miller Freeman, "The Japanese Question," from the *Great Northern Daily News of Seattle*, a Japanese American newspaper, Jan. 25, 1921. Miller Freeman Archives, University of Washington. The piece is also noteworthy in that it quotes nineteenth-century evolutionary philosopher Herbert Spencer: "If you mix the constitutions of two widely divergent varieties which have become adapted to widely divergent modes of life, you get a constitution which is adapted to the mode of life of neither—a constitution which will not work properly, because it is not fitted for any set of conditions whatever . . . I have for the reasons indicated, entirely approved of the regulations which have been established in America for restraining Chinese immigration. . . . If the Chinese are allowed to settle in America they must either, if they remain unmixed, form a subject race standing in the position, if not of slaves, yet of a class approaching slaves; or they mix and form a bad hybrid. . . . The same thing will happen if there should be any considerable mixture of American or European races with the Japanese."
38. Sucheng Chan, *Asian Americans, an Interpretive History* (Boston: Twayne Publishers, 1991), p. 47. For the gamut of alien land acts, see also Douglas W. Nelson, "The Alien Land Law Movement of the Late Nineteenth Century," *Journal of the West* 9:46–49 (1970).
39. See Magden, *Furusato*, p. 65.
40. See Daniels, *The Politics of Prejudice*, p. 98. The case is *Ozawa v. United States*, 260 U.S. 178 (1922), 43 S.Ct. 65, 67 L.Ed. The facts: "The appellant is a person of the Japanese race born in Japan. He applied, on October 16, 1914, to the United States District Court for the Territory of Hawaii to be admitted as a citizen of the United States. His petition was opposed by the United States District Attorney for the District of Hawaii. Including the period of his residence in Hawaii appellant had continuously resided in the United States for 20 years. He was a graduate of the Berkeley, Cal., high school, had been nearly three years a student in the University of California, had educated his children in American schools, his family had attended American churches and he had maintained the use of the English language in his home. That he was well qualified by character and education for citizenship is conceded." The court responded: "The effect of the conclusion that the words 'white person' means a Caucasian is not to establish a sharp line of demarcation between those who are entitled and those who are not entitled to naturalization, but rather a zone of more or less debatable ground outside of which, upon the one hand, are those clearly eligible, and outside of which, upon the other hand, are those clearly ineligible for citizenship. Individual cases falling within this zone must be determined as they arise from time to time by what this court has called, in another connection (*Davidson v. New Orleans*, 96 U.S. 97, 104), 'the gradual process of judicial inclusion and exclusion.' The appellant, in the case now under consideration, however, is clearly of a race which is not Caucasian and therefore belongs entirely outside the zone on the negative side. A large number of the federal and state courts have so decided and we find no reported case definitely to the contrary. These decisions are sustained by numerous scientific authorities, which we do not deem it necessary to review. We think these decisions are right and so hold."
41. The case is *Terrace v. Thompson*, 263 U. S. 197, 44 S. Ct. 15, 68 L. Ed. 255 (1923). The facts of the case: "Terrace owned land in Washington which he desired to lease for 5

years to Nakatsuka, a Japanese alien who had not declared his intention of acquiring American citizenship. Under the Anti-Alien Land Law of Washington of 1921, it was made a criminal offense to sell or lease land to any alien who had not declared his intention of acquiring citizenship, and Thompson, the attorney general of the state, threatened to apply the full force of the Act against Terrace if the sale was made to Nakatsuka. Terrace challenged such action and filed to enjoin Thompson from enforcing the act." The court answered the plaintiffs' claims regarding the equal-protection clause thus: "The rights, privileges, and duties of aliens differ widely from those of citizens; and those of alien declarants differ substantially from those of nondeclarants. The inclusion of good faith declarants in the same class with citizens does not unjustly discriminate against aliens who are ineligible or against eligible aliens who have failed to declare their intention. The classification is based on eligibility and purpose to naturalize. Two classes of aliens inevitably result from the naturalization laws—those who may and those who may not become citizens. The rule established by Congress on this subject, in and of itself, furnishes a reasonable basis for classification in a state law withholding from aliens the privilege of land ownership as defined in the act. It is obvious that one who is not a citizen and cannot become one lacks an interest in, and the power to effectually work for the welfare of, the state, and, so lacking, the state may rightfully deny him the right to own and lease real estate within its boundaries. The quality and allegiance of those who own, occupy and use the farm lands within its borders are matters of highest importance and affect the safety and power of the state itself."

42. See Magden, *Furusato*, pp. 65–66; Daniels, *The Politics of Prejudice*, pp. 98–103; and Page Smith, *Democracy on Trial: The Japanese American Evacuation and Relocation in World War II* (New York: Simon and Schuster, 1995), p. 50.
43. See Audrie Girdner and Annie Loftis, *The Great Betrayal: The Evacuation of Japanese-Americans During World War II* (London: The Macmillan Company, 1969), p. 364.
44. See Flewellen, *Shirakawa*, pp. 76–79.
45. See Nishinoiri, "Japanese Farms in Washington," pp. 78–79, and 102–05. See also Asaichi Tsushima, *Pre-WWII History of Japanese Pioneers in the Clearing and Development of Land in Bellevue* (Bellevue: Private printing, 1991), p. 45.
46. See Nishinoiri, "Japanese Farms in Washington," pp. 9–11, 61–89, for complete details on the Alien Land Law prosecutions that followed the 1921 law, and the key cases that formed the legal precedents upholding the laws. See also Rademaker, "The Ecological Position of the Japanese Farmers in the State of Washington," pp. 29–32. See also Magden, *Furusato*, pp. 62–64.
47. See Rademaker, "The Ecological Position of the Japanese Farmers in the State of Washington," pp. 35–36.
48. See Tanaka, *The Nikkei on Bainbridge Island, 1883–1942*, pp. 113–14, and Modell, *The Economics and Politics of Racial Accommodation*, p. 151.
49. See Rademaker, "The Ecological Position of the Japanese Farmers in the State of Washington," pp. 35–39.
50. See Daniels, *The Politics of Prejudice*, p. 88. See also Modell, *The Economics and Politics of Racial Accommodation*, p. 151, and Tanaka, *The Nikkei on Bainbridge Island, 1883–1942*, pp. 111–17.
51. See *A Hidden Past: An Exploration of Eastside History* (Seattle: *Seattle Times* Publishing, 2000), "Meydendauer Whalers: Bellevue was one of the last active whaling ports in the United States," pp. 57–59.
52. Much of this is recounted in McDonald, *Bellevue*, pp. 84–118. Hennig described his father's vineyard operation in an interview with the author.
53. This characterization is drawn from the author's interviews with subjects who were involved in agriculture in Bellevue at that time. They uniformly described the farming scene in Bellevue as dominated by the Japanese, though they hardly were the only farmers on the Eastside. They also uniformly said that the truck farms were solely Japanese operations.

54. This figure, mentioned by McDonald, *Bellevue* (p. 90), was substantiated by nearly every person the author interviewed when discussing the Bellevue agricultural situation.
55. See McDonald, *Bellevue*, pp. 77–79, and *A Hidden Past*, "Great Escapes: The Eastside was the place to be on a sunny Saturday in the early 1920s," pp. 52–53.
56. See McDonald, *Bellevue*, pp. 113–15.
57. See Tsushima, *Pre-WWII History of Japanese Pioneers*, p. 83.
58. See Gregory Roberts, "Before Pearl Harbor," *Seattle Post-Intelligencer*, Friday, May 25, 2001, p. C1.
59. Densho Project Visual History Interview: Tom Matsuoka, May 7, 1998, segment 8.
60. Ibid., segments 10–11.
61. Tyrus Matsuoka (author's phone interview, Feb. 16, 2002) confirmed his father named him for Cobb, "long before he knew what kind of man he was," referring to Cobb's notorious racism.
62. Densho Project Visual History Interview: Tokio Hirotaka, Toshio Ito, and Joe Matsuzawa, May 21, 1998, segment 16.
63. Densho Project Visual History Interview: Chizuko Norton, April 27, 1998, segment 4.
64. Densho Project Visual History Interview: Rae Takekawa, May 8, 1998, segment 14.
65. Densho Project Visual History Interview: Chizuko Norton, April 27, 1998, segment 8.
66. Ibid., segments 7–14.
67. See Tsushima, *Pre-WWII History of Japanese Pioneers*, pp. 24–30.
68. One of these teachers, a Mrs. Kaneji Takekawa, later became Rae Matsuoka's mother-in-law.
69. For more on the Courier League, see Gregory Roberts, "Before Pearl Harbor."
70. Miller Freeman, *The Memoirs of Miller Freeman* (Bellevue: Private printing, 1956), pp. 165–166.
71. Robert F. Karolevitz, *Kemper Freeman, Sr., and the Bellevue Story* (Mission Hill, SD: The Homestead Publishers, 1984), pp. 27–34.
72. Densho Project Visual History Interview: Tom Matsuoka, May 7, 1998, segment 19.
73. Densho Project Visual History Interview: Rae Takekawa, April 27, 1998, segment 11.
74. Author's interview with Tom Matsuoka, March 11, 1992. For all interview quotations in this text, see "A Note On Sources," after the Epilogue.

Chapter 3: "A Jap is a Jap"

1. See Peter Irons, *Justice at War* (New York: Oxford University Press, 1962), p. 20.
2. See Greg Robinson, *By Order of the President: FDR and the Internment of Japanese Americans* (Cambridge, Mass.: Harvard University Press, 2001), pp. 32–43.
3. Franklin D. Roosevelt, "Roosevelt Says," *Macon Telegraph*, April 30, 1925. Available online at http://www.cviog.uga.edu/Projects/gainfo/FDRedito.htm#anchor440429.
4. See Robinson, *By Order of the President*, pp. 54–57, and Tetsuden Kashima, *Judgment Without Trial: Japanese American Internment During World War II* (Seattle: University of Washington Press, 2003), p. 16.
5. See Kashima, *Judgment Without Trial*, pp. 55–57.
6. See Kashima, *Judgment Without Trial*, pp. 38–39, and *Personal Justice Denied*, pp. 471–75.
7. *Personal Justice Denied: Report of the Commission on Wartime Relocation and Internment of Civilians* (Seattle: University of Washington Press, 1996), pp. 52–53. See also Kashima, *Judgment Without Trial*, pp. 40–41, and Daniels, *The Decision to Relocate the Japanese Americans* (Malabar, Fla.: Robert E. Krieger Publishing Co., 1986), pp. 8–9.
8. See Kashima, *Judgment Without Trial*, pp. 27–29; and Louis Fiset, *Imprisoned Apart: The World War II Correspondence of an Issei Couple* (Seattle: University of Washington Press, 1997), p. 28. For more on the compilation of the dossiers, see Committee on Wartime Relocation and Internment of Civilians, *Personal Justice Denied*, pp. 53–55 and 471–78, as well as Carol Van Valkenburg, *An Alien Place: The Fort Missoula, Montana Detention Camp 1941–1944* (Missoula, Mont.: Pictorial Histories Publishing Co., 1995), pp. 35–36.

9. See Fiset, *Imprisoned Apart*, pp. 28–29, and Irons, *Justice at War*, p. 22.
10. Department of Justice, Press Releases, Dec. 8 and Dec. 13, 1941; Feb. 16, 1942. See also FBI, Memorandum for the Director, April 6, 1943, "Re: Apprehension of Japanese Individuals" (FBI document from Freedom of Information Reading Room, Custodial Detention, pt. 1a, pp. 141 and 174), which lists the number of Seattle detainees.
11. Densho Project Visual History Interview: Rae Takekawa, May 8, 1998, segment 14.
12. "Ban on Japanese In Busses Is Corrected," *Seattle Times*, Dec. 9, 1941, p. 3.
13. "Sailor's Wife Leads Glass-Smashing Mob, Blacking Out Lights," *Seattle Times*, Dec. 9, 1941, pp. 1–3.
14. "30 Enemy Planes Fly Over S.F.," *Seattle Times*, Dec. 9, 1941, p. 2.
15. See Roger Daniels, *The Decision to Relocate the Japanese Americans* (Malabar, Fla.: Robert E. Krieger Publishing Co., 1986), pp. 14–15. See also Audrie Girdner and Annie Loftis, *The Great Betrayal: The Evacuation of Japanese-Americans During World War II* (London: The Macmillan Company, 1969), pp. 6–7.
16. See "Coast Blacked Out," *Post-Intelligencer*, Dec. 9, 1941, p. 1. Subheads on the page read: "Mystery Planes Routed At S.F." and "Big Formation Turned Back At Golden Gate". The lead paragraph reads: "SAN FRANCISCO, Dec. 8. (AP)—An apparent attempt by Japanese warplanes to bomb the San Francisco Bay area was reported tonight by Brig. Gen. William Ord Ryan of the Fourth Intercepting Command, who said a large number of aircraft were turned back at the Golden Gate." The dispatch included this update, though: "WASHINGTON, Dec. 9 (AP)—The war department said early today it has 'no information of the report that any enemy planes attempted an attack on the West Coast and no means of verifying it at this time.'"
17. See Page Smith, *Democracy on Trial: The Japanese American Evacuation and Relocation World War II* (New York: Simon & Schuster, 1995), p. 106. See also Girdner and Loftis, *The Great Betrayal*, pp. 6–7.
18. See Daniels, *The Decision to Relocate the Japanese Americans*, pp. 14–15.
19. See Girdner and Loftis, *The Great Betrayal*, pp. 6–7; and Daniels, *The Decision to Relocate the Japanese Americans*, pp. 14–15.
20. See Burl Burlingame, *Advance Force Pearl Harbor: The Imperial Navy's Underwater Assault on America* (Honolulu: Pacific Monograph), pp. 344–52.
21. See Bert Webber, *Retaliation: Japanese Attacks and Allied Countermeasures on the Pacific Coast in World War II* (Corvallis: Oregon State University Press, 1976), pp. 29–32, 53–67. See also Burlingame, *Advance Force Pearl Harbor*, p. 346. See also Daniels, *The Decision to Relocate the Japanese Americans*, pp. 24–25. For contemporary news reports of the incendiary bombs, see also the *Post-Intelligencer*, "Incendiaries Drop in Forested Areas," June 2, 1943, p. A1; "Bombs From Balloons Fell On Oregon," June 11, 1943, p. A1; "N.W. Forests Get Big U.S. Fire Fund," June 4, 1943, p. A1.
22. See Robert C. Mikesh, *Japan's World War II Balloon Bomb Attacks on North America* (Washington, Smithsonian Institution Press, 1973), pp. 7–24, 38, and 67–69; and Webber, *Retaliation*, pp. 93–123.
23. See Klancy Clark de Nevers, *The Colonel and the Pacifist: Karl Bendetsen, Perry Saito, and the Incarceration of Japanese Americans During World War II* (Salt Lake City: University of Utah Press, 2004), pp. 77–83. See also Smith, *Democracy on Trial*, pp. 102–16, and Daniels, *The Decision to Relocate the Japanese Americans*, pp. 14–18.
24. See Girdner and Loftis, *The Great Betrayal*, p. 16.
25. See Smith, *Democracy on Trial*, p. 120.
26. See Daniels, *The Decision to Relocate the Japanese Americans*, p. 42.
27. Ibid., pp. 16–17.
28. Ibid., p. 7.
29. Ibid., p. 15.
30. See Girdner and Loftis, *The Great Betrayal*, p. 17–18.
31. See Smith, *Democracy on Trial*, p. 106. Knox was not known for his circumspection; he later made headlines for a grotesque diplomatic gaffe, when he told Chiang Kai-Shek's

brother-in-law, making an official visit, that the United States would certainly defeat Japan. He patted the man on the back and said, "That's all right, T.V., we'll lick those yellow devils yet." See "Is Knox's Face Red? He Mixed His 'Yellows'," *Seattle Times*, March 4, 1942, p.1.

32. See Daniels, *The Decision to Relocate the Japanese Americans*, p. 12.
33. See Norio Mitsuoka, *Nisei Odyssey: The Camp Years* (Fountain Valley, Calif.: Bowder Printing and Publishing Co., 1991), p. 5.
34. See "Fires Set to Aid Enemy Planes," "Flaming Arrows Planted by 5th Columnists to Guide Foe Toward Seattle," *Post-Intelligencer*, Dec. 11, 1942, p. 1. Buried in the text of the story, on p. 3, was this information: "No details about the flaming arrows on the Olympic Peninsula were disclosed ay the Interceptor Command Headquarters, but Cunningham told the Associated Press that the fires had been set by white men who had been clearing land."
35. See "26 Japanese Girls Leave School Jobs," *Post-Intelligencer*, Feb. 26, 1942, p. 1.
36. These meetings were reconstructed from minutes of the sessions recorded by Freeman's private secretary, and all quotes are taken directly from those minutes. They are from the Miller Freeman Archives at the University of Washington Archival Collection, Seattle; Folder 6, "Minutes," Documents 1, 2, and 3. The *Bellevue American* also carried Whitney's abbreviated account of the first meeting in its Dec. 18, 1941, edition, under the headline: "Special Committee at Work," p. 1.
37. Author's interview with Aramaki, March 14, 1992.
38. In fact, as Morton Grodzins points out in *Americans Betrayed: Politics and the Japanese Evacuation* (Chicago: University of Chicago Press, 1949), pp. 149–52, further memorials passed in 1919 and 1924 stiffening the requirements for obtaining dual citizenship, and "failure to make such a notification was presumption that the newborn child held no Japanese citizenship." Moreover, "The principal charge, linking American citizens of Japanese ancestry with the Japanese government, was that which imputed disloyalty as the result of dual-citizenship status. Probably no claim could have less relevance to matters of allegiance, yet it alone was the principal stock-in-trade of the California Joint Immigration Committee for many years, and it, almost alone, was used as the peg on which the California State Personnel Board hung its 'investigation' and subsequent dismissal of Japanese American employees."
39. See the Miller Freeman Archives at the University of Washington Archival Collection, Seattle; Folder 6, "Minutes," Documents 1, 2, and 3.
40. Densho Project Visual History Interview: Rae Takekawa, April 27, 1998, segment 14.
41. See Van Valkenburg, *An Alien Place*, pp. 41–47. See also Fiset, *Imprisoned Apart*, pp. 36–42. The description of the housing is from Tom Matsuoka interview with the author, Aug. 31, 2000.
42. *Missoulian*, Dec. 20, 1912; cited in Van Valkenburg, *An Alien Place*, p. 46.
43. *Bellevue American*, Nov. 20, 1941, "Bellevue Japanese Buy Defense Bonds," p. 1.
44. See "American-Born Japanese Loyal, Editor Asserts," *Seattle Times*, Dec. 9, 1941, p. 3.
45. See DeNevers, *The Colonel and the Pacifist*, p. 93.
46. See Associated Press dispatch, "Japs Planning Sabotage In U.S. Soon, Says Solon," *Seattle Post-Intelligencer*, March 7, 1942, p. 9.
47. See "Whites Try to Buy Them Out at Low Price, Say Japanese," *Seattle Daily Times*, March 21, 1942, p. 12.
48. See "Nisei Citizenship," letter to the editor, *Seattle Post-Intelligencer*, Feb. 28, 1942, p. 8.
49. Associated Press dispatch, "Japs? 'Get Tough'—Solon," *Seattle Post-Intelligencer*, March 22, 1942, p. 7.
50. See "Japs Reside Near Vital Plants Here," *Seattle Daily Times*, March 5, 1942, p. 1. The day before, the *Times* had also run a front-page Associated Press piece headlined: "Areas Vital to Defense in Jap Hands."
51. See Henry McLemore, "This Is War! Stop Worrying About Hurting Jap Feelings," *Seattle Times*, Jan. 30, 1942, p. 6. McLemore, whose columns ran daily in the paper, continued

fulminating periodically against Japanese Americans for the next several months; see, e.g., "Excuse, Please; But What's In Those Jap Text-Books," *Seattle Times*, Feb. 7, 1942, which promulgated the belief that Japanese-American schools were hotbeds of pro-imperial propaganda.

52. See letter to the editor, "Fourteenth Amendment," *Post-Intelligencer*, March 10, 1942, p. 12.
53. See Girdner and Loftis, *The Great Betrayal*, p. 17. See also Smith, *Democracy on Trial*, pp. 107–25.
54. See Smith, *Democracy on Trial*, pp. 107–13. Smith places great weight on Biddle's refusal to accede to DeWitt's request for mass raids, arguing that this would have relieved some of the political pressure and reassured DeWitt at a time when he was sympathetic to citizens' rights. This conclusion, however, strikes the author as highly speculative at best; DeWitt behaved erratically throughout his remaining tenure at the Western Command, and it seems imprudent if not impossible to predict how he would have behaved under this scenario. Certainly, given his predilections, it seems likely that mass evacuation would have been the outcome regardless. See also Daniels, *The Decision to Relocate the Japanese Americans*, pp. 6–8.
55. See Smith, *Democracy on Trial*, pp. 111–13.
56. Army G–2 Information Bulletin, "Japanese Espionage," January 21, 1942, p. 3.
57. See Smith, *Democracy on Trial*, p. 427.
58. Memo, Gen Clark for Judge Advocate GHQ, 24 Jan 42, GHQ file, WDC: Enemy Aliens.
59. See de Nevers, *The Colonel and the Pacifist*, pp. 83–90.
60. See Girdner and Loftis, *The Great Betrayal*, pp. 17–21.
61. See Robinson, *By Order of the President*, pp. 97–124, and de Nevers, *The Colonel and the Pacifist*, pp. 91–114.
62. See Daniels, *The Decision to Relocate the Japanese Americans*, pp. 10–11, and Smith, *Democracy on Trial*, p. 119.
63. See Grodzins, *Americans Betrayed*, pp. 74–75.
64. Ibid., pp. 72–78.
65. See Smith, *Democracy on Trial*, p. 120.
66. *Congressional Record*, December 15, 1941.
67. *Congressional Record*, February 26, 1942.
68. See Masayo Umezawa Duus, *Unlikely Liberators: The Men of the 100th and 442nd* (Honolulu: University of Hawaii Press, 1987), p. 62. See also Girdner and Loftis, *The Great Betrayal*, p. 17.
69. See Smith, *Democracy on Trial*, pp. 121–22.
70. See John Hersey, "A Mistake of Terrifically Horrible Proportions," introductory essay to John Armor and Peter Wright, *Manzanar* (New York: Vintage Books, 1989), pp. 18–21.
71. "Final Recommendation of the Commanding General, Western Defense Command and Fourth Army, Submitted to the Secretary of War," General DeWitt to Secretary of War Stimson, February 14, 1942. See also Smith, *Democracy on Trial*, pp. 123–27.
72. See Mike Masaoka, Tolan Committee Hearings, February 21 and 23, 1942, San Francisco, p. 11137: " . . . with any policy of evacuation definitely arising from reasons of military necessity and national safety, we are in complete agreement. As American citizens, we cannot and should not take any other stand. But, also, as American citizens believing in the integrity of our citizenship[,] we feel that any evacuation enforced on grounds violating that integrity should be opposed. If, in the judgment of military and Federal authorities, evacuation of Japanese residents from the West Coast is a primary step towards assuring the safety of this Nation, we will have no hesitation in complying with the necessities implicit in that judgment. But, if, on the other hand, such evacuation is primarily a measure whose surface urgency cloaks the desires of political or other pressure groups who want us to leave merely from motives of self-interest, we feel that we have every right to protest and to demand equitable judgment on our merits as American citizens."

73. See "Freeman Calls Japan Society '5th Column,'" Seattle Post Intelligencer, Feb. 27, 1942, p. A1.
74. All quotes taken from contemporary newspaper coverage Feb. 27–March 4 of the three days of hearings, by the *Post-Intelligencer:* "Freeman Calls Japan Society '5th Column'"; "Tolan Sees Early Ouster of Japs"; "East Side Doesn't Want Japs, Says: Governor Quizzed on State's Alien Policy"; and the *Seattle Times:* "Mass Ouster of Japanese is Demanded by Att. Gen."; and "Enemy Alien Evacuation Order Held Imminent."
75. See "Army Order Reveals Eventual Ouster of All Coast Japanese," *Seattle Times,* March 3, 1942, p. 1
76. See Dorothy Swaine Thomas and Richard S. Nishimoto, *The Spoilage: Japanese-American Evacuation and Resettlement During World War II* (Berkeley: University of California Press, 1946), pp. 24–25.
77. See Eric L. Muller, *Free to Die for Their Country: The Story of the Japanese American War Resisters in World War II* (Chicago: University of Chicago Press, 2001), pp. 32–33.
78. See Civilian Exclusion Order No. 1, Headquarters, Western Defense Command and Fourth Army, Presidio of San Francisco, California, March 24, 1942.
79. See Daniels, *The Decision to Relocate the Japanese Americans,* p. 54.
80. See Ronald Magden, *Furusato: Tacoma-Pierce County Japanese 1888–1977* (Tacoma: Tacoma Japanese Community Service, 1988), p. 132, 126. See also Daniels, *The Decision to Relocate the Japanese Americans,* 54–55, 71–76. See also Smith, *Democracy on Trial,* p. 427.
81. See Public Proclamation No. 3, Headquarters, Western Defense Command and Fourth Army, Presidio of San Francisco, California, March 24, 1942. See Smith, *Democracy on Trial,* pp. 122–26.
82. See "Jap Given 15 Days For Violating Curfew," *Post-Intelligencer,* April 15, 1942, p. 5.
83. See Anne Stewart, "Japs Accept Army Order With Bewilderment and Obedience," *Seattle Times,* March 22, 1942, p. 6.
84. See Frank Miyamoto, "The Seattle JACL and Its Role in Evacuation," p. 26, File 6.24, Japanese Evacuation and Resettlement Study, Bancroft Library, University of California, Berkeley.
85. See *Seattle Post-Intelligencer,* April 4, 1942, "Keeping Japanese Lands Producing Offers Problem," by Fred Niendorff, p. 14.
86. See Leonard Broom and Ruth Riemer, *Removal and Return: The Socio-Economic Effects of the War on Japanese Americans* (Berkeley: University of California Press, 1949), pp. 82–83.
87. See *Bellevue American,* "200 Workers Needed Now to Care for Crops in Overlake Area," May 28, 1942; and "Workers Needed for Crops," June 11, 1942. Another primary source of information for the author was a collection of papers formerly in the possession of Joe Matsuzawa, whose brother found them in a corner of the old Bellevue Vegetable Growers Association warehouse in Bellevue after the war. They are primarily receipts, but also contain letters of correspondence between the company and their clientele, including claims against the company and counterclaims by it. Arranged chronologically, this is the picture that emerges from the papers. The author wishes to express his gratitude to Mr. Matsuzawa for sharing these papers.
88. See "Operators For Jap Farms Lag," *Post-Intelligencer,* April 2, 1942, p. 6.
89. Densho Project Visual History Interview: Rae Takekawa, May 8, 1998, segment 17.
90. See "Eastsiders in Exile," by Janet Burkitt, from *A Hidden Past: An Exploration of Eastside History* (Seattle: *Seattle Times* Publishing, 2000), pp. 69–71.

Chapter 4: Exile

1. Densho Project Visual History Interview: Tokio Hirotaka, Toshio Ito, and Joe Matsuzawa, May 21, 1998, segment 22.
2. Densho Project Visual History Interview: Seichi Hayashida, Aug. 21, 1998, segment 14.
3. Ibid., segment 15.

4. Densho Project Visual History Interview: Mitsuko Hashiguchi, July 28, 1998, segment 36.
5. Ibid., segment 40.
6. Densho Project Visual History Interview: Seichi Hayashida, Aug. 21, 1998, segment 15.
7. See Page Smith, *Democracy on Trial: The Japanese American Evacuation and Relocation in World War II* (New York: Simon & Schuster, 1995), p. 156.
8. See Smith, *Democracy on Trial*, pp. 161–62.
9. Ibid., pp. 156, 161–62, 181–82, and 218, as well as Roger Daniels, *Concentration Camps: North America: Japanese in the United States and Canada During World War II* (Malabar, Fla.: Krieger Publishing Company, 1993), p. 104. The difference in figures is due to what is being counted and when; the camp populations changed daily as persons died or were born, or released, or transferred.
10. Smith, *Democracy on Trial*, p. 162.
11. Ibid., pp. 176–77.
12. Densho Project Visual History Interview: Tok Hirotaka, Toshio Ito, and Joe Matuszawa, May 21, 1998, segment 26.
13. Densho Project Visual History Interview: Seichi Hayashida, Aug. 21, 1998, segment 21.
14. See Carol Van Valkenburg, *An Alien Place: the Fort Missoula, Montana Detention Camp 1941–1944* (Missoula, Mont.: Pictorial Histories Publishing Co., 1995), pp. 46–50. Also see Louis Fiset, *Imprisoned Apart: The World War II Correspondence of an Issei Couple* (Seattle: University of Washington Press, 1997), pp. 53–59. A photograph of the fishing boat appears on p. 59.
15. Matsuoka told this story twice to the author and another time to the Densho Project, but his best telling of it is the one he gave to Louis Fiset for *Imprisoned Apart*, from which this account is directly taken.
16. See NARA Japanese-American Internee File, 1942–1946, Record Group 210: Records of the War Relocation Authority, File #412297, Takeo Tom Matsuoka, copy of note from Department of Justice File No.146–13–2–82–79.
17. See Van Valkenburg, *An Alien Place*, pp. 65–72. This is an excellent and detailed account of the interrogations, relying on records that were finally unsealed in 1985.
18. See John Tateishi, *And Justice For All: An Oral History of the Japanese American Internment Camps* (Seattle: University of Washington Press, 1984), pp. 66–67.
19. Densho Project Visual History Interview: Rae Takekawa, May 8, 1998, segment 22.
20. Densho Project Visual History Interview: Mitsuko Hashiguchi, July 28, 1998, segment 43.
21. Densho Project Visual History Interview: Rae Takekawa, May 8, 1998, segment 24.
22. See NARA Japanese American Internee File, 1942–1946, Record Group 210: Records of the War Relocation Authority, File #412297: Letter dated Aug. 21, 1943 from the WRA Relocation Officer, Murray E. Stebbins in Havre, to Raymond R. Best, Project Director at Tule Lake.
23. See "200 Workers Needed Now to Care for Crops in Overlake Area," *Bellevue American*, May 28, 1942, p. A1.
24. See "Workers Needed for Crops," *Bellevue American*, June 11, 1942.
25. This account of Western Farm and Produce's operations before and after the internment is derived from two sources: First, from news accounts in the company's early stages in the *Bellevue American*, particularly "200 Workers Needed Now to Care for Crops in Overlake Area," May 28, 1942; and "Workers Needed for Crops," June 11, 1942; and second and most helpfully, from the Joe Matsuzawa collection of papers (see chapter 3, en. 87).
26. See *Personal Justice Denied: Report of the Commission on Wartime Relocation and Internment of Civilians* (Seattle: University of Washington Press, 1996), p. 157.
27. See John Armor and Peter Wright, *Manzanar* (New York: Vintage Books, 1989), p. 75.
28. Densho Project Visual History Interview: Tokio Hirotaka, Toshio Ito, and Joe Matsuzawa Interview, May 21, 1998, segment 28.
29. See Dorothy Swaine Thomas and Richard S. Nishimoto, *The Spoilage: Japanese-American Evacuation and Resettlement During World War II* (Berkeley: University of California Press, 1946), pp. 25–26. See also Smith, *Democracy on Trial*, p. 223.

30. See, e.g., letter to the editor, *The Missoulian*, from Mrs. Walter Luke, Feb. 27, 1942, in which she warned that bringing Japanese laborers to the state would expose Montanans to such dangers as arson, and that local forests and grain fields "could easily be reduced to ashes or our wild game eliminated completely; so there would be little need for roads if those treacherous Japs came here and started their sabotage" (that is, it would wipe out the source of all jobs); and letter from "Joe Kalispell," Feb. 28, 1942, likewise warned of the danger to the forests.
31. See Van Valkenburg, *An Alien Place*, pp. 76–77.
32. The wartime campaign against the internees is described in greater detail in chapter 6, pp. 234–36.
33. Letter, on American Legion letterhead, from H. L. Chaillaux, National American Commission, to Miller Freeman, Feb. 9, 1942, with enclosure describing resolution. Miller Freeman Archives, University of Washington.
34. See Smith, *Democracy on Trial*, pp. 252–58.
35. There have been numerous accounts of the violence at Manzanar, Poston, and Tule Lake. The best is probably Arthur A. Hansen and David A. Hacker, "The Manzanar Riot: An Ethnic Perspective," *Amerasia Journal* (Fall 1974) 2:112–57. See also Audrie Girdner and Annie Loftis, *The Great Betrayal: The Evacuation of Japanese-Americans During World War II* (London: The Macmillan Company, 1969), pp. 318–26. See also Michi Weglyn, *Years of Infamy: The Untold Story of America's Concentration Camps* (New York: Morrow Quill Paperbacks, 1976), pp. 156–73; Daniels, *Concentration Camps: North America*, pp. 104–26. *Personal Justice Denied* also describes the incidents on pp. 178–79 and 245–52, as does Thomas and Nishimoto, *The Spoilage*, pp. 45–52.
36. See Thomas and Nishimoto, *The Spoilage*, p. 56.
37. See Dorothy Matsuo, *Boyhood to War: History and Anecdotes of the 442nd RCT* (Honolulu: Mutual Publishing of Honolulu, 1992), p. 43.
38. Probably the most thorough account of the Tule Lake discord appears in Thomas and Nishimoto, *The Spoilage*, especially pp. 72–146.
39. Densho Project Visual History Interview: Seichi Hayashida, August 21, 1998, segment 30.
40. See Weglyn, *Years of Infamy*, pp.156–73, which provides a detailed account of the Tule Lake violence. See also Thomas and Nishimoto, *The Spoilage*, pp. 113–46; Girdner and Loftis, *The Great Betrayal*, pp. 318–26, and Smith, *Democracy on Trial*, p. 299.
41. Densho Project Visual History Interview: Seichi Hayashida, August 21, 1998, segments 30–31.
42. See Smith, *Democracy on Trial*, pp. 310–21. Thomas and Nishimoto, *The Spoilage*, also discuss the yes-yes respondents who chose to stay, pp.103–04.
43. For a detailed discussion of the reasons that many "yes-yes" signees, as well as conservatives who disagreed with the newcomers, chose to remain at Tule anyway, see Thomas and Nishimoto, *The Spoilage*, pp. 88–102.
44. Densho Project Visual History Interview: Chizuko Norton, April 27, 1998, segment 24.
45. See Thomas and Nishimoto, *The Spoilage*, pp. 114–15; Girdner and Loftis, *The Great Betrayal*, pp. 326–27, and Smith, *Democracy on Trial*, p. 323.
46. See *Personal Justice Denied*, p. 176 and 248–49, and Girdner and Loftis, *The Great Betrayal*, pp. 324–25.
47. Densho Project Visual History Interview: Chizuko Norton, April 27, 1998, segment 27.
48. See Thomas and Nishimoto, *The Spoilage*, pp. 271–73.
49. The most thorough account of the repatriation debacle appears in Thomas and Nishimoto, *The Spoilage*, pp. 333–61. See also *Personal Justice Denied*, pp. 251–52, and Smith, *Democracy on Trial*, pp. 331–33, 414.
50. Densho Project Visual History Interview: Chizuko Norton, April 27, 1998, segment 28.
51. See Roger Daniels' trenchant observation in *Concentration Camps USA: Japanese Americans and World War II* (New York: Holt, Rinehart & Winston, 1972), p. 96: "That these areas were still vacant land in 1942, land that the ever-voracious pioneers and developers had either passed by or abandoned, speaks volumes about their attractiveness."

52. Smith, *Democracy on Trial*, pp. 352–53.
53. Author's interview with Ed Suguro. He was describing life at Tule Lake, but the breakdown he describes was similarly described in nearly every Nisei's testimony from a variety of camps.
54. Smith, *Democracy on Trial*, pp. 310–21.

Chapter 5: Going For Broke

1. See Thelma Chang, *'I Can Never Forget': Men of the 100th/442nd* (Honolulu: Sigi Productions, 1991), p. 102.
2. See Roger Daniels, *The Decision to Relocate the Japanese Americans* (Malabar, Fla.: Robert E. Krieger Publishing Co., 1986), p. 82.
3. See John Hersey, "A Mistake of Terrifically Horrible Proportions," introductory essay to John Armor and Peter Wright, *Manzanar* (New York: Vintage Books, 1989), pp. 56–58. See also Page Smith, *Democracy on Trial: The Japanese American Evacuation and Relocation in World War II* (New York: Simon & Schuster, 1995), pp. 315–16. See also the Commission on Wartime Relocation and Internment of Civilians, *Personal Justice Denied: Report of the Commission on Wartime Relocation and Internment of Civilians* (Washington, D.C., 1982), pp. 216–18.
4. See Hersey, "A Mistake," pp. 59–60, and Roger Daniels, *Concentration Camps: North America: Japanese in the United States and Canada During World War II* (Malabar, Fla.: Krieger Publishing Company, 1993), pp. 278–79, and *Personal Justice Denied*, pp. 215–23.
5. See Audrie Girdner and Annie Loftis, *The Great Betrayal: The Evacuation of Japanese-Americans During World War II* (London: The Macmillan Company, 1969), pp. 279–84. As they observe on p. 324: "The radicals were not the majority . . . but they acted as the majority in the absence of a group who were willing to defy them."
6. See Fair Play Committee Bulletin #3 (March 1, 1944), which went on to announce that the FPC members would not register or appear for the draft. (A copy of this bulletin can be found on the Web at http://www.pbs.org/conscience/resistance/we_hereby_refuse/02_fpc_1.html.)
7. See particularly Eric L. Muller, *Free to Die for their Country: The Story of the Japanese American Draft Resisters in World War II* (Chicago: University of Chicago Press, 2001), which explores the Clark matter in detail on pp. 124–30. See also Frank Abe's remarkable film for PBS, *Conscience and the Constitution*, which explored the resisters' story. Abe also maintains a Web site (http://www.pbs.org/conscience/index.html) that is an excellent resource for historical research on this topic, as well as the related matter of JACL behavior during the war period.
8. See Chester Tanaka, *Go For Broke: A Pictorial History of the Japanese American 100th Infantry Battalion and the 442nd Regimental Combat Team* (Redmond, Calif.: Go For Broke Inc., 1982), pp. 26–44.
9. See Associated Press story of Oct. 21, 1943, cited in John Tsukano, *Bridge of Love* (Honolulu: Hawaii Hosts, 1985), pp. 195–97.
10. See Masayo Umezawa Duus, *Unlikely Liberators: The Men of the 100th and 442nd* (Honolulu: University of Hawaii Press, 1987), pp. 151–52.
11. Densho Project Visual History Interview: Tokio Hirotaka, Toshio Ito, and Joe Matsuzawa, May 21, 1998, segment 38.
12. Another 22 were awarded the Medal of Honor in June 2000 by President Clinton; only seven of the men honored were alive at the time. The name of the federal courthouse in Seattle was subsequently renamed in honor of one of the posthumous honorees, William K. Nakamura of Seattle, who was killed July 4, 1944, during a battle near Castellina.
13. See Matsuo, *Boyhood to War: History and Anecdotes of the 442nd RCT* (Honolulu: Mutual Publishing of Honolulu, 1992), p. 139; Chang, *'I Can Never Forget'*, p. 19; and Smith, *Democracy on Trial*, p. 342.

14. There are many vivid accounts of this battle, but the best is probably in Matsuo, *Boyhood to War*, pp. 98–103.
15. Ibid., pp. 109–10.
16. See Chang, *'I Can Never Forget'*, pp. 32–33. The author also visited Bruyeres in 1995 and was regaled with enthusiastic retellings of the liberation from several villagers, including the town's elderly mayor. Their annual festival, which draws a number of Nisei veterans to the picturesque village in October, is viewed with considerable fondness, as are the veterans themselves. A pleasant and striking memorial constructed by the veterans' families and friends is atop one of the nearby ridges where some of the fighting took place.
17. Ibid., p. 38.
18. See Tanaka, *Go For Broke*, pp. 92–93.
19. Anonymous 442nd veteran, quoted in Tanaka, *Go For Broke*, p. 85.
20. See Tsukano, *Bridge of Love*, pp. 259–67, and Matsuo, *Boyhood to War*, pp.112–13.
21. For a couple of discussions of the perception that the 442nd was used as cannon fodder, see Matsuo, *Boyhood to War*, pp. 102–05, and Smith, *Democracy on Trial*, pp. 389–90. This characterization, while controversial, appears through much of the oral literature on the 442nd. Upon being awarded the Medal of Honor by President Clinton in June 2000 for his heroism in the Vosges Mountains, 442nd veteran George Sakato told reporters: "As a unit we were used like cannon fodder."
22. See *Personal Justice Denied*, p. 260.
23. See Smith, *Democracy on Trial*, pp. 391–92.
24. Ibid., p. 391.
25. War Relocation Authority report, Impounded People: Japanese Americans in the Relocation Centers, 1946, cited in Smith, *Democracy on Trial*, pp. 391–92.
26. See *Personal Justice Denied*, pp. 213–243. See also Smith, *Democracy on Trial*, pp. 267, 310–15.
27. See *Personal Justice Denied*, pp. 227–28.
28. See Robert G. Kaufman, *Henry M. Jackson: A Life in Politics* (Seattle: University of Washington Press, 2000), pp. 35–37, and the Warren G. Magnuson Archives, University of Washington Archives, 3181–2, box 6, folders 53–58; and box 7, folder 44–45, which contain much of Magnuson's correspondence with constituents on the "Japanese question." Magnuson, as pointed out in chapter 6, was also in regular correspondence with Miller Freeman on the Japanese question, and those letters may also be found in WGM archives in 3181–2, box 6, folders 46–47.
29. See Sucheng Chan, *Asian Americans: An Interpretive History* (New York: Twayne Publishers, 1991), pp. 135–37.
30. Ibid., pp. 137–38.
31. The ruling is *Ex Parte Mitsuye Endo*, 323 U.S. 283 (1944).
32. See Smith, *Democracy on Trial*, pp. 368–71.
33. See *Personal Justice Denied*, pp. 240–41.
34. Ibid., p. 395.

Chapter 6: The Long Road Home

1. This account is drawn from two sources: Whitney's own, relatively brief, report in the American of June 24, 1943, headlined, "Excitement Prevails as Rumors Spread—No Japanese in This Area"; and a more detailed account in the *Post-Intelligencer* of June 27, 1943, p. 5, by Doug Welch, headlined "Bellevue 'Jap' Only Chinese: Woo Boo, Farmer Whose Truck Balked, Startles Suburb."
2. See, e.g., "Japan Plans Attack On Pacific Coast, Magnuson Asserts," *Post-Intelligencer*, Sunday, June 13, 1943, p. 1.
3. See "Coast Visits By U.S.-Jap Soldiers Hit," *Post-Intelligencer*, May 6, 1943, p. 1.
4. The draft of the speech can be found in the Henry M. Jackson Archives, University of Washington Archives, 3560–2156/31. It is also cited, along with a brief discussion of

Jackson's early attitudes toward Japanese Americans, in Robert G. Kaufman, *Henry M. Jackson: A Life in Politics* (Seattle: University of Washington Press, 2000), pp. 35–37.

5. See *Personal Justice Denied: Report of the Commission on Wartime Relocation and Internment of Civilians* (Seattle: University of Washington Press, 1996), pp. 224–26.
6. See "Japs Drill in Internment Camp To Aid Coast Attack," *Seattle Post-Intelligencer*, Friday, June 11, 1943, p. 1.
7. See Page Smith, *Democracy on Trial: The Japanese American Evacuation and Relocation World War II* (New York: Simon & Schuster, 1995), p. 312.
8. See "Demand for Return of Freed Japs Made," *Seattle Post-Intelligencer*, June 24, 1943, p. 12.
9. See "Aged Japs Plotted Oregon Forest Fires," *Seattle Post-Intelligencer*, June 11, 1943, p. 8.
10. See "Jap Inquiry Bares Shameful Facts," *Seattle Post-Intelligencer*, June 20, 1943, p. 1.
11. See "Jap Internees Get Best Food, Dies Charges," *Seattle Post-Intelligencer*, June 1, 1943, p. 12.
12. Probably the best overview of the Dies Committee's colorful career is August Raymond Ogden, *The Dies Committee, A Study of the Special House Committee For The Investigation Of Un-American Activities, 1938–1944* (Washington: Catholic University Press, 1945).
13. See chapter 4, p. 219.
14. See Audrie Girdner and Annie Loftis, *The Great Betrayal: The Evacuation of Japanese-Americans During World War II* (London: The Macmillan Company, 1969), p. 361.
15. See Lucile McDonald, *Bellevue: Its First 100 Years* (Bellevue: Bellevue Historical Society, 2000), p. 115.
16. Letter is in Miller Freeman Archives, University of Washington: Box 11, Folder 15. Archives also contain letters to Justice Department and FBI officials complaining of activities by various Japanese; see e.g., File 3–23, letter to Sen. Homer R. Bone, June 25, 1943; File 4–19, letter to Department of Justice; File 4–22, letters from FBI acknowledging receipt of letters reporting un-American activities; letter from H.B. Fletcher, Agent in Charge, FBI Seattle, denying request for list of names of Japanese students enrolled at Washington State College.
17. Letter from M. J. Hopkins, Rolling Bay, Bainbridge Island, to Miller Freeman, April 26, 1945. Miller Freeman Archive, University of Washington, Box 11, Folder 13.
18. See "Japs 'Bleed' Leased Farms, Says Bainbridge Economist," *Japanese Exclusion League Journal*, June 1945, p. 1.
19. See "A Program That All Can Back!," *Japanese Exclusion League Journal*, June 1945, p. 4.
20. See Lambert Schuyler, *The Japs Must Not Come Back!* (Winslow, Wash.: Heron House, Publishers, 1945), pp. 4–5.
21. Ibid., p. 8.
22. Ibid., pp. 11–15.
23. See "Anti-Jap League Solicits Membership Fund at Meet," *Seattle Star*, April 3, 1945, p. 7.
24. See "Anti-Jap League Bans Opposition," *Seattle Times*, April 3, 1945, p. 11.
25. See "Pearl Harbor Unit Will Be Organized," *Seattle Times*, April 3, 1945, p. 11; and Girdner and Loftis, *The Great Betrayal*, p. 399.
26. "Editorial," *Bellevue American*, April 5, 1945, p. A1.
27. See "To Hold Town Meeting at Bellevue School Next Thursday, April 19," *Bellevue American*, April 12, 1945, p. A1.
28. Robert F. Karolevitz, *Kemper Freeman, Sr., and the Bellevue Story* (Mission Hill, SD: The Homestead Publishers, 1984), pp. 80–82.
29. Ibid., p. 82.
30. See *Bellevue American*, March 10, 1946.
31. Figures derived from Asaichi Tsushima, *Pre-WWII History of Japanese Pioneers in the Clearing and Development of Land in Bellevue* (Bellevue: Private printing, 1991), pp. 16–17, 35–40, and newspaper and oral accounts of the evacuation.

32. See United States Census Bureau figures for Seattle in 1940 and 1950. See also Calvin F. Schmid, Charles E. Nobbe, and Arlene E. Mitchell, *Nonwhite Races: State of Washington* (Olympia: Washington State Planning and Community Affairs Agency, 1968), pp. 11–12; 19–20; 24–25; 32–37; 62–63; and Calvin F. Schmid and Wayne W. McVey, Jr., *Growth and Distribution of Minority Races in Seattle, Washington* (Seattle: Seattle Public Schools, 1964), pp. 14–15, and figures 1:10 and 1:11. The 1950 U.S. Census also provides the first tract figures for rural King County, including Bellevue. Although a comparison with the 1940 population thus is not possible, it is clear that any nonwhite population that may have existed in Bellevue before the war vanished by 1950; the two Bellevue tracts (KC–66 and KC–67) combined record only 161 nonwhites in 1950, from a total combined population of 6,660.
33. See Linda Tamura, *The Hood River Issei: An Oral History of Japanese Settlers in Oregon's Hood River Valley* (Urbana/Chicago: University of Illinois Press, 1993), pp. 226–33.
34. See Leonard Broom and Ruth Riemer, *Removal and Return: The Socio-Economic Effects of the War on Japanese Americans* (Berkeley: University of California Press, 1949), p. 109.
35. Densho Project Visual History Interview: Chizuko Norton, April 27, 1998, segment 30.
36. Densho Project Visual History Interview: Rae Takekawa, May 8, 1998, segment 27.
37. Densho Project Visual History Interview: Tom Matsuoka, May 7, 1998, segment 31.
38. Densho Project Visual History Interview: Rae Takekawa, May 8, 1998, segment 32.
39. Densho Project Visual History Interview: Seichi Hayashida, August 21, 1997, segment 14.
40. See Smith, *Democracy on Trial*, pp. 392–93.
41. See Deborah K. Lim, "Research Report prepared for Presidential Select Committee on JACL Resolution #7," 1990, "IIA: JACL Position on Legal Test Cases: (4) Change of Policy": "Official communication of a policy change appears in the March 4, 1943, Bulletin #7, to all JACL leaders and National Board members from National Secretary Masaoka. On page two under the heading of Civil Rights Committee, Masaoka informs the recipients of the Bulletin that the government has been making disturbing claims regarding the unassimilability of Japanese Americans, effect of dual citizenship on allegiance of the Nisei, schooling and indoctrination of Japanese Americans and so forth."
42. The best overall discussion of the major legal cases involving Japanese-American civil rights in World War II is Peter Irons, *Justice at War* (New York: Oxford University Press, 1962). See also Suchen Chang, *Asian Americans: An Interpretive History* (New York: Twayne Publishers, 1991), pp. 139–40.
43. As Roger Daniels points out in *Concentration Camps: North America: Japanese in the United States and Canada During World War II* (Malabar, Fla.: Krieger Publishing Company, 1993), p. 170, McCarran-Walter was actually "one of the most reactionary pieces of national legislation. . . . This act, passed over President Truman's veto, subjected visiting scholars to all kinds of indignities, and was in many other ways a typical measure of the era of Senator Joseph R. McCarthy and cold war hysteria. But within this abominable piece of legislation was a significant redeeming principle: total exclusion of Asians from immigration naturalization was ended."
44. See particularly Daniels, *Concentration Camps: North America*, pp. 162–63.
45. See Lucile McDonald, *Bellevue: Its First 100 Years* (Bellevue: Bellevue Historical Society, 2000), pp. 147–50.

Epilogue: The Internment: Race, Memory, and Meaning

1. See "N.C. Congressman Says Internment of Japanese-Americans during World War II Was Appropriate," Associated Press, Feb. 5, 2003.
2. See Nick Maheras, "Groups Call on Coble for Apology," *High Point Enterprise*, Feb. 7, 2003.
3. See Eric Muller, *Is That Legal?*, http://www.isthatlegal.org, entries for 2/7/2003, 2/8/2003, and 2/9/2003.

4. See *Personal Justice Denied: Report of the Commission on Wartime Relocation and Internment of Civilians* (Seattle: University of Washington Press, 1996), p. 89.
5. See Ben Pershing, "Asian-American Members Unhappy With Coble Letter," *Roll Call*, Feb. 13, 2003
6. See Niraj Warikoo, "Arabs in U.S. Could Be Held, Official Warns," *Detroit Free Press*, July 20, 2002. Available online at http://www.freep.com/news/metro/civil20_20020720.htm.
7. See Michelle Malkin, *In Defense of Internment: The Case for "Racial Profiling" in World War II and the War on Terror* (Washington: Regnery Publishing, Inc., 2004), especially pp. viii-xxxv, 17–51, and 65–85.
8. See Tetsuden Kashima, *Judgment Without Trial: Japanese American Imprisonment during World War II* (Seattle: University of Washington Press, 2003), especially pp. 14–66.
9. See Anita Ramasastry, "Do Hamdi and Padilla Need Company: Why Attorney General Ashcroft's Plan to Create Internment Camps forSupposed Citizen Combatants Is Shocking and Wrong." FindLaw, Aug, 21, 2002. Available online at http://writ.news.FindLaw.com/ramasastry/20020821.html.
10. See, e.g., James Ridgeway, "John Ashcroft's New America," *Village Voice*, Oct. 2, 2001: "[T]he racial profiling that allows the government to keep tabs on [more than seven million American Muslims] may be the modern equivalent of a concentration camp." Further examples can be found in David Cole, "Enemy Aliens," *Stanford Law Review*, vol. 54, no. 953 (2002), p. 997: "The post-9/11 response constitutes a reprise of some of the worst mistakes of our past." See also Susan M. Akram and Kevin R. Johnson, "Race, Civil Rights, and Immigration Law After September 11, 2001: The Targeting of Arabs and Muslims," *NYU Annual Survey of American Law*, vol. 58, no. 295 (2002), p. 337: "the September 11 dragnet carried out by the federal government [against Arab and Muslim aliens] resembles the Japanese internment during World War II."
11. See John Leo, "The Internment Taboo," *U.S. News and World Report*, Sept. 27, 2004, p. 74.
12. See Daniel Pipes, "Why the Japanese Internment Still Matters," *New York Sun*, Dec. 28, 2004.
13. See Eric L. Muller, "Inference or Impact? Racial Profiling and the Internment's True Legacy," *Ohio State Journal of Criminal Law*, vol. 1, no. 1, November 2003.
14. See "Detaining Minority Citizens, Then and Now," *Chronicle of Higher Education*, Feb. 15, 2002.
15. See Fred Korematsu, "Do we really need to relearn the lessons of Japanese American internment?," *San Francisco Chronicle*, Sept. 16, 2004. Available online at http://www.sfgate.com/cgi-bin/article.cgi?file=/chronicle/archive/2004/09/16/EDGP28P0T11.DTL.

Bibliography

Armor, John, and Peter Wright. *Manzanar.* New York: Vintage Books, 1989.

Broom, Leonard, and Ruth Riemer. *Removal and Return: The Socio-Economic Effects of the War on Japanese Americans.* Berkeley: University of California Press, 1949.

Burlingame, Burl. *Advance Force Pearl Harbor: The Imperial Navy's Underwater Assault on America.* Honolulu: Pacific Monograph, 1992.

Chan, Sucheng. *Asian Americans: An Interpretive History.* Boston: Twayne Publishers, 1991.

Chang, Thelma. *'I Can Never Forget': Men of the 100th/442nd.* Honolulu: Sigi Productions, 1991.

Chin, Art. *Golden Tassels: A History of the Chinese in Washington, 1857–1977.* Seattle: n.p., 1977.

Chuman, Frank. *The Bamboo People: The Law and Japanese-Americans.* Del Mar, Calif.: Publisher's Inc., 1976.

Committee on Wartime Relocation and Internment of Civilians, *Personal Justice Denied: Report of the Commission on Wartime Relocation and Internment of Civilians.* Seattle: University of Washington Press, 1996.

Daniels, Roger. *The Politics of Prejudice: The Anti-Japanese Movement in California and the Struggle for Japanese Exclusion.* Berkeley: University of California Press, 1961.

———. *The Decision to Relocate the Japanese Americans.* Malabar, Fla.: Robert E. Krieger Publishing Co., 1986.

———. *Concentration Camps: North America: Japanese in the United States and Canada During World War II.* Malabar, Fla.: Krieger Publishing Company, 1993.

———. *Concentration Camps USA: Japanese Americans and World War II.* New York: Holt, Rinehart & Winston, 1972.

Darrow, George M. *The Strawberry: History, Breeding and Physiology.* Washington: U.S. Department of Agriculture, 1965.

de Nevers, Klancy Clark. *The Colonel and the Pacifist: Karl Bendetsen, Perry Saito, and the Incarceration of Japanese Americans During World War II.* Salt Lake City: University of Utah Press, 2004.

Duus, Masayo Umezawa. *Unlikely Liberators: The Men of the 100th and 442nd.* Honolulu: University of Hawaii Press, 1987.

Fiset, Louis. *Imprisoned Apart: The World War II Correspondence of an Issei Couple.* Seattle: University of Washington Press, 1997.

Flewelling, Stan. *Shirakawa: Stories from a Pacific Northwest Japanese American Community.* Auburn: White River Valley Museum, 2002.

Freeman, Miller. *The Memoirs of Miller Freeman.* Bellevue: Private printing, 1956.

Galpin, C. J., and Veda B. Larson. *Farm Population of Selected Counties: Composition, Characteristics and Occupations in Detail for Eight Counties, Comprising Tsego County, N.Y., Dane County, Wis., New Madrid and Scott Counties, Mo., Cass County, N. Dak., Wake County, N.C., Ellis County, Tex., and King County, Wash.* Washington: Department of Commerce and the Census Bureau, 1924.

Garreau, Joel. *Edge City: Life on the New Frontier.* New York: Doubleday and Co., 1992.

Girdner, Audrie, and Annie Loftis. *The Great Betrayal: The Evacuation of Japanese-Americans During World War II.* London: The Macmillan Company, 1969.

Grant, Madison. *The Passing of the Great Race, or The Racial Basis of European History.* New York: Charles Scribner's Sons, 1922.

Grodzins, Morton. *Americans Betrayed: Politics and the Japanese Evacuation.* Chicago: University of Chicago Press, 1949.

Irons, Peter. *Justice at War.* New York: Oxford University Press, 1962.

Iwata, Masakazu. *Planted in Good Soil: A History of the Issei in the United States Agriculture.* 2 vols. New York: P. Lang, 1990.

Karolevitz, Robert F. *Kemper Freeman, Sr., and the Bellevue Story.* Mission Hill, South Dakota: The Homestead Publishers, 1984.

Kaufman, Robert G. *Henry M. Jackson: A Life in Politics.* Seattle: University of Washington Press, 2000.

LeWarne, Charles Pierce. *Utopias on Puget Sound 1885–1915.* Seattle: University of Washington Press, 1995.

Magden, Ronald. *Furusato: Tacoma-Pierce County Japanese 1888–1977.* Tacoma: Tacoma Japanese Community Service, 1988.

Malkin, Michelle. *In Defense of Internment: The Case for 'Racial Profiling' in World War II and the War on Terror.* Washington: Regnery Publishing Inc., 2004.

Matsuo, Dorothy. *Boyhood to War: History and Anecdotes of the 442nd RCT.* Honolulu: Mutual Publishing of Honolulu, 1992.

McDonald, Lucile. *Bellevue: Its First 100 Years.* Bellevue, Wash.: Bellevue Historical Society, 2000.

Mikesh, Robert C. *Japan's World War II Balloon Bomb Attacks on North America.* Washington: Smithsonian Institution Press, 1973.

Mitsuoka, Norio. *Nisei Odyssey: The Camp Years.* Fountain Valley, Calif.: Bowder Printing and Publishing Co., 1991.

Modell, John. *The Economics and Politics of Racial Accommodation: The Japanese of Los Angeles, 1900–1942.* Urbana/Chicago: University of Illinois Press, 1963.

Muller, Eric L. *Free to Die for their Country: The Story of the Japanese American Draft Resisters in World War II.* Chicago: University of Chicago Press, 2001.

Niiya, Brian, ed. *The Encyclopedia of Japanese-American History.* Los Angeles: The Japanese-American National Museum, 2001.

Nishinoiri, John Isao. *Japanese Farms in Washington.* Master's thesis, University of Washington, 1926.

Norton, Henry Kittredge. *The Story of California From the Earliest Days to the Present.* Chicago: A.C. McClurg & Co., 1924.

Ogden, August Raymond. *The Dies Committee, A Study Of The Special House Committee For The Investigation Of Un-American Activities, 1938–1944.* Washington: Catholic University Press, 1945.

Rademaker, John Adrian. "The Ecological Position of the Japanese Farmers in the State of Washington." Ph.D. diss., University of Washington, 1939.

Robinson, Greg. *By Order of the President: FDR and the Internment of Japanese Americans.* Cambridge, Mass.: Harvard University Press, 2001.

Sandmeyer, Elmer C. *The Anti-Chinese Movement in California.* Urbana: University of Illinois Press, 1973.

Schmid, Calvin F., Charles E. Nobbe and Arlene E. Mitchell. *Nonwhite Races: State of Washington.* Olympia: Washington State Planning and Community Affairs Agency, 1968.

Schmid, Calvin F., and Wayne W. McVey, Jr. *Growth and Distribution of Minority Races in Seattle, Washington.* Seattle: Seattle Public Schools, 1964.

Schuyler, Lambert. *The Japs Must Not Come Back!* Winslow, Wash.: Heron House, Publishers, 1945.

Seattle Times staff. *A Hidden Past: An Exploration of Eastside History.* Seattle: Seattle Times Publishing, 2000.

Selden, Steven, and Ashley Montagu. *Inheriting Shame: The Story of Eugenics and Racism in America.* New York: Teachers College Press, Advances in Contemporary Educational Thought Series, Vol. 23, 1999.

Smith, Page. *Democracy on Trial: The Japanese American Evacuation and Relocation in World War II.* New York: Simon and Schuster, 1995.

Stoddard, Lothrop. *The Rising Tide of Color Against White World Supremacy.* New York: Charles Scribner's Sons, 1922.

Takami, David. *Divided Destiny: A History of Japanese Americans in Seattle.* Seattle: University of Washington Press, 1998.

Tamura, Linda. *The Hood River Issei: An Oral History of Japanese Settlers in Oregon's Hood River Valley.* Urbana/Chicago: University of Illinois Press, 1993.

Tanaka, Chester. *Go For Broke: A Pictorial History of the Japanese American 100th Infantry Battalion and the 442nd Regimental Combat Team.* Redmond, Calif.: Go For Broke Inc., 1982.

Tateishi, John. *And Justice For All: An Oral History of the Japanese American Internment Camps.* Seattle: University of Washington Press, 1984.

Tanaka, Stefan Akio. *The Nikkei on Bainbridge Island, 1883–1942: A Study of Migration and Community Development.* Master's thesis, University of Washington, 1977.

Thomas, Dorothy Swaine, and Richard S. Nishimoto. *The Spoilage: Japanese-American Evacuation and Resettlement During World War II.* Berkeley: University of California Press, 1946.

Tsukano, John. *Bridge of Love.* Honolulu: Hawaii Hosts, 1985.

Tsushima, Asaichi. *Pre-WWII History of Japanese Pioneers in the Clearing and Development of Land in Bellevue.* Bellevue, Wash.: Private printing, 1991.

Van Valkenburg, Carol. *An Alien Place: The Fort Missoula, Montana Detention Camp 1941–1944.* Missoula, Mont.: Pictorial Histories Publishing Co., 1995.

Watanabe, James. *The History of the Tacoma Japanese translated from Tacoma Nihonjin Hattenshi.* Tacoma: Pierce County Historical Society, n.d.

Weglyn, Michi. *Years of Infamy: The Untold Story of America's Concentration Camps.* New York: Morrow Quill Paperbacks, 1976.

Webber, Bert. *Retaliation: Japanese Attacks and Allied Countermeasures on the Pacific Coast in World War II.* Corvallis: Oregon State University Press, 1976.

Wilson, Robert A., and Bill Hosokawa. *East to America: A History of the Japanese in the United States.* New York: William and Morrow Co., 1980.

Woodroffe, Pamela J. *Vashon Island's Agricultural Roots.* iUniverse, 2002.

Index

Alien Land Laws, 56–7, 61–6, 84, 228, 241, 258–60
Anti-Asian sentiment, 12, 13, 18, 19, 205, 208, 254, 257
  see also Japanese Americans; "Yellow Peril"
Anti-Japanese League, 57, 61, 91, 206, 208
Arab Americans, 237–40, 245–48, 272
Aramaki, Akira, 32, 40, 42, 44, 81, 94, 111, 112, 114–16, 135–6, 159, 171, 217, 222, 229, 251, 263
Aramaki, Hikotara, 32, 94
Aramaki family, 228
Asian Exclusion Act, 64, 72, 149, 208, 224, 241
Asiatic Exlusion League, 19, 56, 61, 255

baseball, 70, 71, 85, 86, 94, 146, 159
442nd Battalion, 181–94, 197, 198, 204, 213, 223, 224, 252, 269
Bechtel, Barbara, 2, 9
Bechtel, Isaac, 28, 29
Bellevue American, 111, 119, 139, 140, 155–6, 201, 202, 203, 212, 213, 214, 263, 270
Bellevue Japanese Association, 40
Bellevue Square, 6, 215, 226–8
Bellevue Vegetable Growers Association, 88, 89–90, 94, 98, 137, 157, 265
Bendetsen, Karl R. (Maj./Col.), 109, 119, 121–4, 126, 132, 176, 177, 241
Biddle, Francis (Atty. Gen.), 121, 123–5, 194, 195, 264
Bovee, Charles W. 135, 170–1, 202–3, 213, 220, 224, 226

California Gold Rush, 11, 254
Cano Numoto Collection, 34, 42, 82, 87
Central Pacific Railroad, 11, 12
Chelsvig, Ethel, 104, 262
Chinese Exclusion Act of 1882, 12, 18
Clark, Chase A., 179, 268
Clark, Mark (Gen.), 108, 122, 193
Cleveland, Grover, 13
Clinton, William Jefferson, 268, 269
Constitution (U.S.), 120, 124, 164, 178–9, 195–6, 210, 212–13, 243–5, 247–9, 268
Coolidge, Calvin, 64
Crandell, George H., 201, 202, 205, 211, 224

Daniels, Roger, 66, 243, 246, 249, 273
Densho Project, 41, 77, 88, 251, 253, 256, 257, 261, 263, 265, 266, 267, 268, 271
DeWitt, John (Lt. Gen.), 104–9, 119, 121–8, 130, 132–4, 176–7, 193, 207, 239, 241–4
Dies Committee, 204–5, 270
Ditty, James S., 92, 215
Douglas, Malcolm, 64–5

"Edge City," 5, 254
Endo, Mitsuye, 195–6, 269
"enemy aliens," 102, 108–9, 117, 123, 125, 147, 163, 164, 178, 272
Ex Parte Mitsuye Endo, 196, 269
Executive Order 9066, 127, 243, 249
Fair Play Committee, 178–9
Federal Bureau of Investigation, 97–9, 102–4, 105, 107–8, 115, 117, 122, 126, 148, 203, 206, 207, 270
"Fifth Column," 109, 126, 128, 236, 240, 265
Food for Freedom program, 136
Fort Missoula, 117, 118, 134, 147–50, 152, 195, 266
Freeman, Kemper, 104, 116, 214–5, 227, 270
Freeman, Miller, 6, 20–2, 55–61, 63, 91–3, 104, 111–17, 128–9, 206–8, 212–15, 225–6, 242–3, 256, 259, 261, 263, 265, 267, 269, 270, 273
  anti-Japanese crusade, 6, 21, 55–61, 63, 111–17, 128–9, 206–8, 212, 213, 242–3, 259, 265, 270

Anti-Japanese League, 57, 61, 91, 206, 208
and Mercer Island Floating Bridge, 92–3, 225, 226
Pacific Fisherman, 20–2
and "special committee," 111–17
Tolan hearings, 128–9, 206
white supremacy, 58–61
"Yellow Peril," 22, 91, 112–13, 256
Fretheim, Einar, 103–4

"Gentlemen's Agreement," 20, 21, 24, 27, 55–6, 64, 128
Grant, Madison, 58, 61, 258
Great Northern Railroad, 23–4, 221
Gullion, Allen (Prvst. Marshl. Gen.), 108–9, 121, 122–3, 176

Hashiguchi, Mitsuko, 69, 74–5, 76, 79–80, 85, 103, 139, 143, 144, 150–51, 220–21, 229, 253, 266
Hashiguchi, Mutsuo, 133, 139, 140, 158, 220, 229, 140
Hashiguchi family, 173, 221
Hawaii, 23, 25, 26, 99, 100, 106, 109, 120, 125, 126, 129, 147, 176, 190
alleged "fifth column" activity, 109, 126
and 100th Battalion, 176, 179–82
and Pearl Harbor, 96, 97, 98
Hayashi, Kanji, 111, 112, 113, 114, 115, 116
Hayashida, Fumiko, 130
Hayashida, Seichi, 140, 141, 142–3, 144, 146, 165, 171, 173, 174, 222, 253, 265, 266, 267
Hayashida family, 167
Hearst, William Randolph, 17, 19, 256
Hennig, Adolph, 67, 75, 260
Hennig, Robert, 69, 75, 85–6, 90–1, 213–14, 253
Hirabayashi, Gordon, 243, 244
Hirotaka, Kazue
see Kazue Hirotaka Matsuoka
Hirotaka, Tatsunosuke, 32, 70
Hirotaka, Tokio, 90, 111, 113, 114, 116, 135, 136, 141, 146, 152, 154, 218, 229, 251, 253, 256, 261, 265, 266, 268
Hirotaka family, 70, 152, 218, 220, 228
Hoover, J. Edgar, 124, 126

1790 Immigration Act, 12, 15, 55
1870 Immigration Act, 224
see also McCarran-Walter Act
Inatsu, Masami, 111, 116, 191, 192, 201
internment camps, 1–2, 7, 102, 121–7, 129–130, 141–155, 157–75, 192, 194–5, 202, 212, 214, 216, 220, 222–3, 230–1, 235–9, 246, 250, 266, 270
agitation at, 161–7
see also Japanese American Citizens League (JACL)
and Arab Americans, 240, 246–8, 272
and children, 142, 147, 149, 151
defense of, 230–1, 237–40, 272
definition of "suspect," 102
description of, 157–9, 168, 169–70
see also Manzanar; Pinedale; Poston, Arizona; Tule Lake
Executive Order 9066, 243
see also Franklin D. Roosevelt; War Relocation Authority (WRA)
hired laborers, 151–5, 159–161
"no-no boys," 163–6
and young people, 146–7, 158, 170–1, 175
see also 442nd Battalion
racism, 241–3, 249, 250
see also John DeWitt; Miller Freedman
recreation, 146–8, 159, 171, 266
and revisionist history, 240, 241
see also Michelle Malkin
September 11, 2001, 7, 235–8, 245–7, 249, 250, 253, 272
Ito, Alice, 153, 251, 253
Ito, Itaro, 33, 42
Ito, Tosh, 33, 42, 78, 81, 103, 110, 115, 138, 142, 158, 159, 235, 236, 237, 251, 253, 256, 261, 265, 266, 268
Ito family, 75, 153, 228

Jackson, Henry, 203–4, 207, 269, 270
"Jap," 6, 15, 16, 17, 30, 59–60, 62, 75, 81, 85, 97, 109–10, 120–1, 125, 127, 129, 137, 160–1, 198, 201–4, 208, 209–13, 217–20, 222, 242, 258, 261, 263, 265, 267, 269, 270
Japan, 14–16, 23, 25–7, 32, 35–40, 43–5, 49, 51, 55, 60, 66, 71, 84, 86, 94–5, 99–100, 107, 109, 112–16, 129, 148, 162–7, 170, 180, 201, 208–9, 214, 229–31, 241, 243, 263
culture, 27, 43–4, 82, 84, 86
"*see* "picture brides"
"Gentlemen's Agreement," 55
and Hitler, Adolph, 95
"MAGIC" cables, 101–2
and Matsuoka, Tom 23, 95–6, 148
reaction to Alien Land Laws, 5, 64
Sino-Japanese War, 95
supersubs, 105, 106, 122, 262

Tachibana spy ring, 101
Tokugawa Period, 25
Japan Society of Seattle, 128, 129
Japanese American Citizens League, 133–4, 158, 161–2, 164–5, 176, 195, 223–4, 236, 238, 245, 253, 268, 271
Japanese American Courier, 86, 119
Japanese Americans (Nikkei), 2, 6, 7, 9, 10, 11, 14–16, 31, 33, 41, 50, 54, 158, 165, 216, 237, 240, 242, 246, 248, 254, 255, 256, 257, 260
and Alien Land Laws, 62–5
alleged spy activity, 122, 123, 126, 208
anti-Japanese campaign, 66, 84, 123, 224
anti-Japanese hysteria, 109–12, 118, 119, 124, 126
see Miller Freeman
anti-Japanese laws, 63–6
anti-Japanese sentiment, 17–20, 22, 29, 54–55, 56, 58–9, 60–3, 101, 126, 128, 197–9, 201, 204, 205, 207–13, 217–23, 230, 239, 241–2, 270, 271
see "Yellow Peril"
baseball, 70, 71
Buddhism, 43, 70, 134, 169, 170, 252
children, 74–9, 81–5, 86, 89,101, 103
citizenship, 63, 100, 115, 116, 123, 127, 140, 141, 142, 148, 162, 223–4, 242, 244, 263
see Japanese American Citizens League
culture, 43, 44, 49
Christianity, 40, 43, 70, 164
"enemy aliens," 102, 108, 123
evacuation of, 119–30, 129, 132–4, 136, 137, 139–141, 144, 145, 241, 264, 265, 270
exclusion of, 17, 27, 43–4, 56, 57, 58, 63, 64, 80, 205–8, 210, 258
Executive Order 9066, 243
farmers, 2, 32, 36, 49, 50, 60, 63–7, 68, 89–91, 110, 122, 132, 133, 135, 136, 155, 206, 214–17, 221, 222, 226, 227–8, 242, 257–60
see truck farming
"fifth column," 126, 128, 142, 265
Freeman, Miller, 20–2, 32
haiseki, 80, 81
home raids, 108
immigrants, 11–18, 21, 22, 24–7, 56, 60
internment, *see* internment camps
Issei, 7, 35, 39, 43, 44, 47, 49, 50, 51, 52, 53, 54, 56, 65, 66, 70, 71, 72, 76, 83–4, 86, 89, 94, 100, 111–13, 115, 119, 122, 127, 128, 132, 142, 146, 147, 149, 151, 159, 162–5, 171, 173–4, 197–8, 205, 229, 257, 258, 266
Japanese language, 112, 113, 115
Japanese language schools, 84, 98, 107, 113, 129, 150, 167
Kibei, 117, 122, 162, 164, 167
land clearing, 32, 38, 39, 40–2
land ownership, 63, 65, 66, 259, 260
language, 43, 79, 82–4, 147
and mobility, 49, 50
Nisei, 7, 32, 54, 64–6, 70, 72–4, 76, 78, 79, 82–6, 89, 100–5, 109, 263, 111–14, 117, 119, 122, 124, 127, 128, 132, 133, 134, 138, 142, 149, 151, 157–9, 161–4, 166–7, 170–1, 173–7, 191, 193, 214, 217, 218, 220, 222, 227–30, 235–7, 242, 249, 251–3, 268, 271
Nisei soldiers, 175–95, 269
see 442nd Battalion
Ozawa vs. U.S., 63
"picture brides," 27, 32, 37, 56, 57, 64, 72
post-Pearl Harbor treatment, 99, 100,133, 201–4, 214, 220–2, 241–2
property rights, 64
race relations and, 76, 78, 80
and racism, 16, 17, 20, 40, 53, 57, 132, 241–2
relocation of, 109, 119–21, 123, 127, 212, 261–3
Sansei, 74, 223
Seinenkai, 83–4
and September 11, 2001, 235–8, 250, 271, 272
stereotypes of, 50, 54, 61, 107, 109, 123, 128, 129, 241
Tolan Hearings, 127–130
and "tradition," 33, 35, 40, 43, 162
Japanese Exclusion League, 205, 208–9, 211, 212, 214, 217
Japanese Exclusion League Journal, 208–9, 270
Johnson, Albert, 60, 62, 63
Justice Department (U.S.), 102, 108, 125, 148, 149, 167, 206, 243, 244, 245, 270

Knox, Frank, 109, 126, 262, 263
Korematsu, Fred, 243–6, 250, 272
Kurita, Ryutan, 33, 35, 65, 228

Lake Washington, 5, 10, 27–30, 68, 92–93, 206

"MAGIC" cables, 101–2

Magnuson, Warren, 204, 206, 207, 269
Malkin, Michelle, 240–2, 246–7, 249, 274
Manzanar, 131, 132, 145, 157–8, 162, 204, 266, 267
Mathewson, Beatrice, 28–9, 75–6, 253, 256
Matsuoka, James, 44, 47, 160
Matsuoka, John, 1–4, 7, 44, 47, 50–1, 53, 94, 160–1, 227, 253
Matsuoka, Kanju, 22–4, 26–7, 47–8, 50, 94
Matsuoka, Kazue Hirotaka, 72–4, 83, 86, 97, 118, 134–5, 138, 152–4, 220, 228, 231–3
Matsuoka, Tats, 74, 86, 88
Matsuoka, Tom Takeo, 7, 9, 10, 23, 24, 26, 27, 40, 44–5, 47, 48, 54, 72–5, 83–6, 89–90, 94–6, 97, 102, 114, 115, 117, 118, 119, 138, 147–54, 165, 191, 218–20, 228–9, 231–4, 251–3, 261, 256, 257, 266, 271
  and baseball, 70, 71, 85–6, 261
  and Bellevue Vegetable Growers Association, 89, 94
  and FBI, 97–9
  and land clearing, 40, 42
  and Pearl Harbor, 96, 97, 261
Matsuoka, Tori, 23, 26
Matsuoka, Tyrus, 74, 85, 88, 90, 110, 144, 151, 253, 261
Matsuoka family, 86, 88, 135, 152–53, 159, 169, 197, 218–20
Matsushita, Rose, 80–1, 142, 158, 220, 222–3, 229, 230, 235, 252, 253
Matsuzawa, Hichiro, 36–7, 94
Matsuzawa, Joe, 36–7, 78, 86, 95, 110, 143, 144, 146, 162, 163,174, 178, 180, 181, 183, 191, 202, 204, 220, 228, 229, 251–52, 253, 256, 261, 265, 266, 268
McCarran-Walter Act, 224, 271
McCloy, John, 123–4, 176, 181, 239
McLemore, Henry, 120–1, 263, 264
Mercer, Aaron, 28
Mercer Island Floating Bridge, 92–3, 214, 225–6
Microsoft, 5, 6, 227
Minidoka, 2, 158, 165, 167–8, 170–2, 175, 177, 179, 198, 221
Miyamoto, Frank, 134, 265
Mizokawa family, 228
Munson, Curtis, 101–2
Muromoto, Kim, 175, 188, 190–3, 198, 229, 252
Muromoto family, 228
Myer, Dillon, 159–61, 176, 194, 206

Nakamura, George, 187
Niendorff, Fred, 136–7
Nishimura, Michi (Tsushima), 35, 82, 98, 99, 119, 171, 192, 229, 230, 252
Nishimura, Tom, 229, 252
Northern Pacific Railroad, 30, 89, 91
North, Chizuko, 37, 76, 81, 83, 166–7, 173, 217, 253, 256, 261, 267, 271
Norton, Henry Kittredge, 11, 254
Numoto, Cano, 67, 68, 89, 93, 142, 171–2, 229, 251, 252
  see Cano Numoto Collection
Numoto, May, 171–2
Numoto, Tokuo, 33, 70
Numoto, Tsuruichi, 33, 34
Numoto family, 228

Office of Naval Intelligence, 99, 101–2
  and "MAGIC" cables, 101–2
Ozawa v. United States, 63
Ozawa, Takao, 63

Pacific Fisherman, 20–2
  see Miller Freeman
Pearl Harbor, 96, 97, 98, 102–3, 104–5, 108–9, 111, 118–19, 123–5, 130, 162, 177, 180, 201, 205, 211, 213, 230, 231, 235–7, 242–3, 249, 262, 270
  and anti-Japanese hysteria, 104, 109, 111, 177, 201, 205, 211, 242–3
  100th Battalion, 180
  "enemy aliens," 123–5
  home raids, 108
  and internment of Italian nationals, 118–19
  September 11, 2001, 235–7, 249
Phelan, James Duval, 18–19, 22, 58, 125
"picture brides," 27, 32, 37, 56, 57, 64, 72
Pinedale, 143–4, 148, 150, 155, 160, 171, 177, 181
  see internment camps
Poston, Arizona, 157, 162, 165, 204–5
  see internment camps

racial profiling, 7, 239–40, 247, 249, 272
revisionist history, 240–2, 249
Roosevelt, Franklin D., 99, 100, 101,103, 109, 119, 123–7, 162–3, 176, 179, 194–6, 211, 238, 241, 243, 246, 249, 261
  and Bush, George W. 245–6, 249
  and internment camps, 119, 123–7, 194–6, 241, 243
  and white supremacy, 99–100

Roosevelt, Theodore, 20, 21, 256
  see "Gentlemen's Agreement"

Sakamoto, James, 86, 119
San Francisco Chronicle, 19, 255
San Francisco Examiner, 19, 256
Sandbo, Patricia, 80, 140, 253
Schuyler, Lambert, 210, 270
Seattle Post-Intelligencer, 17, 93, 104, 110, 120–1, 128, 131, 136, 203, 225, 261, 262, 263, 265, 269, 270
Seattle Star, 54–6, 59, 60, 93, 258, 270
Seattle Times, 22, 93, 104, 110, 120, 262, 264, 270, 274
September 11, 2001, 7, 235–8, 245–7, 249, 253, 272
Shiraishi, Mitsi, 39, 41, 78, 80, 86, 89, 95, 133, 134, 135, 138, 142, 169, 170–1, 213, 218, 228, 230, 231, 252
Shiraishi family, 167, 218
Sino-Japanese War, 95
Social Darwinism, 6–7
Stark, Harold (Adm.), 108
Stillwell, Joseph (Maj. Gen.), 105, 193, 223
Stimson, Henry, 123–7, 176, 194, 196
Stoddard, Lothrop, 58, 61, 258, 259
Strawberries, 26, 27, 30, 51, 52, 136–8, 156, 208
  Bellevue Strawberry Festival, 6, 53–4, 68–9, 75–7, 155, 157, 206, 209, 227, 228, 248
  farmers, 31, 33, 34, 35, 37, 39, 40, 42, 47, 66, 67, 68, 208, 216
  see truck farming
  and Issei character, 52–3
  strawberry paradigm, 53
  as symbol, 54
  and sugar industry, 23, 25
Suguro, Ed, 142, 144, 151, 166, 173, 217, 251, 268
Suguro, Togoro, 37, 166
Suguro family, 77, 228
Suzzallo, Dr. Henry M., 92

Takano, Komaji, 111, 113, 115, 116
Takekawa, Rae Matsuoka, 42, 72–4, 79, 96, 97, 103, 118, 127, 134, 149, 146, 150, 152, 154, 219, 220, 232–4, 251, 252, 253, 261, 262, 263, 266, 271
Takeshita, Haruji, 30, 38
Takeshita family, 64
Tamaye, Enji, 37, 78, 165, 166, 217
Tanino, Ryomi, 177–8, 181–2, 184–6, 188, 192–3, 252
Tateishi, John, 235–40, 253, 275
Thompson, L. L., 65
Tolan hearings, 127–30, 206
truck farming, 38, 48–9, 51, 52, 49, 66–7, 76, 89, 137, 216, 260
Truman, Harry, 193, 198, 271
Tsushima, Asaichi, 31, 35, 36, 38, 82, 84, 98, 99, 102, 115, 150, 229, 251, 254, 256, 261, 270
Tsushima, Michi, *see* Michi Tsushima Nishimura
Tsushima family, 228
Tule Lake, 150–2, 157–8, 160, 162, 164, 166, 167, 171, 173, 175, 177, 193, 194, 198, 204, 217, 266, 267, 268
  see internment camps

Van Valkenburgh, H. C., 155–7, 267

Wallgren, Mon, 124, 194, 203
War Department (U.S.), 107, 108, 109, 123, 127, 162, 176, 180, 194, 243, 244
War Relocation Authority (WRA), 144–6, 148, 150, 152, 154, 157–9, 161–3, 165, 168, 170, 176, 193, 194, 196, 203–5, 212, 266, 269
Western Farm and Produce, Inc., 155–57
  see Bellevue Vegetable Growers Association
White River Journal, 16–17
White River Valley, 15–17, 24, 31, 50, 53, 76, 86, 89, 136, 139, 156, 160, 165, 205
white supremacy, 12, 43–4, 51, 57–8, 99, 125, 209–10, 241, 258, 259
Whitney, A. J., 111, 116, 203, 212–3, 269
World War I, 124, 141, 204
World War II, 1, 7, 9, 181, 260
  see 442nd Battalion; Pearl Harbor

Yabuki, Alan, 85, 143, 174, 191, 197, 199, 216, 252
Yabuki, Kameiji, 38–9, 70, 119, 138
Yabuki, Kiyo, 81, 98, 175, 177, 183, 185–6, 187, 188, 198–9, 217–18, 252
Yabuki, Terumatsu, 39, 98, 99, 102, 150
Yabuki family, 162, 228
Yamasaki, Toranosuke, 40–2
Yasui, Masuo, 149–50
Yasui, Minoru, 149, 195, 243, 244
"Yellow Peril," 19, 21–2, 91, 99, 105, 107, 112, 122, 206, 223, 241–2, 256